Self-Harm Behavior *and* Eating Disorders

SELF-HARM BEHAVIOR and EATING DISORDERS

Dynamics, Assessment, and Treatment

EDITED BY

JOHN L. LEVITT, PH.D.
RANDY A. SANSONE, M.D.
LEIGH COHN, M.A.T.

 Brunner-Routledge
Taylor & Francis Group

NEW YORK AND HOVE

Published in 2004 by
Brunner-Routledge
270 Madison Avenue
New York, NY 10016
www.brunner-routledge.com

Published in Great Britain by
Brunner-Routledge
27 Church Road
Hove, East Sussex
BN3 2FA
www.brunner-routledge.co.uk

Brunner-Routledge is an imprint of the Taylor & Francis Group.
Printed in the United States of America on acid-free paper.

10 9 8 7 6 5 4 3 2 1

Library of Congress Cataloging-in-Publication Data

Self-harm behavior and eating disorders: dynamics, assessment, and treatment / edited by John L. Levitt, Randy A. Sansone, Leigh Cohn.
    p. ; cm.
Includes bibliographical references and index.

ISBN 0-415-94698-0 (hardback : alk. paper)

1. Self-mutilation. 2. Self-injurious behavior. 3. Eating disorders—Complications. 4. Eating disorders.
[DNLM: 1. Eating Disorders—complications. 2. Self-Injurious Behavior—complications. 3. Eating Disorders—psychology. 4. Eating Disorders—therapy. 5. Self-Injurious Behavior—psychology. 6. Self-Injurious Behavior—therapy. WM 165 S464 2004] I. Levitt, John L., 1951-II. Sansone, Randy A., 1953-III. Cohn, Leigh. IV. Title.

    RC552.S4S456 2004
    616.85'82—dc22

                                                                                    2004006592

Editors

John L. Levitt, Ph.D., is the director of the Eating Disorders and Violence and Abuse Programs of Alexian Brothers Behavioral Health Hospital. He has delivered over 100 papers and workshop presentations locally and nationally with a particular emphasis upon the development and application of the Self-Regulatory Approach for treating patients with complex, multi-compulsive eating disorder. He is co-author of one book, co-editor of another book, and has over 35 published works. He is also on the editorial board of *Eating Disorders: The Journal of Treatment and Prevention.*

Randy A. Sansone, M.D., is a professor in the departments of Psychiatry and Internal Medicine at Wright State University School of Medicine in Dayton, Ohio, and director of Psychiatry Education at Kettering Medical Center. He has authored over 125 published papers and 14 book chapters, and is on the editorial boards of *Eating Disorders: The Journal of Treatment and Prevention* and *Violence and Victims.*

Leigh Cohn, M.A.T., is founder and editor-in-chief of *Eating Disorders: The Journal of Treatment and Prevention* and publisher of Gürze Books, which specializes in eating disorders publications and education. He is co-author or co-editor of several books, including *Making Weight: Healing Men's Conflicts with Food, Weight, and Shape,* (Gürze Books, Carlsbad, CA, 2000); *Bulimia: A Guide to Recovery* (Gürze Books, Carlsbad, CA, 1999); and *Sexual Abuse and Eating Disorders* (Brunner-Routledge, New York, 1996). He is also the publisher of *Eating Disorders Review* and *Eating Disorders Today.*

Contents

Inside My Wounds

BY M. M.

My parents divorced when I was 7 years old and my younger sister, Megan and I lived with our father, because my mother drank too much and had terrible mood swings. She couldn't make it on her own and died in a car accident a few years later. She had been drinking and slammed into a tree, and the police speculated that she probably did it on purpose.

When we weren't in school, Megan and I spent most of our time at our grandparents' house. They treated us harshly, like we were a nuisance, and I tried to be invisible around them. My father worked long hours and we saw little of him in those days. I think he preferred it that way. When he looked at us, he probably saw Mom and that just made him feel badly.

During my year in 6th grade, Dad knocked up Marie, a woman with three other kids, and decided to marry her. I suppose he loved her, though with Dad, it's always hard to tell what he's thinking. Suddenly, I had to switch schools, slept alone in a converted garage in Marie's house, and began having random nighttime visits from Jeremy, my 16-year-old step-brother.

Jeremy was a bastard. He threatened to kill Megan, who shared a bunk bed with our stepsister, if I ever told anyone about what he did to me. I hated him, but I hated myself even more because not only did I let him abuse me, but I also got excited about it. I never knew when Jeremy would show up, and I'd usually lie in bed praying that he would not come into the garage, but secretly hoping that he might. I felt guilty and ashamed.

By the end of 7th grade, I spent most weekends with friends drinking and binge eating. One of the girls taught me how to stick my finger down my throat to throw up, and by mid-8th grade I was binging and vomiting at least a couple of times every week. One thing about living in a home with six kids is that no one notices when food is missing. Who wouldn't want to eat as much as they could without gaining weight? Actually, though, if truth be told, I especially liked the way it felt when I threw up. I'd feel the pressure building inside of me, delaying the moment until I could wait no longer. What a rush! I'd see the half-digested food in the toilet, and for just that instant, I felt totally clean and pure. But soon after, I always felt worse, like I was crazy and would probably end up dead like my mother. That's why I didn't drink too often—only on weekends now and then—because I feared becoming an alcoholic like her.

Jeremy went away to college the same year I entered high school, and I did feel somewhat relieved to have him out of the house. Still, I would always lay in bed thinking about him and the horribly exciting things he did to me. I used to pinch myself real hard until the thoughts of him left and I could only think of the pain. That's when I would eventually fall asleep.

I took an art class that year, and we used matte knives to cut out frames for our drawings. I remember feeling powerful clasping the knife in my hand. I even joked with the other kids at my table, imitating a street gangster and saying, "Mess with me and I'll cut you up." We all laughed, but the knife seemed to fit me perfectly, and I stuck it in my book bag unseen. That first night, I played with it unconsciously while doing my homework. When I got in bed, I held it under the covers, and scratched at the insides of my thighs. I can't honestly say that I thought about Jeremy while I did that, but my heart raced and my mind was as numb as it gets when I'm binging.

I continued just scratching the surface for a few months or longer, up until Jeremy's Spring Break, when he came home for a week. I kept thinking that if he tried to screw me, I'd cut off his dick. As it happened, he avoided me all week long. He wouldn't even look at me. Then, on the Saturday night before he returned to college, he came into my room. It was way past midnight, and I was kind of out-of-it from drinking that night. While he was inside of me, I thought about reaching for the blade, which was hidden under the mattress, but I just couldn't bring myself to do it.

The next day was the first time I drew blood. I kept going over the same scratch again and again, berating myself for not stopping him the night before. Finally, I pushed down a little harder, and a thin red line appeared. It didn't hurt. The blood looked like it was ink from a red pen, and I disappeared into it. The cut was my punishment and my salvation, and cutting became an almost nightly ritual.

Some of the deeper wounds became scars, and I wore them with pride as if they were medals of valor. However, most of the time I barely cut the skin, usually just breaking the outer layer and bringing out only specks of blood. I took to wearing long sleeves to hide the markings on my arms, and I never wore shorts or bathing suits. Although a few of my friends were aware of my bulimia, no one knew about my cutting.

During particularly stressful times, I might spend two or three hours caught up in a session. At those times, I felt both peaceful and alive in a way that is hard to describe. It was as if no one and nothing else existed other than the shiny metal blade and my soft, pale flesh. If I could be that focused on my schoolwork, I would have been a straight-A student; but, of course, only while I cut did I maintain such a high level of concentration.

The next couple of years are a blur to me, now. I continued binging and vomiting, perhaps with even greater frequency; I also kept cutting, although with increasing severity, and sometimes would burn myself with candles. I'm not sure why, but Jeremy stopped abusing me. He had an apartment at school and pretty much quit coming home over vacations. He also had a few girlfriends, so I guess he was content with just doing it to them. I didn't exactly miss his stinking breath and coarse hands, but I did feel more and more invisible and alone. Megan seemed to fit into Dad's second family pretty easily, but I never belonged, and by the end of my senior year in high school, I doubted that I would live to see the age of 20.

I thought I could make a fresh start of my life by going away to college halfway across the country. I threw away my secret collection of knives and razor blades, and I entered the freshman dorm with great hope. However, before long, I had my head in the toilet and a new knife—one of those long camping knives that comes with a holster. I hadn't been cutting for more than a week or two when my roommate unexpectedly walked in on me while I thought she was in class. She opened the door, saw me pulling the edge across my forearm and screamed. I quickly put the knife under my pillow and pulled down my sleeve, but the cat was out of the bag.

That may have been the best thing that ever happened to me. My roommate contacted the residence assistant on our floor and they had a kind of intervention with me. I agreed to see the campus psychologist, and I've been in therapy ever since. I passed my 21st birthday with over a year and a half of sobriety. I've only binged a few times, but haven't for more than 3 months. I completely stopped cutting, and I know that I will never get that desperate again. I have learned new ways of coping with stress, and I'm starting to feel pretty good about myself at times. That's my story, and I hope it helps whoever reads it.

Acknowledgments

I am pleased to have this opportunity to acknowledge some of the sources that have contributed to the development of this book. There are so many people who have contributed to my professional development over the last 25 years that I could not even do them justice by listing them. But thank you. I am in debt to all those patients with whom I have been fortunate enough to interact over the years. They have certainly taught me much of what I know. I would like to thank my colleagues and friends at Alexian Brothers Behavioral Health Hospital for supporting my efforts to develop treatment programs for these patients. I want to specially acknowledge my relationship with Dr. Randy Sansone. He can write with the best of them. He has been a strong professional support, colleague, and friend. Thank you for the opportunity to work with you. Leigh Cohn is a special guy and has been the foundation of many of Randy's and my professional efforts over the last several years. I greatly appreciate the opportunities that you have provided and look forward to our continuing relationship. Finally, I want to thank my wife Janet and my children. Janet is my life-mate, and often the first editor of my writings. You are indeed special. And to my children Lance and Drew, thanks for keeping me on my toes. And to my "babies," Taylor and J.T., thanks for being my inspiration.

John L. Levitt

Participating in this project has rekindled my sincere appreciation of the many mentors and colleagues whom I have encountered on my academic journey. While there are too many to individually note, several merit public acknowledgment. First, I would like to thank Paul Rodenhauser, my first academic mentor, for his continuing friendship and ongoing encouragement and support of my research and writing endeavors. I would like to thank Mike W. Wiederman for his friendship, superb writing expertise, and imparting to me his unique philosophies about research. I would like to acknowledge Kettering Medical Center, a genuinely supportive academic environment that relentlessly prioritizes teaching, education, and research. I would also like to recognize both John Levitt and Leigh Cohn, two outstanding colleagues who have facilitated a true sense of mutuality in my work with them. Finally, I would like to thank my wife, Lori, who has played many roles in my academic life, including co-researcher, co-author, and co-presenter—*mi amor para siempre.*

Randy A. Sansone

Thanks to John and Randy for including me in this project. Their enthusiasm, expertise, and vision were matched by their hard work, superb writing, and thorough editing. I also acknowledge Rachel Ravitsky, the managing editor of *Eating Disorders: The Journal of Treatment and Prevention,* and the editorial board of that publication, in which portions of this book first appeared.

Leigh Cohn

Introduction

Over the last 20 years, the literature in the field of eating disorders has been expanding at a rapid rate. There are currently two significant professional journals, one empirically based newsletter, and a newsletter for family members and significant others of individuals with eating disorders. Yet, this is just a fraction of the material currently being published in the field. What has become increasingly clear is that patients with eating disorders represent a complex, heterogeneous group who require extensive study and understanding (Garner & Garfinkel, 1997).

Patients who present with eating disorder symptoms are extremely diverse. Imagine a group of patients who have become so alienated from their bodies that they purge food, aggressively diet or restrict, exercise compulsively, and/or regularly terrorize themselves with punitive messages about their appearance, worth, and value. Imagine, yet, that a significant number also intentionally attack and inflict injury to their bodies, sometimes permanently, by burning, cutting, or scratching themselves, or undertaking some other form of bodily harm. Imagine, subsequently, the relationship that any of these individuals has with their body self or psychological self, or the degree of isolation, lack of safety, unhappiness, or fear that they must experience. Clearly, any information that might help these patients live their lives without the intense drive to attack their bodies is important.

Initially, the subgroup of patients with eating disorder who self-injured generally went unrecognized in the eating disorder literature. When the intersection between self-injury and eating disorders was in fact discussed, self-injury (i.e., self-mutilation) was examined either in the context of one of many prognostic indicators (Garfinkel & Garner, 1982, p. 346) or as one of many behavioral characteristics encountered in a disordered personality, such as borderline personality disorder (Johnson & Connors, 1987). Similarly, the self-injury literature, rather than specifically exploring the subgroup of patients who presented with a current or past history of an eating disorder, primarily viewed the eating disorder symptoms as further manifestations of self-injury. Only recently has the actual relationship between self-injury and eating disorders been more prominently investigated (Levitt & Sansone, 2002).

In 2002 Levitt and Sansone, in conjunction with Leigh Cohn, edited a special issue of *Eating Disorders: The Journal of Treatment and Prevention.* This journal issue was entirely devoted to scholarly works that explored the relationship between self-injury and eating disorders. Several important concepts emerged from this special issue. First, the prevalence of self-injury among patients with eating disorders is quite significant (Sansone & Levitt, 2002). Second, few assessment tools currently exist that explore both self-injury and eating disorders, and their interaction (Sansone & Sansone, 2002). Third, patients with eating disorders, as a group, have an interesting and unique relationship with self-injury behaviors that requires considerable study and understanding (Favaro & Santonastaso, 2002; Wonderlich, Myers, Norton, & Crosby, 2002). Finally, specific treatment approaches for the eating disorder/self-injury population need to be developed (Claes, Vandereycken, & Vertommen, 2002).

This book is an effort toward the next step in exploring and treating patients with eating disorder who self-injure. As with any initial endeavor, it will hopefully open doors for further scientific inquiry and clinical exploration. We believe that those patients with eating disorder who self-injure represent a somewhat different group of patients from those who do not self-injure. This book is intended to stimulate the examination of this complex group of patients from various perspectives. For example, what makes this group unique and why do they so intensely use their bodies as a tool, a weapon, and an object? We want the reader to share an appreciation of the struggle facing the patient with eating disorder who has to deal with these symptoms every day, the researcher who is trying to understand these complicated patients, and the practitioner who is working to help reduce the fear and pain in their lives.

In order to achieve these goals, we have structured the book in the following manner. It is organized into four general areas. In the first area, Epidemiology, we broadly examine the intersection of eating disorder and self-injury as it is encountered in the general populations. In the second section, Psychodynamics, we discuss some of the relationships between eating disorders and self-injury in the context of psychological functioning. In the third section, Assessment, we present some of the current information on assessing this population, including the introduction of an assessment tool that may be useful for clinical practice.

In the fourth section, we focus on Treatment. It is no accident that the largest section in the book is on treatment. We believe that the ultimate impact of this effort should ideally be to treat patients suffering from self-injury and eating disorder symptoms, and to improve their ability to function without being dependent on these behaviors. In the preparation of this book, we recognized that the special issue of the *Journal* offered a number of articles that contained important information. In revised format, we have incorporated several of these articles (now chapters) throughout the book.

We attempt to capture the subject matter in a variety of ways. For example, we have included several examples of patient works throughout the book in the form of clinical vignettes or original writings. There are also several research studies that examine the components of self-injury in patients with eating disorders. There are articles describing clinical approaches to treatment written by both clinical researchers and practicing clinicians. The type of diversity found in this book mirrors the diversity currently found in the self-injury and eating disorder literature. We believe that this work reflects our current understanding of this group of individuals as well as the enormous questions and areas yet unexplored. The ultimate goal of this book is for us, the therapeutic community, to improve our understanding and treatment of this substantial group of patients with eating disorders.

John L. Levitt, Ph.D.

Randy Sansone, M.D.

Leigh Cohn, M.A.T.

References

Claes, L., Vandereycken, W., & Vertommen, H. (2002). Therapy-related assessment of self-harming behaviors in eating disordered patients: A case illustration. *Eating Disorders: The Journal of Treatment and Prevention, 10,* 269–279.

Favaro, A., & Santonastaso, P. (2002). The spectrum of self-injurious behavior in eating disorders. *Eating Disorders: The Journal of Treatment and Prevention, 10,* 215–225.

Garfinkel, P. E., & Garner, D. M. (1982). Anorexia nervosa: A multidimensional perspective. New York: Brunner/Mazel.

Garner, D. M., & Garfinkel, P. E. (Eds.) (1997). *Handbook of treatment for eating disorders* (2nd ed.). New York: Guilford Press.

Johnson, C., & Connors, M. E. (1987). *The etiology and treatment of bulimia nervosa: A biopsychosocial perspective.* New York: Basic Books.

Levitt, J. L., & Sansone, R. A. (2002). Searching for the answers: Eating disorders and self-harm. *Eating Disorders: The Journal of Treatment and Prevention, 10,* 189–191.

Sansone, R. A., & Levitt, J. L. (2002). Self-harm behaviors among those with eating disorders: An overview. *Eating Disorders: The Journal of Treatment and Prevention, 10,* 205–213.

Sansone, R. A., & Sansone, L. A. (2002). Assessment tools for self-harm behavior among those with eating disorders. *Eating Disorders: The Journal of Treatment and Prevention, 10,* 193–203.

Wonderlich, S., Myers, T., Norton, M., & Crosby, R. (2002). Self-harm and bulimia nervosa: A complex connection. *Eating Disorders: The Journal of Treatment and Prevention,10,* 257–267.

Epidemiology

CHAPTER 1

The Prevalence of Self-Harm Behavior among Those with Eating Disorders

RANDY A. SANSONE AND JOHN L. LEVITT

Introduction

In this chapter, we discuss the prevalence of self-harm behavior (SHB) among individuals with eating disorders. Using the Medline and Psy-INFO databases, we discovered that large epidemiological studies on the prevalence of SHB among those with eating disorders are not currently available. However, we summarize available data from existing studies, examining suicide attempts versus other forms of self-injury among the various diagnostic subgroups. We found that the prevalence of suicide attempts among outpatient bulimics is 22% ($N = 1308$), inpatient bulimics 39% ($N = 260$), alcoholic bulimics 54% ($N = 76$), and outpatient anorexics 11% ($N = 497$). The prevalence of self-injury among outpatient bulimics is 25% ($N = 574$), inpatient bulimics 25% ($N = 260$), and outpatient anorexics 22% ($N = 288$). We discuss the possible implications of these findings for clinical practice and future research.

SHB is known to occur among a subgroup of individuals with eating disorders. From a clinical perspective, SHB among those with eating disorders has been associated with early histories of abuse (Fullerton, Wonderlich, & Gosnell, 1995; van der Kolk, McFarlane, & Weisaeth, 1996), dissociation (Brown, Russell, Thornton, & Dunn, 1999), "multi-impulsivity" (Fichter, Quadflieg, & Rief, 1994), personality disorders (Yates, Sieleni, & Bowers, 1989) including borderline personality disorder (Sansone, Fine,

& Nunn, 1994; Schmidt & Telch, 1990), greater severity of psychiatric illness (Herzog, Keller, Lavori, Kenny, & Sacks, 1992; Newton, Freeman, & Munro, 1993), and more refractoriness to eating-disorder treatment (Nagata, Kawarada, Kiriike, & Iketani, 2000).

In the eating disorder literature, there are several available studies examining the prevalence of SHB among those with eating disorders. The majority focus on suicide attempts. Studies exploring other forms of self-injury are typically vague about the definition of such behavior. In addition, the explicit association between eating disorders and SHB is unclear. Likewise, the basic texts or "handbooks" on eating disorders (e.g., Garner & Garfinkel, 1997) are relatively silent about SHB. However, when SHB *is* discussed, it is primarily in the context of descriptive or prognostic indicators (e.g., Garner & Fairburn, 1988; Hsu, 1990; Johnson & Connors, 1987).

In contrast, in the literature on self-injury, there are several studies that describe the prevalence of comorbid eating disorders as well as provide more speculation on the association between eating disorders and self-harm/self-injury. Regarding comorbidity, for example, Favazza (1987) asserts that as many as 50% of self-mutilators have a history of anorexia or bulimia nervosa. Levenkron (1998) maintains that, in our society, the percentage of cutters and the percentage of individuals with anorexia nervosa is similar. Conterio and Lader (1998) found that 61% of self-injurers reported a current or past eating disorder, while Walsh and Rosen (1988) found that, compared with non-mutilators, self-mutilating teenagers were significantly more likely to have an eating disorder. As for the psychological relationship between self-injury and eating disorder symptoms, Conterio and Lader (1998), Miller (1994), and Favazza (1987) view eating disorder symptoms as self-injury equivalents.

In this chapter, we review the available comorbidity data for these two phenomena and summarize trends, given the interrelationship(s) between SHB and eating disorders. We collected studies for review by entering various search terms into two databases, Medline (back to 1966) and PsyINFO (back to 1967). Entered search terms for SHB were "suicide attempts, self-harm behavior, self-mutilation, self-destructive behavior." These search terms were cross-referenced with the eating disorder terms, "anorexia nervosa, bulimia nervosa, eating disorders." For each resulting article, we determined the number of subjects in the sample, treatment setting (e.g., inpatient, residential, outpatient setting), eating disorder diagnoses of subjects, type(s) of SHB examined, and prevalence of the designated SHB in the study population.

Before presenting findings, several caveats are worth noting. First, some relevant articles may not have been included due to the search parameters that we selected. As an example, we encountered one clinical overview article that presented the frequency of suicide attempts within a specific study population, but SHB was not emphasized in the title or abstract of the article.

Second, we excluded articles with less than 20 subjects or those printed in foreign languages (e.g., Italian, Hebrew). Third, when a single population was examined by investigators for two or more different SHBs (e.g., suicide attempts, self-mutilation), the authors and sample were listed twice or more in Table 1.1, as we wished to identify each SHB.

Fourth, most articles did not describe non-suicidal forms of SHB beyond, for example, "self-mutilation" or "self-injury." Therefore, for the majority of entries, we are unable to describe the specific behaviors such as cutting, burning, hitting oneself, and so forth, and their corresponding prevalence. Fifth, several investigators did not separate out SHB as a function of specific eating disorder diagnoses. Likewise, some did not specify the treatment setting. While these latter types of articles are included in Table 1.1, they could not be included in the summary of self-harm data by eating disorder diagnosis or treatment setting.

Sixth, several articles dichotomized an initial study population into specific clinical sub-samples to examine a particular feature (e.g., those with alcohol abuse versus those without, those with early-onset versus late-onset bulimia). This sub-sample approach may have excluded some subjects who were in the initial, broader sample. However, if the sub-samples were diagnostically defined by the type of eating disorder pathology, they were included in the data summary.

Finally, several articles and corresponding samples originated from the same authorship group, each with a different publication date. It was, thus, not possible for us to determine if each individual article represented a new and distinct group of subjects. For the preceding reasons, we conservatively describe the following summary of available information on SHB among those with eating disorders as an *overview*. A summary of the articles that we encountered on SHB among individuals with eating disorders, alphabetized by first author, is shown in Table 1.1.

Suicide Attempts in Bulimia Nervosa

In examining the prevalence of suicide attempts among individuals with bulimia nervosa, note that the largest number of studies in Table 1.1 relates to *outpatients*. These studies (Bulik, Sullivan, & Joyce, 1999; Favaro & Santonastaso, 1996; Favaro & Santonastaso, 1998; Fullerton, Wonderlich, &

TABLE 1.1 Studies of Self-Harm Behavior among Those with Eating Disorders*

First Author (Year)	N	Sample Characteristics	Eating Disorder Population	Self-Harm Behavior	Prevalence
Bulik (1997)	60	OP	BN, no ETOH	Suicide attempts	11 (18.3%)
Bulik (1997)	54	OP	BN, ETOH	Suicide attempts	26 (48.1%)
Bulik (1999)	152	OP	BN	Suicide attempts	47 (30.9%)
Bulik (1999)	70	OP	AN	Suicide attempts	19 (27.1%)
Demitrack (1990)	30	IP	AN, BN	Suicide attempts/ self-mutilation	14 (46.7%)
Favaro (1995)	259	OP	AN, BN, EDNOS	Suicide attempts	33 (12.7%)
Favaro (1996)	126	OP	BN, P	Suicide attempts	26 (20.6%)
Favaro (1998)	125	OP	BN, P & NP	Self-injury	27 (21.6%)
Favaro (1998)	125	OP	BN, P & NP	Suicide attempts	23 (18.4%)
Favaro (1998)	125	OP	BN, P & NP	Hair pulling	44 (35.2%)
Favaro (2000)	155	OP	AN-R	Suicide attempts	7 (5%)
Favaro (2000)	155	OP	AN-R	Cutting	20 (13%)
Favaro (2000)	155	OP	AN-R	Hair pulling	50 (32%)
Favaro (2000)	81	OP	AN-BP	Suicide attempts	8 (10%)
Favaro (2000)	81	OP	AN-BP	Cutting	22 (27%)
Favaro (2000)	81	OP	AN-BP	Hair pulling	36 (44%)
Fichter (1994)	196	IP	BN	Suicide attempts	78 (39.8%)
Fichter (1994)	196	IP	BN	Self-mutilation	47 (24.0%)
Fullerton (1995)	98	OP	AN	Suicide attempts	10 (10.2%)
Fullerton (1995)	243	OP	BN	Suicide attempts	70 (28.8%)
Fullerton (1995)	353	OP	ED, NOS	Suicide attempts	82 (23.2%)
Garfinkel (1980)	68	?	AN-BP	Suicide attempts	16 (23.5%)
Garfinkel (1980)	68	?	AN-BP	Self-mutilation	6 (8.8%)
Garfinkel (1980)	73	?	AN-R	Suicide attempts	5 (6.8%)
Garfinkel (1980)	73	?	AN-R	Self-mutilation	1 (1.4%)
Gleaves (1993)	535	Residential	AN, BN, EDNOS	Suicide attempts	110 (20.6%)
Gleaves (1993)	535	Residential	AN, BN, EDNOS	Self-injury	105 (19.6%)
Herzog (1992)	41	OP	AN	Suicide attempts	4 (9.8%)
Herzog (1992)	98	OP	BN	Suicide attempts	13 (13.3%)
Jacobs (1986)	40	OP	AN	Suicide attempts/ self-injury	14 (35.0%)
Lacey (1993)	112	OP	BN, NL WT	Overdosed	20 (17.9%)
Matsunaga (2000)	64	IP	BN	Suicide attempts	23 (35.9%)
Matsunaga (2000)	64	IP	BN	Self-harming	19 (29.7%)

TABLE 1.1 (Continued)

First Author (Year)	N	Sample Characteristics	Eating Disorder Population	Self-Harm Behavior	Prevalence
Mitchell (1986)	185	OP	BN	Self-injurious behavior	60 (32.4%)
Mitchell (1986)	185	OP	BN	Suicide attempts	32 (17.3%)
Mitchell (1987)	44	OP, early/late onset	BN	Suicide attempts	7 (15.9%)
Mitchell (1990)	25	OP	BN, OW	Suicide attempts	14 (56%)
Mitchell (1990)	25	OP	BN, OW	Self-injury	15 (60.0%)
Mitchell (1990)	25	OP	BN, NL WT	Suicide attempts	4 (16.0%)
Mitchell (1990)	25	OP	BN, NL WT	Self-injury	5 (20.0%)
Nagata (2000)	29	OP	AN-R	Suicide attempts	2 (6.9%)
Nagata (2000)	29	OP	AN-R	Self-mutilation	4 (13.8%)
Nagata (2000)	23	OP	AN-BP	Suicide attempts	7 (30.4%)
Nagata (2000)	23	OP	AN-BP	Self-mutilation	8 (34.8%)
Rossotto (1997)	71	BN + SA, BN-SA, OP	BN	Suicide attempts	16 (22.5%)
Schmidt (1990)	23	College students	BN	Suicide attempts	0 (0.0%)
Suzuki (1994)	22	IP/OP	BN, ETOH	Suicide attempts or wrist cutting	15 (68.2%)
Suzuki (1994)	22	IP/OP	BN, no ETOH	Suicide attempts or wrist cutting	7 (31.8%)
Welch (1996)	102	OP	BN	Overdose	20 (19.6%)
Welch (1996)	102	OP	BN	Cutting or burning	27 (26.5%)

*Studies with $N > 20$

Note: AN = anorexia nervosa; AN-B = anorexia nervosa, binge-eating/purging type; AN-R = anorexia nervosa, restricting type; BN = bulimia nervosa; EDNOS = eating disorder, not otherwise specified; IP = inpatient; OP = outpatient; ETOH = alcohol; NL WT = normal weight; OW = overweight; SA = substance abuse

Gosnell, 1995; Herzog et al., 1992; Lacey, 1993; Mitchell, Boutacoff, Hatsukami, Pyle, & Eckert, 1986; Mitchell, Hatsukami, Pyle, Eckert, & Soll, 1987; Mitchell, Pyle, Eckert, Hatsukami, & Soll, 1990; Rossotto, 1997; Welch & Fairburn, 1996) encompass a total of 1,308 outpatients diagnosed with bulimia nervosa. (The study by Schmidt & Telch [1990] was excluded from the preceding summary because participants were college students; our summary reflects clinical populations, only.) The prevalence of suicide attempts in this collective outpatient sample was 22% ($n = 292$).

With regard to suicide attempts among *inpatients* with bulimia nervosa, only two studies were available (Fichter et al., 1994; Matsunaga, Kiriike,

Iwasaki, et al., 2000). Among the 260 subjects studied, 101 (39%) reported suicide attempts. Note that compared with outpatient bulimics, the prevalence of suicide attempts among inpatient bulimics is substantially higher.

Suicide Attempts in Bulimia Nervosa and Comorbid Alcohol Abuse

Only two studies in the literature (Bulik, Sullivan, Carter, & Joyce, 1997; Suzuki, Higuchi,Yamada, Komiya, & Takagi, 1994) examine bulimic subjects with alcohol abuse. In one study, Bulik and colleagues (1997) exclusively examined outpatients, while in the second, Suzuki and colleagues (1994) examined both inpatients and outpatients. In combining the subjects from these two studies and treatment settings together, 54% of 76 alcoholic bulimics reported suicide attempts compared with 22% of 82 non-alcoholic bulimics. It is interesting to note that, in these two studies, the rate of suicide attempts among those without alcohol abuse (22%) is nearly identical to the rate we encountered for bulimic outpatients in general (i.e., 23%).

Self-Injury in Bulimia Nervosa

The majority of studies exploring self-injury among bulimic individuals did not identify specific behaviors such as cutting oneself, burning oneself, etc. Among *outpatient* populations (Favaro & Santonastaso, 1998; Lacey, 1993; Mitchell et al., 1986; Mitchell et al., 1990; Welch & Fairburn, 1996), 25% of 574 individuals with bulimia nervosa reported self-injury. Among studies of *inpatients* with bulimia nervosa (Fichter et al., 1994; Matsunaga et al., 2000), 25% of 260 individuals reported self-injurious behavior. Note that the prevalence of self-injury in both populations is identical.

Suicide Attempts in Anorexia Nervosa

Several studies have examined the prevalence of suicide attempts among *outpatients* with anorexia nervosa (Bulik et al., 1999; Favaro & Santonastaso, 2000; Fullerton et al., 1995; Herzog et al., 1992; Nagata et al., 2000). Among a total of 497 subjects, 11.3% reported such attempts. Two studies differentiated the diagnostic subtype of anorexia nervosa (Favaro & Santonastaso, 2000; Nagata et al., 2000). Surprisingly, we were unable to locate any studies of suicide attempts among inpatients with anorexia nervosa.

Self-Injury in Anorexia Nervosa

We found two articles describing self-injury (i.e., cutting, self-mutilation) in anorexia nervosa (Favaro & Santonastaso, 2000; Nagata et al., 2000). Among 288 outpatients, 22.2% reported such behavior.

Discussion

Among those suffering from bulimia nervosa, the prevalence of suicide attempts varies from a low of 22% among outpatients, to 39% among inpatients, to 54% among those with comorbid alcohol abuse. One conclusion from these findings is that the treatment setting, to some degree, is predictive of the prevalence of suicide attempts, with inpatient populations demonstrating a much higher prevalence of such behavior than outpatient populations. Consequently, clinicians practicing in inpatient and partial hospital programs need to be especially alert to the issues of hopelessness and suicide. In addition to direct clinical inquiry, two assessment measures may be helpful—the Beck Depression Inventory (BDI; Beck, 1967) and the Beck Hopelessness Scale (BHS; Beck, Weissman, Lester, & Trexler, 1974). These instruments, and others similar to them, may be useful for initial assessment as well as ongoing evaluation.

Our findings also indicate that comorbid alcohol abuse appears to meaningfully heighten the risk of suicide attempts among bulimic individuals. We found a similar relationship among a mixed cohort of eating-disordered women (Sansone, Fine, & Nunn, 1994). In this study, we explored three study cells of women—those with an eating disorder only, substance abuse only, and both eating disorder and substance abuse. Using the Self-Harm Inventory (SHI; Sansone, Wiederman, & Sansone, 1998), a 22-item measure of self-harm, we determined that the prevalence of SHB was substantially higher for the comorbid group with both an eating disorder and substance abuse. Specifically, the mean number of reported SHBs for the eating disorder–only group was 9.45, for the substance abuse–only group 9.24, and for the comorbid group 15.88. In this same study, we also examined the prevalence of borderline personality using the Diagnostic Interview for Borderlines (Kolb & Gunderson, 1980). The prevalence of borderline personality among the eating disorder–only group was 36%, the substance abuse–only group 36%, and the comorbid group 94%. These data suggest that, among those with bulimia nervosa, character pathology may be a substantial contributory variable to SHB as well as a heightened risk of suicide attempts. Because of these findings, practitioners need to be particularly alert to SHB among bulimics who also use substances. We recommend the use of the SHI, along with several other easy-to-repeat assessment measures, such as the BDI and BHS, for ongoing evaluation of these populations.

The current review indicates that the frequency of suicide attempts among outpatients with anorexia nervosa is 11%. This percent is considerably lower than the prevalence found in both outpatient and inpatient populations of those with bulimia nervosa. The associated types of character pathology reported for these diagnostic groups might, in part, explain this. In this regard, among those with anorexia nervosa, particularly the restricting type, there appears to be a high prevalence of Cluster C personality disorders (Dennis & Sansone, 1997). The fearful, anxious, and inhibited nature of this cluster of personality disorders may be protective against overt SHB. In contrast, among those with bulimia nervosa or the binge-eating/purging type of anorexia nervosa, there appears to be a high prevalence of Cluster B personality disorders (Dennis & Sansone, 1997), which are highlighted by impulsivity. Among the Cluster B disorders, borderline personality may be the most frequent disorder (Dennis & Sansone, 1997); this is the only personality disorder in *DSM-IV* (American Psychiatric Association, 1994) that has a criterion for suicide attempts. As a caveat, while the rate of suicide attempts in anorexia nervosa is substantially lower, clinicians should remain alert to the fact that it is still relatively high and, like bulimic populations, should be evaluated in an ongoing fashion throughout treatment.

We wish to emphasize that the presence of personality disorder is likely to be but one of several contributory factors to SHB among individuals with eating disorders. Early histories of abuse and the presence of dissociative defenses, as well as highly chaotic family environments, lack of sufficient parental support, extensive psychosocial stressors, genetic predisposition, and severe mood disorders on Axis I, may also confer significant risk.

According to our review, the self-injury rate among those with bulimia nervosa (both inpatients and outpatients) appears to be around 25%. Realistically, it is somewhat risky to compare this prevalence among those with anorexia nervosa, as there are no available inpatient samples and only two outpatient samples. Whether these two disorders will demonstrate a similar prevalence of SHB, or whether personality and other variables will be protective in anorexia nervosa, remains unknown.

Our findings are subject to a number of potential limitations, many of which we noted earlier. We wish to emphasize: (1) the relatively small numbers of studies and subjects in this area; (2) the probable lack of disclosure of suicide attempts and/or self-injury by some participants due to embarrassment or fears of stigmatization; and (3) the vague definitions of self-injury in many studies (e.g., scratching oneself versus cutting oneself versus lacerating oneself to the point of requiring stitches). In addition, comparisons of SHB among eating-disorder diagnostic groupings were compromised by largely unequal samples. Finally, the role of culture must be factored into these summaries. Several studies were non-U.S. samples (e.g., Italy, Japan, Germany), and whether certain types of SHB emerge in all cultures (e.g., cutting behavior in the United States versus India) is unknown.

Clearly, future studies need to explore among eating disorder populations the prevalence of SHB in more detail as well as the role and function of this behavior. From the present data, it is apparent that researchers must factor in the eating-disorder diagnostic subtypes. In addition, studies need to *simultaneously* explore possible contributory variables (e.g., abuse histories, personality pathology, dissociative tendencies, perceived parental support, family environment stability, psychosocial stressors, Axis I disorders such as depression) to SHB, use broader measures of SHB, assess lifelong physical damage caused by self-harm, and determine the social cost of such behavior (e.g., lost days of work), if any. Likewise, cross-cultural studies are needed in this area, particularly to determine whether culture influences the specific manifestation of SHB within a given racial, ethnic, religious, or geographic group. Undoubtedly, SHB is a very complex psychological issue among patients with eating disorders. Sadly, it appears to be prevalent to a substantial degree in most clinical populations of such patients.

References

American Psychiatric Association. (1994). *Diagnostic and statistical manual of mental disorders* (4th ed.). Washington, DC: Author.

Beck, A. T. (1967). *Depression: Causes and treatment.* Philadelphia, PA: University of Pennsylvania Press.

Beck, A. T., Weissman, A., Lester, D., & Trexler, L. (1974). The measurement of pessimism: The Hopelessness Scale. *Journal of Consulting and Clinical Psychology, 42,* 861–865.

Brown, L., Russell, J., Thornton, C., & Dunn, S. (1999). Dissociation, abuse and the eating disorders: Evidence from an Australian population. *Australian and New Zealand Journal of Psychiatry, 33,* 521–528.

Bulik, C. M., Sullivan, P. F., Carter, F. A., & Joyce, P. R. (1997). Lifetime comorbidity of alcohol dependence in women with bulimia nervosa. *Addictive Behaviors, 22,* 437–446.

Bulik, C. M., Sullivan, P. F., & Joyce, P. R. (1999). Temperament, character and suicide attempts in anorexia nervosa, bulimia nervosa and major depression. *Acta Psychiatrica Scandinavica, 100,* 27–32.

Conterio, K., & Lader, W. (1998). *Bodily harm: The breakthrough treatment program for self-injurers.* New York: Hyperion.

Demitrack, M. A., Putnam, F. W., Brewerton, T. D., Brandt, H. A., & Gold, P. W. (1990). Relation of clinical variables to dissociative phenomena in eating disorders. *American Journal of Psychiatry, 147,* 1184–1188.

Dennis, A. B., & Sansone, R. A. (1997). Treatment of patients with personality disorders. In D. M. Garner & P. E. Garfinkel (Eds.), *Handbook of treatment for eating disorders* (2nd ed.) (pp. 437–449). New York: Guilford.

Favaro, A., Magnavita, N., & Santonastaso, P. (1995). Suicide attempts by outpatients with eating disorders. *Rivista di Psichiatria, 30,* 47–51.

Favaro, A., & Santonastaso, P. (1996). Purging behaviors, suicide attempts, and psychiatric symptoms in 398 eating disordered subjects. *International Journal of Eating Disorders, 20,* 99–103.

Favaro, A., & Santonastaso, P. (1998). Impulsive and compulsive self-injurious behavior in bulimia nervosa: Prevalence and psychological correlates. *Journal of Nervous and Mental Disease, 186,* 157–165.

Favaro, A., & Santonastaso, P. (2000). Self-injurious behavior in anorexia nervosa. *Journal of Nervous and Mental Disease, 188,* 537–542.

Favazza, A. R. (1987). *Bodies under siege: Self-mutilation in culture and psychiatry.* Baltimore: Johns Hopkins University Press.

Fichter, M. M., Quadflieg, N., & Rief, W. (1994). Course of multi-impulsive bulimia. *Psychological Medicine, 24,* 591–604.

Fullerton, D. T., Wonderlich, S. A., & Gosnell, B. A. (1995). Clinical characteristics of eating disorder patients who report sexual or physical abuse. *International Journal of Eating Disorders, 17,* 243–249.

Garfinkel, P. E., Moldofsky, M. D., & Garner, D. M. (1980). The heterogeneity of anorexia nervosa. *Archives of General Psychiatry, 37,* 1036–1040.

Garner, D. M. & Fairburn, C. G. (1988). Relationship between anorexia nervosa and bulimia nervosa: Diagnostic implications. In D. M. Garner & P. E. Garfinkel (Eds.), *Diagnostic issues in anorexia nervosa and bulimia nervosa* (pp. 56–79). New York: Brunner/Mazel.

Garner, D. M., & Garfinkel, P. E. (Eds.) (1997). *Handbook of treatment for eating disorders* (2nd ed.). New York: Guilford Press.

Gleaves, D. H., & Eberenz, K. P. (1993). Eating disorders and additional psychopathology in women: The role of prior sexual abuse. *Journal of Child Sexual Abuse, 2,* 71–81.

Herzog, D. B., Keller, M. B., Lavori, P. W., Kenny, G. M., & Sacks, N. R. (1992). The prevalence of personality disorders in 210 women with eating disorders. *Journal of Clinical Psychiatry, 53,* 147–152.

Hsu, L. K. G. (1990). *Eating disorders.* New York: Guilford Press.

Jacobs, B. W., & Isaacs, S. (1986). Pre-pubertal anorexia nervosa: A retrospective controlled study. *Journal of Child Psychology and Psychiatry, and Allied Disciplines, 27,* 237–250.

Johnson, C., & Connors, M. E. (1987). *The etiology and treatment of bulimia nervosa: A biopsychosocial perspective.* New York: Basic Books.

Kolb, J. E., & Gunderson, J. G. (1980). Diagnosing borderline patients with a semi-structured interview. *Archives of General Psychiatry, 37,* 37–41.

Lacey, J. H. (1993). Self-damaging and addictive behaviour in bulimia nervosa: A catchment area study. *British Journal of Psychiatry, 163,* 190–194.

Levenkron, S. (1998). *Cutting: Understanding and overcoming self-mutilation.* New York: W. W. Norton.

Matsunaga, H., Kiriike, N., Iwasaki, Y., Miyata, A., Matsui, T., Hagata, T., Yamagami, S., & Kaye, W. H. (2000). Multi-impulsivity among bulimic patients in Japan. *International Journal of Eating Disorders, 27,* 348–352.

Miller, D. (1994). *Women who hurt themselves.* New York: Basic Books.

Mitchell, J. E., Boutacoff, L. I., Hatsukami, D., Pyle, R. L., & Eckert, E. (1986). Laxative abuse as a variant of bulimia. *Journal of Nervous and Mental Disease, 174,* 174–176.

Mitchell, J. E., Hatsukami, D., Pyle, R. L., Eckert, E. D., & Soll, E. (1987). Late onset bulimia. *Comprehensive Psychiatry, 28,* 323–328.

Mitchell, J. E., Pyle, R. L., Eckert, E. D., Hatsukami, D., & Soll, E. (1990). Bulimia nervosa in overweight individuals. *Journal of Nervous and Mental Disease, 178,* 324–327.

Nagata, T., Kawarada, Y., Kiriike, N., & Iketani, T. (2000). Multi-impulsivity of Japanese patients with eating disorders: Primary and secondary impulsivity. *Psychiatry Research, 94,* 239–250.

Newton, J. R., Freeman, C. P., & Munro, J. (1993). Impulsivity and dyscontrol in bulimia nervosa: Is impulsivity an independent phenomenon or a marker of severity? *Acta Psychiatrica Scandinavica, 87,* 389–394.

Rossotto, E. (1997). Bulimia nervosa with and without substance use disorders: A comparative study. *Dissertation Abstracts International: Section B, 58,* 4469.

Sansone, R. A., Fine, M. A., & Nunn, J. L. (1994). A comparison of borderline personality symptomatology and self-destructive behavior in women with eating, substance abuse, and both eating and substance abuse disorders. *Journal of Personality Disorders, 8,* 219–228.

Sansone, R. A., Wiederman, M. W., & Sansone, L. A. (1998). The Self-Harm Inventory (SHI): Development of a scale for identifying self-destructive behaviors and borderline personality disorder. *Journal of Clinical Psychology, 54,* 973–983.

Schmidt, N. B., & Telch, M. J. (1990). Prevalence of personality disorders among bulimics, nonbulimic binge eaters, and normal controls. *Journal of Psychopathology and Behavioral Assessment, 12,* 169–185.

Suzuki, K., Higuchi, S., Yamada, K., Komiya, H., & Takagi, S. (1994). Bulimia nervosa with and without alcoholism: A comparative study in Japan. *International Journal of Eating Disorders, 16*, 137–146.

van der Kolk, B. A., McFarlane, A. C., & Weisaeth, L. (Eds.) (1996). *Traumatic stress: The effects of overwhelming experience on mind, body, and society.* New York: Guilford Press.

Yates, W. R., Sieleni, B., & Bowers, W. A. (1989). Clinical correlates of personality disorder in bulimia nervosa. *International Journal of Eating Disorders, 8*, 473–477.

Walsh, B. W., & Rosen, P. M. (1988). *Self-mutilation: Theory, research & treatment.* New York: Guilford Press.

Welch, S. L., & Fairburn, C. G. (1996). Impulsivity or comorbidity in bulimia nervosa. A controlled study of deliberate self-harm and alcohol and drug misuse in a community sample. *British Journal of Psychiatry, 169*, 451–458.

CHAPTER 2

Dying to Live: Eating Disorders and Self-Harm Behavior in a Cultural Context

MERVAT NASSER

If people get sick
Of living in
The same old place,
Why not of living
In the same old skin?

"I'm a runaway" by Fernando Pessoa
In: Honig & Brown, 1998

And I, stepping from this skin
Of old bandages, boredoms, old faces
Step to you from the black car of lethe
Pure as a baby

Sylvia Plath, 1981

Suffering for a Purpose: Body Rites and Body Art

For various cultural purposes, damage to one's body, by others or by one-self, has been a longstanding theme in human history. The explanations have been diverse, while the theme has been a seeming constant—even in the mythical literature.

Dismemberment: The Myth of Osiris

The story of Osiris is central to ancient Egyptian mythology. It is a story written in graphic body language of death fighting to overcome death. In an address to Ra in *The Book Of The Dead*, Osiris says, "What is this I am bound for? No water there, no breath, twice deep, twice dark, twice vacant. There one lives by the piece of the heart." Ra replies, "I have given you divinity in place of water and air." Osiris, the son of Ra, is a god who undergoes a mythical dismemberment of his body (prior to his resurrection) to convey, metaphorically, the psychological dismemberment that constitutes (as they threaten) the construction of the subjective human consciousness (Hare, 1999).

Body Flaying

Historically, flaying entails a number of contradictory messages that bridge the gap between art, philosophy, and medicine. In examining the symbolism of the skin as a cultural border between self and the world, Benthian (2002) discusses body flaying as follows. Through the inflicted violence, the body transcends its cutaneous boundary in an attempt to depict more than a naked body. As a form of torture, flaying represents the most extreme inscription of power. In the culture of medicine, body dissection was an accepted practice to produce knowledge. Flaying a person alive was an archaic sacrificial ritual among pre-Columbian Mexican cultures and was also common among the Scythians, Persians, and Assyrians. In the European visual arts, the theme of flaying an individual was taken from both classical and Christian sources. Examples include the punitive flaying of Marsyas, the satyr who challenged Apollo to a musical contest and lost, as well as the flaying of Bartholomew (thus elevating him to martyrdom), which was punishment for converting Polimius (the brother of the Armenian king Astyagus) to Christianity (Benthien, 2002).

Flagellation

Flagellation has longstanding roots in history. Oddly, this behavior is still practiced today. Through flagellation, the re-enactment of martyrdom is still experienced among Shia Muslims on the day of remembrance of the martyrdom of El Hussein. El Hussein, the son of the apostle Ali, was denied the right to rule after Mohamed's death. He was killed in a famous battle in Karballa'a (Iraq) and his corpse was beheaded. Like the head of St. John the Baptist for Christians, the head of El Hussein symbolizes for Muslims both justice and truth. In the festival of El Hussein's remembrance, devout Shia Muslims inflict on their bodies the most horrendous forms of pain, including the ritual of "tatbir," which consists of striking the head with a sword as well as other forms of self-abuse, including body beating, flagellation with knives, whipping, and blood letting. All is done to relive El Hussein's agony and to transcend the body to the ultimate goals of the soul.

In addition to its cultural underpinnings, the observance of symbolic flagellation by some Shia Muslims living in Britain today is interpreted as a way of reaffirming their own identity in the face of a continued sense of oppression (Addley, 2003). In confusing times, these rituals, albeit apparently cruel, carry referential memories of bygone stability and give newly invented identities a false tribal/ethnic authenticity (Nasser & DiNicola, 2001).

Other Forms of Culturally Related Mutilation

In the present-day United Kingdom, minority groups practice other traditional ethnic rituals. For example, some African immigrants living in Britain insist on performing tribal initiation rituals such as the mutilation of female genitals (i.e., clitoridectomy). This practice is explained as a reaction to the deadlocks of contemporary society, an answer to a sense of disillusionment and disbelief. In performing these rituals, the body is trying to find within itself a place of anchorage to hold on to and to maintain a sense of a stable identity (Salecl, 2001).

Some Hindus perform an extreme yogic tradition called Sadhus in which the body is subjected to strict discipline through pain tolerance by lying on beds of thorns, hanging upside down by the legs all day, or piercing holes into the body. Another ritual, called *kavandi-bearing*, is not performed by Sadhu professional holy men but by ordinary people in India. Usually done during a festival held in February that carries the name of "trials by the spears of Shiva," a framework is placed around the body and locked on, and sharp rods with points are stuck into the skin, which probe deeper into the skin with movement (Vale, 1989, pp. 6–24). Many of these practices embrace body suffering as a way of transcending the flesh and elevating the soul.

Ascetic Starvation

Ascetic starvation, or starving for spiritual or cultural principles, may be perceived as a form of body negation—a voluntary act that deliberately denies the body its basic need for nourishment. The objective is to liberate the soul from the somatic and material preoccupations of the body in the hope that it will finally reach spiritual purity. "Make a supreme effort to root out that self-love from your heart and to plant in its place this holy self hatred. This is the royal road by which we turn our back on mediocrity, and which leads us without fail to the summit of perfection." (Raymond of Capua, 1330–1399, translated by Kearns & Glazier, 1980). Medieval sainthood and ascetic self-starvation, occasionally described as the so-called "holy anorexics," have recently become central to the discourse on the history of the evolution of the modern anorexic phenomenon (Bell, 1985).

Bodyworks and Body Performance Art: The Modern Primitive

In line with the modern phenomenon of anorexic self-starvation, body-works and body performance art took center stage by the early 1970s. In this art form, the body is subjected to certain techniques, some of which are very brutal. A well-known example of this is Orlan's "bloody meta-morphosis." Orlan is a contemporary French artist who voluntarily under-goes continual surgery to shape her face to the ideal of beauty found in classic Renaissance painting (e.g., Botticelli's Venus or Leonardo's Mona Lisa). Orlan describes her work as multiple identities inscribed by the surgeon's knife into the flesh (Benthien, 2002; Salecl, 2001).

In a recent art exhibition held at Selfridges, London, under the name of Body Craze, observers could see suspension performances of men swing-ing through the air hanging by their nipples and artists swimming through broken glasses. Attendees could also get measured for ultra-fitting jeans, up to the millimeter, in a scanner! This exhibition is based on the concept of "modern primitives," which is currently so much in vogue. The concept deals with the growing revival of highly visual and sometimes shocking primitive body modification practices. The phenomenon is attributed to a universal feeling of being dislocated in a multicultural world that preaches diversity but continues to behave according to a monocultural ethos. It is a reflection of the powerlessness to change the world, pushing individuals to change, instead, what they have power over—their own bodies.

Vale (1989) researched the phenomenon of the "modern primitives." From that work, the following quotes obtained from conversations held with artists who use the human body as the canvas for their own artistic expression are presented to illustrate the psychological matrix of this form of art.

> I wanted work that was inspired by traditional tribal designs, but contemporary too. An abstract in the sense that it was not rigidly symbolic of any religious or cultural references. (Jane Handel, pp. 77)

A tattoo is an affirmation that this body is yours to have and enjoy while you are here. Nobody else can control what you do with it; that is why tattooing is such a big thing in prison, it is an expression of freedom. (Don ED Hardy, pp. 53)

Obviously, the number one problem today is identity. If you don't have an identity, you try to re-create your life in such a way that you think you have some. How do you do that? Tattoo some weird design on your stomach. (Monte Canasta, pp. 129)

The act of doing piercing and surrendering to the experience is a transcendental spiritual activity; you can learn to separate your consciousness from your body. That makes it possible for you to push a needle through. You don't feel the pain; the body is the one that feels the pain. (Fakir Musafar, pp. 10)

Contemporary cosmetic surgery surpasses any primitive society in the scope and persistence of bodily correction: from the puberty rite of orthodontia, to adult hair implants and silicone breast enlargements, from nose jobs and liposuction to the last, final face-lift. (Wes Christensen, pp. 89)

These quotes highlight a sense of "self-transformation" experienced by those who undergo such practices. In the last quote, there is an emphasis on the "plasticity" of the body throughout the ages. In playing with new forms of "tribalism," body artists are trying to challenge the idea of a stable identity and to affirm a kind of new identity grounded in the body. In other words, the body becomes the site where all identities are written.

It Is My Body and I Do What I Want To—The Clinical Context

The preceding historical, cultural, religious, and artistic rituals involve purposeful aspects of self-injury or self-harm. In psychiatric terminology, the act of deliberate self-harm invites a multitude of clinical expressions including deliberate self–injury, self-inflicted violence, self attack, self-cutting, deliberate nonfatal acts, symbolic wounding, and parasuicide. The possibility of death inherent in all of these forms of self-harm makes them appear to us as "*failures to achieve death.*" However, in clinical practice we realize only too well that the act of self-harm is not meant as an attempt to achieve death, but rather an attempt to draw attention to one's plight or to scream for help. Paradoxically, this means that the act is not *the pursuit of death, but a defiance of it*. In other words, it is "hanging on by the skin of one's teeth," which echoes Parveen Adams's own words that the "*cut/wound is just a boundary between life and death*" (Adams, 1998, p. 63).

Self-damage, to save oneself or to adapt, suggests that any cut or wound in the skin can serve contradictory functions; some of them may even restore life, as is the case when medicine enters the body through a wound for healing purposes. Body wounding for medicinal purposes was a historically accepted form of treatment. During the nineteenth century, for instance, an invention called the "life awakener," a club studded with needles, was meant to puncture the body to rid it of its poisons (Benthien, 2002). And yet, the cut can also be the site where death is realized in an accident or an act of self-harm (Takemoto, 2001).

This contradiction also emerges in the relationship between self-harm and eating pathology. Self-mutilation, like self-starvation, is said to be a plea for recognition (Hewitt, 1997). Fasting is, in a way, a form of body deprivation that is meant to exercise control over the need for food; which in due course may lead to physical harm or even death. The clinical literature is full of cases of self-starvation associated with a variety of "adaptive" self-harming behaviors that border on self-torture. For example, a recent case report describes an individual with anorexia nervosa who was in the habit of using cold baths and blood-letting as means of controlling her mental anguish in the same way that self-starvation did (Morgan & Lacey, 2000). Indeed, the notion of multi-impulsive bulimia nervosa was advanced to highlight a subgroup of eating-disorder sufferers who engage in additional self-damaging behaviors, such as self-cutting, overdosing, or substance misuse (Lacey & Evans, 1986).

The voice of self-cut skin is also said to be a very specific language for indicating childhood trauma, especially childhood sexual abuse, where the act of testifying involves knives, razor blades, or broken glass, secretively and ritualistically, to cut the skin (Kilby, 2001 & McLane, 1996). Indeed, childhood adversity and sexual abuse have strong links with eating disorders to the extent that some perceive an eating disorder as prima facie evidence of prior sexual abuse. Notwithstanding this extreme notion, there is still a substantial body of empirical work that demonstrates an association between childhood abuse and disordered eating (Palmer et al., 1990; Schmidt, Humfress, & Treasure, 1997). In these situations, self-harm functions as a language that articulates past trauma by repeating it, in the present, as pain. This is illustrated in a self-harmer's own description of their act. "When I could not find the words to describe it, cutting had become the language to describe the pain, communicating everything I felt" (Pembroke, 1994, p. 35).

Sadomasochism appears to psychologically underpin all forms of self-harm. This dynamic is bravely dealt with in the controversial movie *The Piano Teacher*. The movie, which won the top award at the Cannes film festival in 2001, is based on a novel by the Austrian writer Elfriede and is brought to life by the German playwright Michael Haneke. *The Piano Teacher* is described as a dance of "self-annihilation" that addresses the deepest and most disturbing of human feelings. The heroine is Professor Erika Kohut, who gives piano lessons to advanced students at the Vienna Conservatory. Since childhood, Erika was expected to give up everything for the sake of music. She obsessively follows this arduous path to achieve ultimate control and perfection. She is, however, a character that one feels has just come out of the clinical psychiatric literature. She is a secret pornography addict and self-mutilator who resides in an apartment with her hysterically possessive mother (Denby, 2002).

In one of the movie's most difficult scenes, Erika sits on the edge of the tub at home and cuts her genitalia with a razor. It is a kind of self-purifying ritual that is done with extreme emotional detachment and absolute disregard to the physical pain she inflicts on herself. Yet, she hurries to respond to her mother's shouted request to come to the dinner table, while the blood is still dripping between her thighs!

The Dialectic of Body/Voice in Minority Groups

Eating disorders have been largely considered unique to Western culture. However, cross-cultural research has recently challenged this notion, indicating that eating disorders are emerging in societies, races, and cultures that were, for a long time, presumed immune to this pathology (Nasser, 1997; Nasser et al., 2001). Eating disorders and their association with self-harm behavior and substance misuse have just begun to receive comparable attention from some researchers concerned with the role played by "culture" in the whole phenomenon.

In a study of self-harm behavior conducted on both Black and White patients with either binge eating disorder or bulimia nervosa, Dohn and colleagues (2002) found elevated rates of symptoms to be more connected to a history of abuse or childhood trauma regardless of the patient's diagnostic status or ethnicity.

Hunter and Harvey (2002) compared rates of self-harm behavior among indigenous populations in Australia, New Zealand, Canada, and the United Sates. They concluded that the vulnerability of the young populations to self-harm behavior was attributed to the impact of cultural breakdown. This demonstrates how young people are influenced by the cultural changes and the circumstances that surround them. In line with these findings, Native American youth in Alaska were shown to have a higher vulnerability to life-threatening behaviors than their White counterparts (Frank & Lester, 2002).

Hospital-based analyses of admissions data, as well as surveys carried out in school settings, suggest that young Asian women born in the United Kingdom are at a higher risk for attempted suicide and self-harm behavior as compared with White and African-Caribbean young women (Merrill & Owens, 1986, 1988; Mumford & Whitehouse, 1988). The results of these studies have been explained as a by-product of acculturation into Western cultures (Burke, 1976; Hodes, 1990; Merrill & Owens, 1988). "Culture clash" explanations have also been applied to cultural and religious customs that place high demands on young Asian women living in the United Kingdom (Soni-Raleigh & Balarajan, 1992). In a more recent study, the higher rates of deliberate self-harm among young Asian women in Britain have been seen as an expression of disconnection and reaction to the sense of cultural alienation felt by this particular group (Bhugra, 2002).

In a qualitative analysis of interviews conducted on young Asian women with self-harm behavior in East London, a Bengali Muslim woman described her self-harm behavior within a context of a distressful and emotionally painful situations; cutting was perceived as a way of communicating and releasing this distress.

> When I start cutting myself… all my anger gets channelled into the cut and I look at the blood and I think it's a release. From emotional pain to physical, and the physical is at least over and done with. The emotional is so hard to deal with. (as cited in Marshall & Yazdani, 2000)

The description of self-harm behavior in this case applies to the patient's smaller culture in which she lives and negotiates, but could also apply to the prevailing culture at large. In this regard, eating disorders may be seen as extreme forms of behavior that are symptomatic of an underlying culturally universal human distress. The distress is caused by the loss of the relationship of oneself to others and is in reaction to a sense of confusion, disorganization, and disharmony felt by those who need to be on the inside of the system and, yet, are always outside it. This sense of rejection, or "not fitting in," is common to ethnic minority groups, who turn to their bodies not only to voice distress but also to negotiate this distress through body language (Nasser, 1997). In the same vein, Katzman and Lee (1997) suggest disconnection as an underlying problem in eating disorders and proposed it, along with transition and oppression, as a new model for thinking about the relationship between culture and eating disorders.

Self-cutting behaviors in young populations have similar sociocultural dynamics to eating disorders and therefore invite similar cultural interpretations (DiNicola & Epstein, 1998). DiNicola suggests that people who cut themselves

> do it as an outlet for interpersonal conflict and a mental anguish. It is a mental dissociation and the body speaking its mind. And while it is easily mistaken for suicide, the sufferers often make a plea for living on their own terms. In other words, as in eating disorders, we see people crossing frontiers and borders and we can read their bodies like passports, being imprints of their travels and travails. (Nasser & DiNicola, 2001, p.183)

"Fatal Identities"

In a translated book entitled *Fatal Identities*, Amin Maalouf (1999) examines the impossibility of postmodern humanity to live in its own skin. His analysis applies more to the immigrant predicament, although he quite rightly sees that the psychological fate is no longer exclusive to the smaller communities of minority groups living in predominantly White European or North American societies. According to Maalouf (1999), minority groups tend to be defined through a monochromatic lens; although in reality they live in societies that are described as multicultural. The same monochromatic lens continues to be operational within the immigrant-inherited cultural setting as defined by family values, religion, and concepts of geographic nationalities. This impossible position of not being able to "fit" into one camp or the other, combined with the denied right to integrate elements of either camp and create a "new self," forces minority groups to resort to extreme and often dangerous positions in an attempt to redefine themselves. This ultimately creates what I refer to in *Culture and Weight Consciousness* as "subcultures of extremism." Some of these extreme stances will involve the "body" and include attempts to mutilate the skin—the very symbol that condemned the person in the first instance to the fate of marginalization and non-acceptance.

> I wanted to be beautiful when I was 16, when I was deeply insecure about the way I looked in a homogenized race. I wanted to fit in. Being half Egyptian and half Japanese made me feel an outsider whatever I do. I wanted to look fragile and controlled like a Japanese beauty. There is a Japanese saying that is "the life of a flower is beautiful. Short lived and painful." So, I decided to fast every day, I had a strong desire to disappear. I measured the thickness of my legs when standing naked in front of a mirror. I squeezed my legs together, and measured the thickness not by looking at my actual legs but by looking at the negative space in between my legs. No matter how big the hollow space in between, it was simply not

enough. (Note: this is from a patient of mine who is an Egyptian/ Japanese Muslim patient, who resides in the United Kingdom and who sees herself as a Zen Buddhist; the description is of her anorexic experience.)

This patient's wish to become "invisible" (i.e., to no longer live in the lived-in body) represents her wish to "disappear without dying." Body denial is often synonymous with all of the lofty ideas associated with self-denial and is indicative of her ethnic Japanese cultural notions of beauty and purity. It is a pursuit of the ascetic which, at the same time, implies a constant search for self-definition. Through the act of starvation, the patient attempts to reproduce a newer self even if it means negation of current self (Nasser & DiNicola, 2001).

"While I was cutting, I felt more in control, whereas before I'd cut, I sort of felt like, Oh God, there is nothing I can control" (Bengali Muslim patient in the United Kingdom describing her self-cutting behavior; citation from Marshall & Yazdani, 2000). In this example of a young Asian woman in the United Kingdom, the body is rendered as a last site for exercising a degree of self-determination. The patient sees the self-cutting behavior as a method of controlling others as it is a behavior that others cannot control; this, in turn, gives the patient an illusory sense of being more in control of her life. For any clinician, the issue of control (or lack of it) is a familiar dynamic in anorexic texts.

In the two cases illustrated here, the self seems to be playing a dangerous game in an attempt to defy and challenge self and others, to establish a point of departure from reality that is also firmly grounded in reality, and to articulate the internal anguish into the externally visible. Within this decipherable language lies the hope that they and their predicaments will finally be noticed!

Reconnecting Body to Voice: Dialectical Solutions

Where do we go from here? How we get back to a clinical perspective and address the meanings that such behaviors have for the patient? How can we reconcile the paradoxes and make sense of identifiable and unhealthy social forces? How can we assist the patient to achieve the desired internal transformation and to succeed in overcoming her sense of disconnection and enable her to reconnect body to voice (Nasser & Katzman, 1999)?

Within dialectical theory, the self is viewed as a process in which individual identity develops in relation to others. Reality is not seen as static, but is composed of internal opposing forces (thesis and antithesis) out of whose synthesis evolves a new set of opposing forces. The constant transaction between parts of self, and between self and others, results in an ever-changing identity. The issues of wholeness and interconnectedness are, therefore, paramount features in the dialectical theory of the self.

Dialectical Behavior Therapy (DBT) (Lineman, 1993) is a treatment that is born out of this tradition. It has been used with some success in the treatment of borderline personality disorder and has recently been advocated for use in treating patients with eating disorders, particularly the multi-impulsive type. DBT enshrines the dialectical theory of the self and refers to a broad way of thinking that emphasizes wholeness, interconnectedness of the world, and the potential for the reconciliation of opposites. It is a constantly evolving technique that has recently incorporated some ethnic philosophies drawn from Zen Buddhism with its emphasis on "mindfulness." The aim is to prepare the individual for change while negotiating the need to accept what cannot be changed from the traumatic experiences of the past (Palmer & Birchall, 2002).

Conclusion

In this chapter, I have given many descriptive accounts of bodies engaged in intentional and deliberate self-harm behaviors. The boundary between the aesthetic and ascetic, the normal and abnormal, the palatable and grotesque, the sacred and profane, has become increasingly blurred. Such behaviors are dictated by cognitions that are trying to explore the limits of the body to speak its mind—to make the body, in the end, "mind in flesh." If we continue to give the body attributes of the mind, and the mind attributes of the body, without realizing it, we will fall into the same old Cartesian trap that is responsible in the first place for this body/mind dualism. The answer is to try to see the self as an integrated being and refer to it as neither mind nor body, but as a "lived body" (Ledder, 1990). Perhaps through such an integrative model, we can begin to understand why people engage in such behaviors and consciously inflict harm on their own bodies.

Self-harming experiences, in all forms, do test the limits of normality and rationality. Their main motive is to go beyond ordinary consciousness to possibly attain greater consciousness. The expansion of awareness is then hoped to ultimately free the body (and its mind) from the pain of existence that, in the first instance, caused the flesh to voice its suffering. In Being and Nothingness, Sartre (1966) speculated that pain consciousness is a projection toward a further consciousness, which would be empty of all pain. At the beginning of this chapter, I noted that in ancient Egyptian mythology, Osiris had to undergo metaphorical dismemberment in order to have the necessary consciousness to re-member himself. Osiris is dead, but the metaphor lives on. He is everyman.

References

Adams, P. (1998). Cars and scars. *New Formations, 35*, pp. 60–72.
Addley, E. (2003, June 28). A glad day for mourning. *The Guardian Weekend*, pp. 20–25.
Bell, R. M. (1985). *Holy anorexia.* Chicago: Chicago University Press.
Benthian, C. (2002). *Skin, on the cultural border between self and the world.* (Translated by Thomas Dunlap.) New York: Columbia University Press.
Bhugra, D. (2002). Suicidal behaviour in South Asians in the UK. *Crisis, 23*, pp. 108–113.
Body Craze. (2003). London May 7-31, Selfridges & Co. www.bodycraze.co.uk
Burke, A. W. (1976). Attempted suicide among Asian immigrants in Birmingham. *British Journal of Psychiatry, 128*, pp. 528-533.
Denby, D. (2002). *The piano teacher.* Quoted from the *New Yorker*, http://www.kino.com/pian-oteacher.
DiNicola, V., & Epstein, I. (1988). Self–mutilation in adolescents. *Parkhurst Exchange*, October, pp. 75-80.
Dohm, F. A., Striegel-Moore, R. H., Wilfley, D. E., Pike, K. M., Hook, J., & Fairburn, C. G. (2002). Self-harm and substance use in a community sample of Black and White women with binge eating disorder or bulimia nervosa. *International Journal of Eating Disorder*s, *32*, pp. 389–400.
Frank, M. L., & Lester, D. (2002). Self-destructive behaviours in American Indian and Alaska Native high school youth. *American Indian & Alaskan Native Mental Health Research, 10*, pp. 24–32.
Hare, T. (1999). *Remembering Osiris: Number, gender, and the word in ancient Egyptian representational systems.* Palo Alto, CA: Stanford University Press.
Hewitt, K. (1997). *Mutilating the body: Identity in blood and ink.* Bowling Green, OH: Bowling Green University Popular Press.
Hodes, M. (1990). Overdosing as communication: A cultural perspective. *British Journal of Medical Psychology, 63*, pp. 319–333.
Honig, E. & Brown, S. M. (Eds.) (1998). *Poems of Fernanndo Pessoa.* San Francisco: City Lights Books.
Hunter, E., & Harvey, D. (2002). Indigenous suicide in Australia, New Zealand, Canada, and the United States. *Emergency Medicine, 14*, pp. 14–23.
Katzman, M. A., & Lee, S. (1997). Beyond body image: The integration of feminist and trans-cultural theories in understanding of self- starvation. *International Journal of Eating Disorders, 22*, pp. 385–394.
Kilby, J. (2001) Carved in skin, bearing witness to self harm. In S. Ahmed & J. Stacey (Eds.), *Thinking through the skin. Transformations: Thinking through feminism* (pp. 124–141). New York: Brunner & Routledge.
Lacey, J. H., & Evans, C. D. H. (1986). The impulsivist, a multi-impulsive personality disorder. *British Journal of Addiction, 81*, pp. 641–649.
Ledder, D. (1990). *The absent body.* Chicago: University of Chicago Press.
Linehan, M. M. (1993). *Cognitive–behavioral treatment of borderline personality disorder.* New York: Guilford Press.
Maalouf, A. (1999). *Les identités meurtrières.* Paris: Bernard Grasset. Arabic translation by Beidon N. Damascus. El Guindy publishing house.
Marshall, H., & Yazdani, A. (2000).Young Asian women and self harm. In J. Ussher (Ed.), *Women's Health: Contemporary International Perspectives* (pp. 26–40). London: British Psychological Society.
McLane, J. (1996). The voice on the skin: Self mutilation and Merleau-Ponty theory of languages. *Hypatia, 11*, pp.107–119.
Merrill, J., & Owens, J. (1986). Ethnic differences in self-poisoning: A comparison of Asian and white groups. *British Journal of Psychiatry, 148*, pp. 708–712.
Merrill, J., & Owens, J. (1988). Self-poisoning among four immigrant groups. *Acta Psychiatrica Scandinavica, 77*, pp. 77–80.

Morgan, J. F., & Lacey, J. H. (2000). Bloodletting in anorexia nervosa: A case study. *International Journal of Eating Disorders, 27,* pp. 483–500.

Mumford, D. B., & Whitehouse, A. M. (1988). Increased prevalence of bulimia nervosa among Asian schoolgirls. *British Medical Journal, 297,* p. 718.

Nasser, M. (1997). *Culture and weight consciousness.* London: Brunner & Routledge.

Nasser M., & DiNicola, V. (2001). Changing bodies, changing cultures: An intercultural dialogue on the body as the final frontier. In M. Nasser, M. Katzman, & R. Gordon (2001), *Eating disorders and cultures in transition* (pp. 171–187). London: Brunner & Routledge.

Nasser, M., and Katzman, M. (1999). Eating Disorders: Transcultural perspectives inform prevention. In N. Piran, M. Levine, & C. Steiner-Adair (Eds.), *Preventing eating disorders: A handbook of interventions and special challenges* (pp. 26–43). Philadelphia: Brunner/Mazel.

Nasser, M., Katzman, M., & Gordon, R. (2001). *Eating disorders and cultures in transition.* London: Brunner & Routledge.

Palmer, B., & Birchall, H. (2002). Dialectical behavior therapy. In J. Treasure, U. Schmidt, & E. van Furth. (Eds.), *Handbook of eating disorders,* 2nd ed. (pp. 271–277). Chichester, England: Wiley.

Palmer, R. L., Oppenheimer, R., Dignon, A., Chaloner, D. A., & Howells, K. (1990). Childhood sexual experiences with adults reported by women with eating disorders: An extended series. *British Journal of Psychiatry, 156,* pp. 699–703.

Pembroke, L. R. (1994). Self-harm: Perspectives from personal experience. London: Survivors speak out. As quoted in Takemoto, T. (2001), Open wounds. In S. Ahmed & J. Stacey (Eds.), *Thinking through the skin. Transformations: Thinking through feminism* (pp. 104–123). New York: Brunner & Routledge.

Plath, S. (1981). *Collected poems.* Ed. Ted Hughes. London: Faber & Faber.

Raymond of Capua (1330–1399). *The life of Catherine of Siena.* Translated, introduced and annotated by C. Kearns & M. Glazier, 1980 (DW. School BX4700 C 4 3 1980).

Salecl, R. (2001). Cut in the body, from citeridectomy to body art. In S. Ahmed & J. Stacey (Eds.), *Thinking through the skin. Transformations: Thinking through feminism* (pp. 21–35). New York: Brunner & Routledge.

Sartre, J. P. (1966). *Being and nothingness: A phenomenological essay on ontology* (H. E. Barnes, Trans.). New York: Washington Square Press.

Schmidt, U. H., Humfress, H., & Treasure, J. L. (1997). The role of general family environment and sexual and physical abuse in the origins of eating disorders. *European Eating Disorders Review, 5,* pp. 184–207.

Soni-Raleigh, V. & Balarajan, R. (1992). Suicide and self-burning among Indians and West Indians in England and Wales. *British Journal of Psychiatry, 161,* pp. 365–368.

Takemoto, T. (2001). Open wounds. In S. Ahmed & J. Stacey (Eds). *Thinking through the skin. Transformations: Thinking through feminism* (pp. 104–123). New York: Brunner & Routledge.

Vale, V. (1989). *Modern Primitives: An investigation of contemporary adornment and ritual.* San Francisco: Research Publications.

Psychodynamics

Impulsive and Compulsive Self-Injurious Behavior and Eating Disorders: An Epidemiological Study

ANGELA FAVARO, SILVIA FERRARA, AND PAOLO SANTONASTASO

The Spectrum of Self-Injurious Behavior

Self-injurious behavior (SIB) is defined as those behaviors that involve the deliberate infliction of direct physical harm to one's own body without the intent to die as a result of the behavior itself (Simeon & Hollander, 2001). Some SIB may be considered "direct," such as skin cutting or severe nail biting, while other types of self-aggressive behaviors are "indirect" (e.g., alcoholism or heavy cigarette smoking; Favazza, 1996). Although in the literature there is an increasing interest in the whole spectrum of SIB, the epidemiology of these phenomena is generally unknown (Favazza, 1998; Simeon & Hollander, 2001).

Favazza and Simeon (1995) have proposed a classification approach to the different types of self-mutilation based on the severity of the consequences of the behavior. These categories are: (a) *major self-mutilation*, which refers to particularly severe acts such as eye enucleation or castration, and are commonly associated with psychotic disorders; (b) *stereotypic self-mutilation*, which refers to repeated acts such as head banging or self-biting, and are usually associated with severe mental retardation; and (c) *moderate/superficial self-mutilation*, which includes behaviors such as skin cutting, scratching, picking or burning, hair pulling, severe nail biting, and other forms of superficial self-injury.

Moderate or superficial SIB can be further divided into two subtypes: compulsive and impulsive (Favazza & Simeon, 1995). Compulsive SIB is usually habitual, repetitive, and "automatic." These behaviors are not associated with conscious intent or an affective experience (Favazza, 1998) and have the typical characteristics of compulsions (i.e., a mounting tension when the individual attempts to resist them and relief of anxiety when the behavior is performed). Compulsive SIB usually has ego-dystonic overtones, despite preventing or reducing anxiety and distress. Hair pulling, skin picking, and severe nail biting are examples of this type of SIB behavior.

On the other hand, impulsive SIB is usually episodic, involves little conscious resistance, and provides some form of gratification beyond reduction of tension or anxiety. Individuals who perform these types of SIB report that the behavior helps to control negative emotions such as depression, loneliness, or depersonalization. Impulsive SIB also satisfies other needs such as self-punishment and the manipulation of others (Favazza, 1998; Vanderlinden & Vandereycken, 1997). The most common behaviors of the impulsive type are skin cutting and burning. In some patients, impulsive SIB can become repetitive and, in these cases, it is best regarded as a separate disorder of impulse control (Favazza, 1998).

The literature reports that SIB is commonly encountered in patients with eating disorder (ED) (Favaro & Santonastaso, 1998, 2000; Lacey & Evans, 1986; Paul, Schroeter, Dahme, & Nutzinger, 2002; Welch & Fairburn, 1996). The relationship between ED and SIB, however, goes beyond simple statistical association. Indeed, the clinical phenomenology of ED shares important overlaps with the phenomenology of SIB. Both are typical of females, and their onset often occurs during adolescence (Favazza, 1996; 1998). Both ED and SIB could be interpreted as being linked to body dissatisfaction, asceticism, or a pervading sense of ineffectiveness which often implies an element of self-punishment (e.g., self-starvation, other body mortification practices such as self-flagellation). Similar to other behaviors typical of adolescence, such as body piercing and tattooing, both SIB and anorexia nervosa appear to be used as a means of taking control and possession of one's own body (Favazza, 1998; Cross, 1993). Since puberty implies uncontrollable changes of the body, adolescence is the time of greatest risk for these types of behaviors. In addition, patients with ED display various types of unhealthy weight-control practices (such as fasting, self-induced vomiting, laxatives, or diuretic abuse) that the patients themselves sometimes define as self-injurious.

Impulsive and compulsive SIB is not mutually exclusive. For example, in subjects with ED who often present with a combination of obsessive-compulsive and impulsive symptoms (Lacey & Evans, 1986; Newton, Freeman,

& Munro, 1993), impulsive and compulsive SIB can coexist (Favaro & Santonastaso, 1998, 2000).

To explain the relationship between impulsive and compulsive traits in patient samples, some authors have hypothesized a unidimensional model that consists of a continuum from compulsivity to impulsivity (Hollander & Wong, 1995). Other authors have proposed orthogonal models in which impulsivity and compulsivity represent separate but often coexisting psychological traits (Lacey & Evans, 1986; McElroy, Pope, Keck, & Hudson, 1995; Rasmussen & Eisen, 1994).

The relationship between SIB and ED is very complex. The ED literature discusses the existence of a subgroup of patients with a *multi-impulsive syndrome* (Lacey & Evans, 1986; Lacey, 1993; Nagata, Kawarada, Kiriike, & Iketani, 2000). This group of patients is characterized by a failure to control eating behavior along with non-ED impulsive behaviors such as alcoholism, the use of illicit drugs, deliberate SIB, suicide attempts, sexual disinhibition, and shoplifting. Other authors hypothesize the existence of a *repetitive self-mutilation syndrome* in which self-mutilative behavior alternates with other impulsive behaviors, including eating disorders (Favazza & Rosenthal, 1993; Favazza, 1998). In a study examining the relationship between deliberate self-harm and bulimia nervosa in a community sample, Welch & Fairburn (1996) observed the existence of a specific link between deliberate self-harm and bulimia nervosa. An association between eating disorders and self-mutilative behavior has also been reported (Favazza, 1996; Parry-Jones & Parry-Jones, 1993). Furthermore, among female self-mutilators, eating disorders are one of the most frequently associated diagnoses (Dulit, Fyer, Leon, Brodsky, & Frances, 1994; Favazza, DeRosear, & Conterio, 1989; Herpertz, 1995).

To better understand the specific relationship between the phenomenon of SIB and that of ED, we have investigated in several studies the relationship between self-destructive behavior and both anorexia nervosa and bulimia nervosa from a dimensional point of view (Favaro & Santonastaso, 1998, 2000). In these studies, we focused on the following SIB behaviors: skin cutting or burning, suicide attempts, substance or alcohol abuse, severe nail biting, hair pulling, and purging behavior such as self-induced vomiting and laxative/diuretic abuse.

In the first study of 125 consecutive patients with bulimia nervosa, 90 subjects with bulimia (72%) reported at least one form of SIB. The principal components analysis allowed us to examine the grouping of different kinds of behavior into one or more dimensions and to study the position of every subject on the dimensions that emerged. The analysis produced a two-factor solution: hair pulling, severe nail biting, and self-induced vomiting loaded on a factor which we called "compulsive SIB," while skin cutting or burning, suicide attempts, substance/alcohol abuse, and laxative/diuretic abuse loaded on another factor that we called "impulsive SIB." These findings suggest two important implications. First, they support the classification of SIB proposed by Favazza & Simeon (1995). Second, they demonstrate that purging behavior belongs to the same dimensions as all the other types of self-injurious behavior (i.e., purging is not a separate dimension). According to our data, the dimensions were *not* correlated (Favaro & Santonastaso, 1998). The impulsive and compulsive classification was also confirmed in a subsequent study (Favaro & Santonastaso 2002).

In a second study, we sampled a consecutive group of 236 patients with anorexia nervosa (155 restricting type and 81 binge eating/purging type; Favaro & Santonastaso, 2000). In this study, we found that the frequency of SIB in anorexia nervosa is similar to that in bulimia nervosa (Favaro & Santonastaso, 2000), except for suicide attempts and substance/alcohol abuse, which were more prevalent among patients with bulimia. This study in anorexia nervosa of the dimensionality of SIB also showed similarities and differences in comparison with our data in bulimia nervosa (Favaro & Santonastaso, 1998). The principal components analysis identified three factors: impulsive SIB (suicide attempts, skin cutting and burning), compulsive SIB (severe nail biting, hair pulling), and purging behavior (self-induced vomiting, laxative/diuretic abuse). The distinction between impulsive and compulsive SIB proposed by Favazza & Simeon (1995) appeared to be confirmed in anorexia nervosa as well as in bulimia nervosa. However, the most important difference between the groups is that in anorexia nervosa, purging behavior formed a third different dimension. What might explain this? Weight control in anorexia nervosa can be considered to be the core feature of the pathology and, probably for this reason, all behaviors with this aim have a different significance and dimensionality. In bulimia nervosa, purging behavior is a "compensation" for loss of control over food intake and might function as a form of self-punishment. On the other hand, purging behavior in anorexia nervosa is not always associated with binging (e.g., 44% of cases with recurrent purging in our sample) and may be considered a means of maintaining an increasing control over food and body even when the patient is not really losing control.

Predictors of the impulsive and compulsive dimensions of SIB may differ in anorexia nervosa and bulimia nervosa. In bulimia nervosa, the presence of compulsive SIB is predicted by a shorter duration of illness and a more accentuated lack of interoceptive awareness; in anorexia nervosa, it is predicted by a younger age and higher obsessionality. Of importance, childhood sexual abuse predicts impulsive SIB in both disorders (Favaro & Santonastaso, 1998, 1999, 2000), supporting the findings reported in the literature (van der Kolk, Perry, & Herman, 1991; Fullerton, Wonderlich, & Gosnell, 1995; Dohm, Striegel-Moore, Wilfley, Pike, Hook, & Fairburn, 2002). Furthermore, higher depression in bulimia nervosa and higher anxiety scores in anorexia nervosa predicted impulsive SIB.

An Epidemiological Perspective

Studies of clinical samples leave many questions about SIB unresolved. Indirect estimations suggest that the incidence of impulsive SIB might be at least 1 case per 1,000 annually (Simeon & Hollander, 2001), but the prevalence rates of impulsive and compulsive SIB in the community is unknown. Moreover, although patients with ED are considered to be at risk for SIB (Paul, Schroeder, Dahme, & Nutzinger, 2002), only one community-based study has investigated the relationship between self-harm behavior and ED (Welch & Fairburn, 1996). It is well known that subjects with ED recruited in clinical settings represent only a percentage of those present in the community (Fairburn, Welch, Norman, O'Connor, & Doll, 1996). Although the study of Fairburn et al. (1996) found no difference in the rates of self-harm between subjects with bulimia nervosa recruited in clinical settings and those recruited in the community, no study to date has assessed the frequency of the whole spectrum of self-injurious behavior in ED.

We planned an epidemiological study to examine some of these important questions. We were particularly interested in the following questions:

1. What is the prevalence of the different types of SIB among young women?
2. Is there a relationship between SIB and ED in the general female population?
3. Is there some type of variability between the prevalence of SIB in subjects with ED recruited in the community versus those recruited in a clinical setting?
4. What are the temperamental correlates of impulsive and compulsive SIB in ED versus the female general population?

In the remainder of this chapter, we report some preliminary findings of a community sample of 453 young women, ages 18–25, residing in an urban area of the city of Padua, in the northeast of Italy. This sample was part of a larger sample recruited to perform a general epidemiological study (Favaro, Ferrara, & Santonastaso, in press). The sample reported here represents about a tenth of the urban population of Padua. All women aged 18–25 years who were listed on registers for the area were sent a letter containing the aims and methods of the research study and an invitation to participate. Within a few weeks, each was contacted by telephone to secure participation, to obtain written informed consent, and to arrange for a clinical interview. All subjects were interviewed for ED using the Structured Clinical Interview for DSM-IV. For SIB, we used a semistructured interview to explore suicide attempts, skin cutting and burning, head or hand banging, self-hitting, self-biting, skin picking or scratching, other types of skin injury, hair pulling, and severe nail biting. The total number of female candidates was 592. We were unable to trace 19 (3.2%), and another 120 (20.3%) refused to be interviewed. We subsequently interviewed 453 subjects (response rate of 76.5%). The prevalence of lifetime ED (including anorexia nervosa, bulimia nervosa, and partial syndromes) was 12.8%. Partial syndromes were defined as reported in Favaro et al. (in press).

Twenty-five percent of the subjects ($n = 113$) reported some type of SIB. Compulsive SIB was reported by 23% of the entire sample, while 5% reported impulsive SIB; 2% reported both types of SIB. These findings are shown in Table 3.1.

Compared with participants without ED, the risk of reporting impulsive SIB was significantly higher among subjects with ED (Odds Ratio = 3.48; 95% C.I. 1.4–8.9; $p = .01$), whereas the risk of having compulsive SIB was similar among both community participants with ED and those without ED (Odds Ratio = 1.5). Among the different types of compulsive SIB,

TABLE 3.1 The Prevalence of Several SIB among Females in a General Population Sample, with Regard to a Diagnosis or Not of Eating Disorder

	Total Sample ($n = 453$)	No Eating Disorder ($n = 395$)	Eating Disorder ($n = 58$)	χ^2
Skin cutting	10 (2.2%)	7 (1.8%)	3 (5.2%)	2.71
Skin burning	2 (0.4%)	2 (0.5%)	0 (0%)	0.30
Self-hitting, head or hand banging	12 (2.6%)	7 (1.8%)	5 (8.6%)	9.20**
At least one impulsive SIB	22 (4.9%)	15 (3.8%)	7 (12.1%)	7.49**
Skin picking	41 (9.1%)	35 (8.9%)	6 (10.3%)	0.14
Severe nail biting	50 (11.0%)	44 (11.1%)	6 (10.3%)	0.03
Hair pulling	24 (5.3%)	16 (4.1%)	8 (13.8%)	9.57**
At least one compulsive SIB	102 (22.5%)	85 (21.5%)	17 (29.3%)	1.76
Suicide attempts	8 (1.8%)	3 (0.8%)	5 (8.6%)	18.2***

Note: SIB = self-injurious behavior.
**$p < .01$; ***$p < .001$.

only hair pulling showed a significant link with the presence of ED (Odds Ratio = 3.79; 95% C.I. 1.5–9.3; p = .004). Subjects with lifetime ED were significantly more likely to report an attempted suicide (Odds Ratio = 12.33; 95% C.I. 2.9–53.1; p = .001). These findings confirm the existence of a specific link between impulsive SIB and ED. The presence of a lifetime diagnosis of ED also seems to indicate a group at significantly higher risk of attempted suicide. On the contrary, with the exception of hair pulling, subjects with ED are not at higher risk of reporting compulsive SIB.

To evaluate the hypothesis of a bias in the prevalence of SIB between subjects with ED recruited in the community and subjects with ED recruited in a clinical setting, we recruited a new sample of patients with anorexia nervosa and bulimia nervosa. These represented a consecutive sample of patients referred to our ED unit. We did not use samples of patients described in our previous studies (Favaro & Santonastaso, 1998, 1999, 2000) because in the evaluation of those samples, we used a previous version of the semistructured interview for the assessment of SIB. This new sample consisted of 296 subjects with bulimia nervosa and 231 with anorexia nervosa. We then excluded all subjects less than 18 or more than 25 years of age, resulting in a final sample of 189 subjects with bulimia nervosa and 132 with anorexia nervosa. The comparison of the clinical and community samples is shown in Table 3.2 and Table 3.3.

We analyzed the data using either chi-square analyses or a Fisher's exact test as appropriate. Because the community ED samples were very small, particularly for anorexia nervosa cases, the power of the statistics was too low to allow us to generalize from our data. However, our findings suggest

TABLE 3.2 The Prevalence of Several SIB in Subjects with Anorexia Nervosa, Recruited in a Clinical Setting or from the Community

	Clinical AN Subjects (n = 132)	Community AN Subjects (n = 13)	Fisher's Exact Test
Skin cutting	19 (14.4%)	2 (15.4%)	Ns
Skin burning	4 (3.0%)	0 (0%)	Ns
Self-hitting, head or hand banging	20 (15.2%)	1 (7.7%)	Ns
At least one impulsive SIB	30 (22.7%)	2 (15.4%)	Ns
Skin picking	42 (31.8%)	1 (7.7%)	Ns (p = .1)
Severe nail biting	22 (16.7%)	1 (7.7%)	Ns
Hair pulling	33 (25.0%)	2 (15.4%)	Ns
At least one compulsive SIB	57 (43.2%)	4 (30.8%)	Ns
Suicide attempts	9 (6.8%)	1 (7.7%)	Ns

Note: AN = anorexia nervosa; Ns = non-significant; SIB = self-injurious behavior.

TABLE 3.3 The Prevalence of Several SIB in Subjects with Bulimia Nervosa, Recruited in a Clinical Setting or from the Community

	Clinical BN Subjects ($n = 189$)	Community BN Subjects ($n = 28$)	χ^2
Skin cutting	37 (19.6%)	1 (3.6%)	*[†]
Skin burning	6 (3.2%)	0 (0%)	Ns[†]
Self-hitting, head or hand banging	42 (22.2%)	3 (10.7%)	1.97
At least one impulsive SIB	59 (31.2%)	3 (10.7%)	5.02*
Skin picking	84 (44.4%)	4 (14.3%)	9.20**
Severe nail biting	34 (18.0%)	2 (7.1%)	Ns[†]
Hair pulling	46 (24.3%)	5 (17.9%)	0.57
At least one compulsive SIB	111 (58.7%)	9 (32.1%)	6.97**
Suicide attempts	22 (11.7%)	4 (14.3%)	Ns[†]

Note: BN = bulimia nervosa, Ns = non-significant, SIB = self-injurious behavior.
*$p < .05$; **$p < .01$.
[†] Fisher's exact test was performed, because more appropriate.

that in both anorexia nervosa and bulimia nervosa, there was little bias in the frequency of suicide attempts, thus confirming the data of Fairburn et al. (1996). In anorexia nervosa, all the behaviors were reported with similar frequencies in both samples. Only skin picking tended to be reported more frequently in the clinical sample than among anorexia nervosa subjects recruited in the community (Fisher's exact test: $p = .1$). For bulimia nervosa, both impulsive and compulsive SIB were significantly more frequent among subjects recruited in the clinical setting than among those recruited from the community. Again, these findings have to be considered preliminary, since the power of the statistical tests is low.

It is noteworthy that skin picking, a behavior that we did not consider in our previous studies, was the SIB that displayed the greatest difference between community and clinical samples in both anorexia nervosa and bulimia nervosa. Pathologic skin picking frequently begins as an urge to touch, scratch, or dig at the skin, often in response to a minor flaw or mild acne. It is a chronic and extensive behavior that leads to significant distress and sometimes to disfiguring skin excoriation. According to two studies (Arnold, McElroy, Mutasim, Dwight, Lamerson, & Morris, 1998; Simeon, Stein, Gross, Islam, Schmeidler, & Hollander, 1997), the face is the most common site of excoriation and few individuals had underlying skin conditions such as acne or eczema. In our community sample, the face was the most common site of excoriation (36% of cases with skin picking), but lips were also very common (22%). Subjects also reported skin picking in other parts of the body or in more than one site (e.g., hands 20%, legs

17%, arms 10%, others 10%). In 15% of cases, underlying acne was present.

In contrast to the community sample, 70% of subjects with anorexia nervosa and 56% of subjects with bulimia nervosa with skin picking reported that acne or some other type of skin problem was the exclusive initiating factor of this type of SIB. In both anorexia and bulimia nervosa, legs were the most common sites of skin excoriation (48 and 43%, respectively). Other common sites were arms (29 and 39%, respectively) and face (17 and 27%, respectively), versus lips (3 and 7%), the scalp (10 and 14%), hands (10 and 14%), or other body parts (10 and 9%).

These differences are quite interesting. It seems that patients with ED tend to produce skin excoriation in parts of the body that are easier to hide. Furthermore, the choice of these sites could also be linked to problems and conflicts with the body, which are usually more focused on body parts other than the face. It is also interesting to note that, although the phenomenology is typically compulsive, this type of SIB is significantly associated with childhood physical and/or sexual abuse. In the general population sample, childhood abuse was present in 17% of individuals with skin picking and 7% of the other subjects (Odds Ratio = 2.72; 95% C.I. 1.1–6.7; $p < .03$); in subjects with anorexia nervosa, childhood abuse was reported in 8% of those who reported skin picking and 4% of the others (Odds Ratio = 2.0; not significant); and in those with bulimia nervosa, the rates of abuse in those with skin picking and those without skin picking were identical to those found in the general population sample (17% vs. 7%; Odds Ratio = 2.57; 95% C.I. 1.2–5.4; $p < .02$). In previous studies performed in ED samples (Favaro & Santonastaso, 1998, 2000; Fullerton et al., 1995) and in other patient samples (van der Kolk et al., 1991), only impulsive SIB was associated with childhood abuse. The association of skin picking with both childhood abuse and ED appears to indicate that this behavior could be considered an index of a severe disorder of the body experience.

Finally, we explored the relationship between different types of SIB and temperamental characteristics found in both the community and ED samples. Temperamental characteristics were investigated by means of the Tridimensional Personality Questionnaire (Cloninger, 1987), which measures four independent temperamental factors: harm avoidance, novelty seeking, reward dependence, and persistence. In a previous sample of patients with anorexia nervosa, we found a significant correlation between impulsive SIB and novelty seeking, and between compulsive SIB and harm avoidance (Favaro & Santonastaso, 2000). These findings seem to be confirmed by the data we present here (Table 3.4). In patients with anorexia nervosa, novelty seeking is significantly higher among subjects with impulsive SIB, or with both impulsive and compulsive SIB, than among all the other subjects.

As in our previous study, patients with anorexia nervosa with compulsive SIB scored significantly higher on the harm avoidance factor (Table 3.4), independently of the presence of impulsive SIB. A similar result was obtained in the general population sample with both the relationship between novelty seeking and impulsive SIB, and that between harm avoidance and compulsive SIB (see Table 3.4). In addition, in the general population sample, a significant difference emerged between subjects with both types of SIB and all the other subjects with regard to the factor reward dependence (Table 3.4), which was significantly higher in this group.

Patients with bulimia nervosa, conversely, appear to display a completely different picture. Only the harm avoidance factor appears to have some link with the presence of SIB. A post-hoc analysis showed that subjects with impulsive SIB scored significantly higher on this factor, independently from the presence of compulsive SIB. These findings about bulimia nervosa are not so easy to interpret. We expected to encounter the relationship between novelty seeking and impulsive behaviors that we found in anorexia nervosa and in the general population sample, since subjects with high novelty seeking are usually described as impulsive and excitable

TABLE 3.4 Temperamental Characteristics among Subjects with Impulsive SIB, Those with Compulsive SIB, and Subjects without Any Type of SIB

	Impulsive SIB	Compulsive SIB	Both SIB	Neither SIB	
General pop. sample	($n = 10$)	($n = 84$)	($n = 11$)	($n = 336$)	F (3, 437)
Novelty seeking	21.2 (3.3)	17.6 (5.3)	18.8 (4.1)	16.3 (5.0)	4.91**
Harm avoidance	18.8 (4.4)	19.4 (6.0)	21.5 (4.8)	17.4 (5.7)	4.24**
Reward dependence	16.0 (4.5)	15.9 (4.0)	18.5 (3.4)	15.5 (3.4)	2.75*
Persistence	4.9 (1.8)	5.6 (2.0)	5.4 (1.9)	5.2 (1.8)	1.17
Anorexia nervosa	($n = 15$)	($n = 58$)	($n = 26$)	($n = 118$)	F (3, 213)
Novelty seeking	17.2 (5.7)	14.6 (5.0)	17.2 (5.1)	14.3 (5.0)	3.31*
Harm avoidance	20.7 (6.2)	23.2 (6.5)	23.7 (6.7)	19.7 (5.8)	6.15**
Reward dependence	14.7 (4.9)	14.4 (4.1)	15.0 (3.7)	13.9 (4.0)	0.59
Persistence	5.4 (2.1)	6.3 (1.6)	6.0 (2.6)	5.9 (1.7)	1.00
Bulimia nervosa	($n = 23$)	($n = 88$)	($n = 50$)	($n = 101$)	F(3, 258)
Novelty seeking	17.2 (5.6)	18.6 (5.1)	18.2 (5.2)	18.7 (5.1)	0.60
Harm avoidance	22.7 (5.0)	20.7 (6.0)	24.2 (4.8)	18.9 (6.3)	10.15***
Reward dependence	14.2 (4.0)	14.9 (3.7)	14.3 (3.7)	15.2 (3.9)	0.86
Persistence	5.5 (2.2)	5.6 (1.9)	5.5 (1.8)	5.6 (1.9)	0.10

Note: SIB = self-injurious behavior.
*$p < .05$; **$p < .01$; ***$p < .001$.

(Cloninger, 1987). The same was true for the relationship between harm avoidance and compulsive SIB. Subjects with high harm avoidance are described as apprehensive, inhibited, and cautious. Obsessive-compulsive disorder and other anxiety disorders have been found to be associated with high scores on the harm avoidance factor (Cloninger, 1996). However, in many studies, harm avoidance appears to be high also in the presence of depression (Cloninger, 1996; Hansenne, Reggers, Pinto, Kjiri, Ajamier, & Ansseau, 1999) and, in bulimia nervosa, depressive symptoms are one of the main predictors of impulsive SIB (Favaro & Santonastaso, 1999). This could be the reason why patients with bulimia and with impulsive SIB showed a significantly higher mean score on this factor. With regard to the novelty seeking finding, we have to consider that bulimia nervosa is a group characterized by high novelty seeking (their mean score was 18.4 ± 5.1), while among subjects in the general population without ED, the mean score was 16.6 ± 5.1 ($t = 4.43$; $p < .0001$). For this reason, the effects of the presence of other impulsive behaviors are probably not appreciable on this variable.

Conclusion

SIB appears to have a specific link with ED. This link has been demonstrated by studies in clinical samples that show a specific relationship between SIB and many important clinical features of ED, and by an epidemiological study performed on a sample representative of the female general population. From a phenomenological point of view, the distinction between impulsive and compulsive SIB demonstrated its validity in all the different studies performed. In bulimia nervosa, both impulsive and compulsive SIB appears to be overrepresented in clinical samples in comparison with subjects with bulimia recruited from the general population. In anorexia nervosa, the frequencies of SIB in the clinical and community samples are more similar. This could be due to the fact that in anorexia nervosa, the rate of subjects who seek treatment is higher than for bulimia nervosa and so the samples may be more similar. The number of subjects with anorexia nervosa in the community sample, however, was too low to draw any conclusions. Finally, among patients with bulimia nervosa, temperamental factors appear to play a different role in the development of SIB in comparison with patients with anorexia nervosa and subjects from the general population. This finding needs further investigation in future studies. Our findings suggest that both types of SIB have a notable clinical impact both in AN and in BN. It seems important that researchers and clinicians consider the presence of both impulsive and compulsive SIB in the assessment and treatment of patients with ED.

References

Arnold, L. M., McElroy, S. L., Mutasim, D. F., Dwight, M. M., Lamerson, C. L., & Morris, E. M. (1998). Characteristics of 34 adults with psychogenic excoriation. *Journal of Clinical Psychiatry, 59,* 509–514.

Cloninger, C. R. (1987). A systematic method for clinical description and classification of personality variants. *Archives of General Psychiatry, 44,* 573–588.

Cloninger, C. R. (1996). Assessment of the impulsive-compulsive spectrum of behavior by the seven-factor model of temperament and character. In J. M. Oldham, E. Hollander, & A. E. Skodol (Eds.), *Impulsivity and compulsivity.* Washington, DC: American Psychiatric Press, pp. 59–95.

Cross, L. (1993). Body and self in feminine development: Implications for eating disorders and delicate self mutilation. *Bulletin of the Menninger Clinic, 57,* 41–68.

Dohm, F. A., Striegel-Moore, R. H., Wilfley, D. E., Pike, K. M., Hook, J., & Fairburn, C. G. (2002). Self-harm and substance use in a community sample of black and white women with binge eating disorder or bulimia nervosa. *International Journal of Eating Disorders, 32,* 389–400.

Dulit, R. A., Fyer, M. R., Leon, A. C., Brodsky, B. S., & Frances, A. J. (1994). Clinical correlates of self-mutilation in borderline personality disorder. *American Journal of Psychiatry, 151,* 1305–1311.

Fairburn, C. G., Welch, S. L., Norman, P. A., O'Connor, M. E., & Doll, H. A. (1996). Bias and bulimia nervosa: How typical are clinic cases? *American Journal of Psychiatry, 153,* 386–391.

Favaro, A., Ferrara, S., & Santonastaso, P. (In press). The spectrum of eating disorders in young women: A prevalence study in a general population sample. *Psychosomatic Medicine.*

Favaro, A., & Santonastaso, P. (1998). Impulsive and compulsive self-injurious behavior in bulimia nervosa: Prevalence and psychological correlates. *Journal of Nervous and Mental Disease, 186,* 157–165.

Favaro, A., & Santonastaso, P. (1999). Different types of self-injurious behavior in bulimia nervosa. *Comprehensive Psychiatry, 40,* 57–60.

Favaro, A., & Santonastaso, P. (2000). Self-injurious behavior in anorexia nervosa. *Journal of Nervous and Mental Disease, 188,* 537–542.

Favaro, A., & Santonastaso, P. (2002). The spectrum of self-injurious behavior in eating disorders. *Eating Disorders, 1,* 215–225.

Favazza, A. R., DeRosear, L., & Conterio, K. (1989). Self mutilation and eating disorders. *Suicide and Life Threatening Behavior, 19,* 352–361.

Favazza, A. R. (1996). *Bodies under siege: Self-mutilation and body modification in culture and psychiatry,* 2nd ed. Baltimore: Johns Hopkins University Press.

Favazza, A. R. (1998). The coming of age of self-mutilation. *Journal of Nervous and Mental Disease, 186,* 259–268.

Favazza, A. R., & Rosenthal, R. J. (1993). Diagnostic issues in self-mutilation. *Hospital and Community Psychiatry, 44,* 134–140.

Favazza, A. R., & Simeon, D. (1995). Self-mutilation. In E. Hollander & D. Stein (Eds.), *Impulsivity and aggression* (pp. 185–200). Sussex, England: John Wiley & Sons.

Fullerton, D. T., Wonderlich, S. A., & Gosnell, B. A. (1995). Clinical characteristics of eating disorder patients who report sexual or physical abuse. *International Journal of Eating Disorders, 17,* 243–249.

Hansenne, M., Reggers, J., Pinto, E., Kjiri, K., Ajamier, A., & Ansseau, M. (1999). Temperament and character inventory (TCI) and depression. *Journal of Psychiatric Research, 33,* 31–36.

Herpertz, S. (1995). Self-injurious behavior: Psychopathological and nosological characteristics in subtypes of self-injurers. *Acta Psychiatrica Scandinavica, 91,* 57–68.

Hollander, E., & Wong, C. M. (1995). Obsessive-compulsive spectrum disorders. *Journal of Clinical Psychiatry, 56* (Suppl. 4), 3–6.

Lacey, J. H., & Evans, C. D. H. (1986). The impulsivist: A multi-impulsive personality disorder. *British Journal of Addiction, 81,* 641–649.

Lacey, J. H. (1993). Self-damaging and addictive behaviour in bulimia nervosa: A catchment area study. *British Journal of Psychiatry, 163,* 190–194.

McElroy, S. L., Pope, H. G., Keck, P. E., & Hudson, J. I. (1995). Disorders of impulse control. In E. Hollander, & D. Stein (Eds.), *Impulsivity and aggression* (pp. 109–136). Sussex, England: John Wiley & Sons.

Nagata, T., Kawarada, Y., Kiriike, N., & Iketani, T. (2000). Multi-impulsivity of Japanese patients with eating disorders: Primary and secondary impulsivity. *Psychiatry Research, 94,* 239–250.

Newton, J. R., Freeman, C. P., & Munro, J. (1993). Impulsivity and dyscontrol in bulimia nervosa: Is impulsivity an independent phenomenon or a marker of severity? *Acta Psychiatrica Scandinavica, 87,* 389–394.

Parry-Jones, B., & Parry-Jones, W. L. I. (1993). Self-mutilation in four historical cases of bulimia. *British Journal of Psychiatry, 163,* 394–402.

Paul, T., Schroeter, K., Dahme, B., & Nutzinger, D. O. (2002). Self-injurious behavior in women with eating disorders. *American Journal of Psychiatry, 159,* 408–411.

Rasmussen, S. A., & Eisen, J. L. (1994). The epidemiology and differential diagnosis of obsessive compulsive disorder. *Journal of Clinical Psychiatry, 55* (Suppl. 10), 5–10.

Simeon, D., & Hollander, E. (2001). *Self-injurious behavior: Assessment and treatment.* New York: American Psychiatric Association.

Simeon, D., Stein, D. J., Gross, S., Islam, N., Schmeidler, J., & Hollander, E. (1997). A double-blind trial of fluoxetine in pathologic skin-picking. *Journal of Clinical Psychiatry, 58,* 341–347.

van der Kolk, B. A., Perry, J. C., & Herman, J. L. (1991). Childhood origins of self-destructive behavior. *American Journal of Psychiatry, 148,* 1665–1671.

Vanderlinden, J., & Vandereycken, W. (1997). *Trauma, dissociation, and impulse dyscontrol in eating disorders.* Bristol: Brunner/Mazel.

Welch, S. L., & Fairburn, C. G. (1996). Impulsivity or comorbidity in bulimia nervosa: A controlled study of deliberate self-harm and alcohol and drug misuse in a community sample. *British Journal of Psychiatry, 169,* 451–458.

CHAPTER 4

Self-Harm and Suicide Attempts in Bulimia Nervosa

CHARLES B. ANDERSON AND CYNTHIA M. BULIK

Self-Harm versus Suicide Attempts in Bulimia Nervosa

The risk of harm associated with eating disorders includes the direct physical consequences of eating disorder symptoms as well as the indirect effects of self-harm behavior, which is exhibited by a substantial minority of individuals. The contribution of associated self-harm behaviors to the relatively high risk of mortality among those with eating disorders has received increasing attention in the literature. In anorexia nervosa, the crude mortality rate ranges from 5.1 to 7.4% (Herzog, Greenwood, Dorer, Flores, Ekeblad, Richards, Blais, & Keller, 2000). In bulimia nervosa, the crude mortality rate is generally lower, ranging from 0.3 to 0.9% (Keel & Mitchell, 1997). Given the potential lethality of self-harm behavior associated with the eating disorders, the ability to distinguish characteristics associated with self-harm behavior without lethal intent from those with lethal intent, as suggested by Simeon, Stein, and Hollander (1995), would help to identify those patients with eating disorders who are at higher risk for mortality.

The current literature examining self-harm and suicidal behavior among individuals with eating disorders frequently examines these behaviors separately. In addition, most studies are unclear as to whether participants engaging in suicidal gestures or behavior are included in the classification of self-harm, or whether participants engaging in suicidal gestures and other self-harm behaviors are included in the classification of suicide attempts. We examined personality and behavioral correlates of self-harm and suicide attempts in women with bulimia nervosa for the purpose of distinguishing how patients at risk for suicide attempts differ from those who engage in self-harm behavior without lethal intent.

It has been suggested that eating disorders themselves constitute a version of self-harm and may exist along a continuum with other self-harm behaviors (Anderson & Bulik, 2002; van der Kolk, Perry, & Herman, 1991). It may be that eating disorders, particularly anorexia nervosa, have an underlying self-destructive purpose similar to that observed in addictive behaviors such as cigarette smoking, drug abuse, and alcohol abuse. While we agree that a continuum of self harm best describes the observed gradations in severity of self-harm behavior among women with bulimia nervosa, the existential salience of suicide attempts demands the consideration of suicidality as qualitatively different from other forms of self-harm behavior. We also recognize that lethal intention does not describe all completed suicides in bulimia nervosa, and that suicidality per se is not a perfect predictor of mortality. For example, in patients presenting with borderline personality disorder, bona fide suicide attempts in bulimia nervosa do not necessarily result in completed suicides. In other cases, self-harm behavior without lethal intention (i.e., suicidal gestures) is sometimes lethal.

The complexity of identifying features associated with lethal versus nonlethal self-harm depends upon an ability to identify differences between those who attempt and those who complete suicide. Longitudinal studies of mortality in eating disorders (Herzog et al., 2000; Keel et al., 2003) have been particularly useful in identifying features associated with completed suicides in anorexia nervosa. However, the low crude mortality rate has thus far precluded meaningful analysis of correlates of mortality in bulimia nervosa. Given the overlap of symptomatology in bulimia and anorexia nervosa, it is likely that characteristics associated with suicidality in anorexia are relevant to bulimia nervosa as well. Acknowledging these limitations, we will examine the results of our research with self-harm and suicide attempts in bulimia nervosa, and discuss them in light of other reported findings found in the literature.

Suicide Attempts in Bulimia Nervosa

Clinical Features

We have previously reported that the clinical and demographic features associated with suicide attempts in bulimia nervosa include lower body mass index, lower past weight, and less incidence of a past history of childhood sexual abuse (Anderson & Bulik, 2002). These results are somewhat inconsistent with the previous findings of an association of a history of childhood sexual abuse with suicide attempts (Favaro & Santonastaso, 1997) and no difference in body mass index between those attempting versus not attempting suicide (Favaro & Santonastaso, 1997). Interestingly, one study of overweight patients with bulimia (Mitchell, Pyle, Eckert, Hatsukami, & Soll, 1990) found that overweight individuals were three times more likely to report a history of suicide attempts. These differences may be reflective of differences in the characteristics of the samples and the relatively small sample sizes in each of the studies, including our own. However, it is possible that our study was somewhat more rigorous in excluding suicidal gestures from inclusion among those attempting suicide, a decision that was indicated by our finding of an association of such gestures with self-harm, as opposed to suicidal behaviors.

Our finding of an association of lower BMI and lower past weight with suicide attempts is intriguing. Low weight status in women with bulimia nervosa could be heterogeneous in origin. Indeed, whereas it may reflect the presence of clinical or subclinical anorexia nervosa (or severe restrictive eating), it could also reflect weight loss secondary to the presence of depression, comorbid substance or alcohol abuse, and/or choice or severity of compensatory behaviors. The possibility that dietary restriction or intensity of compensatory behaviors may be related to suicide attempts in bulimia nervosa is indirectly supported in a study of mortality primarily among participants with anorexia nervosa (Keel et al., 2003). In this study, three out of four suicide completions occurred in participants with anorexia nervosa, restricting type (Keel et al., 2003). An exploration of the features of depression in women with self-harm, as compared to women with suicide attempts, might indicate whether an atypical presentation of depression might have been associated with suicide or self harm.

With respect to histories of childhood sexual abuse, our findings reflect a lower frequency among women with bulimia attempting suicide, compared with those engaging in self-harm or control subjects with bulimia. This finding may, at first, seem counterintuitive, but it is not wholly inconsistent with the literature. For example, Bulik, Sullivan, and Rorty (1989) found a significant association between major depression in women with bulimia and families where childhood sexual abuse was reported, though the association with suicidality did not reach significance. Favaro and Santonastaso (1997), on the other hand, found suicide attempts to be more frequent among women with bulimia with a history of childhood sexual abuse. Again, these differences may be related to the characteristics of the sample (e.g., more rigorous inclusion criteria for suicide attempt in our study). As a caveat, however, the lower percentage of childhood sexual abuse in those attempting suicide in our study actually reflected a substantial proportion of this subsample (40%) and is broadly consistent with an association of a history of childhood sexual abuse with suicide attempts in bulimia nervosa. The greater frequency of childhood sexual abuse in control subjects with bulimia and self-harming women with bulimia is also broadly consistent with the literature (Bulik, Sullivan, & Rorty, 1989; Pope & Hudson, 1989; Wonderlich, Myers, Norton, & Corby, 2002; Zlotnick, Hohlstein, Shea, Pearlstein, Recupero, & Bidadi, 1996).

On measures of severity of bulimic symptoms, we found in our study no differences between those attempting suicide, those engaging in self-harm behavior, or controls. This is somewhat contrary to previous findings associating purging behaviors with suicidality (Favaro & Santonastaso, 1997), but consistent with the findings of Corcos, Taieb, Benoit-Lamy, Paterniti, Jeammet, and Flament (2002) indicating no difference in suicidality between purging and non-purging individuals with bulimia nervosa. Contrary to Corcos et al. (2002), we found no differences in age of onset for disordered eating between those attempting suicide, those engaging in self-harming behavior, and controls.

Axis I and II Comorbidity

In our study, we found that Axis I and Axis II comorbidity was highly associated with differences between control subjects with bulimia and those with self-harm behavior or suicide attempts. However, only social phobia was significantly higher in women with bulimia attempting suicide than those engaging in self-harm behavior or control subjects with bulimia. This suggests that women with bulimia engaging in suicide attempts may be impacted by the effects of a comorbid anxiety disorder that, by definition, has a direct impact on social interactions. One possible effect of comorbid social phobia may be that the quality and quantity of social interactions are compromised to such a degree that social support systems are impacted as well. Our study did not measure aspects of social support systems or the relationship of social support to suicide attempts, but this may well be an area that warrants further investigation.

We also found an association of Cluster A, B, and C personality disorder symptoms and comorbid oppositional defiant disorder in those attempting suicide versus controls; it appears that marked interpersonal deficits may characterize women with bulimia who attempt suicide. Interestingly, in a recent study of factors deemed to be helpful among suicidal patients, social contact and contact with psychiatric services was identified as equally helpful in preventing suicide (Eagles, Carson, Begg, & Naji, 2003). This points to the salience of social support in the prevention of suicide.

Women attempting suicide also differed significantly from controls in the presence of other anxiety disorders including obsessive-compulsive disorder, simple phobia, and panic disorder, each of which is associated with social withdrawal.

An additional factor that may contribute to social phobic, or withdrawing, behaviors may be the presence of comorbid depression and alcohol or other substance abuse. We found an increased lifetime alcohol dependence among individuals with bulimia who attempted suicide, which is consistent with the increased risk of suicide among those with alcohol dependence in the general population (Murphy, 1988; Murphy & Wetzel, 1990; Roy & Linnoila, 1986). A recent study of mortality in eating disorders (Keel et al., 2003) identified severity of alcohol use during the follow-up period as the strongest predictor of mortality in a sample of ten participants with anorexia nervosa and one participant with bulimia nervosa. The standardized mortality rate (SMR) for suicide in this study was 56.9 (95% CI 15.3–145.7), representing a significantly increased risk of mortality in this population. Unfortunately, characteristics of those completing suicide were not separately examined in this study. In addition, all participants who died were diagnosed with comorbid affective disorder. With respect to suicide attempts in bulimia nervosa, our findings are largely consistent with Keel et al. (2003) in identifying a strong association between alcohol dependence and suicide attempts, compared to control subjects with bulimia. In addition, those attempting suicide (and those engaging in self-harming behavior) reported a significant association of comorbid major depressive disorder. This association of depression with suicidality in bulimia nervosa is consistent with the literature (Bulik, Sullivan, & Joyce, 1999). This suggests that a constellation of factors, including comorbid major depression, alcohol dependence, and a combination of Axis II symptoms and anxiety disorders, may influence a person's vulnerability to suicide attempts in bulimia nervosa.

Personality Characteristics

The exploration of personality correlates in suicide attempts among individuals with eating disorders has generally focused on dimensions found in the Temperament and Character Inventory (TCI) (Cloninger, 1987), and on measures of impulsivity, dissociation, and obsessionality.

TCI Findings. With respect to TCI scores, suicide attempts in bulimia nervosa have been found to be associated with high harm avoidance and low self-directedness (Bulik et al., 1999). We have also found suicide attempts to be associated with high harm avoidance and high persistence scores.

High harm avoidance scores are associated with anticipatory worrying, inhibitory apprehension requiring reassurance, inhibited withdrawal from strangers that limits social interaction, preference for quiet inactivity, negative expectations, fatigability, and slow adaptation to change (Cloninger, 1987). In other studies, high harm avoidance scores have been strongly correlated with neuroticism and depression (Hansenne, Reggers, Pinto, Kjiri, Ajamier, & Ansseau, 1999), the presence of personality disorder (Svrakic, Whitehead, Przybeck, & Cloninger, 1993), and high scores in measures of social phobia (Chatterjee, Sunitha, Velayudhan, & Khanna, 1997; Kim & Hoover, 1996). High persistence scores are associated broadly with perfectionism, perseverance, industriousness, and a certain lack of flexibility in responding to environmental challenges. Both persistence and harm avoidance are associated with obsessional qualities and are common to obsessive personality traits and obsessive personality disorder. Collectively, these characteristics are somewhat consistent with the elements of affective disturbance, social withdrawal, and obsessionality discussed in connection with Axis I and II comorbidity. It appears that personality elements related to depression, impaired adaptability to change, pessimistic outlook, and the need for reassurance, coupled with social withdrawal, may combine to create a vulnerability to suicide attempts in women with bulimia nervosa.

Impulsivity/Compulsivity. In the literature, much attention has been given to the dimensions of impulsivity and compulsivity in self-harming behavior and suicidality. Whether impulsivity and compulsivity exist on a continuum or are orthogonal factors remains a focus of current debate. Favaro and Santonastaso (2002) have made a useful distinction between impulsive (e.g., cutting, burning, suicide, alcohol and substance use, laxative and diuretic use) and compulsive self-harm behavior (e.g., hair pulling, nail biting, vomiting). Penas-Lledo, Vaz, Ramos, and Waller (2002) have differentiated between internally directed (i.e., self-harm) and externally directed (e.g., theft, reckless driving, unsafe sex) impulsive behaviors. According to Penas-Lledo et al. (2002), bulimia nervosa is associated with externally directed impulsivity, while internally directed impulsivity (self-harm) is associated with general psychopathology. Penas-Lledo et al. (2002) also suggest that externalizing impulsivity is associated with novelty seeking and internalizing impulsivity with harm avoidance.

Given the broad association of novelty seeking with bulimia nervosa and the observed association of harm avoidance with suicidality in bulimia, one interpretation might be that women with bulimia at risk for suicide attempts exhibit an internalizing form of impulsivity that is marked by high harm avoidance scores. Rather than being broadly associated with self-harm, high harm avoidance may be a specific marker for suicide attempts. The absence of significant differences in novelty seeking between those attempting suicide, engaging in self-harm, or controls suggests that novelty seeking per se may not distinguish between women with bulimia at risk for self-harm and those who are not.

Although Favaro and Santonastaso (2002) and Penas-Lledo et al. (2002) appear to view suicidal behavior as an impulsive spectrum behavior, there is surprisingly little evidence to support an association of trait impulsivity with suicide attempts or self-harming behavior. Only a single study (Paul, Schroeter, Dahme, & Nutzinger, 2002) found an association of impulsivity with self-injuring behavior. In this study, the cognitive impulsivity subscale of the Barratt Impulsivity Scale (Barratt, 1985) was found to be associated with self-injuring women with bulimia. As a follow-up to Anderson and Bulik (2002), we examined the association of cognitive, motor, and nonplanned impulsivity subscales of the Barratt Impulsivity Scale, as well as total impulsivity scores, with self-harm behavior, suicide attempts, and controls in a sample of women with bulimia nervosa. We found no association between total impulsivity scores or the impulsivity subscales of the Barratt Impulsivity Scale with regard to self-harm behavior, suicide attempts, or controls. It is likely that, as an impulsive spectrum disorder, all women with bulimia would differ significantly from control subjects without bulimia on measures of impulsivity. However, it appears that the utility of trait impulsivity scores as a means of distinguishing women with bulimia who engage in self-harm or suicide attempts from those who do not is quite limited.

Body Dissatisfaction/Interoceptive Awareness. Anderson and Bulik (2002) found that women with bulimia engaging in self-harm behavior and suicide attempts each differed from control subjects with bulimia not engaging in self-harm behavior or suicide attempts in measures of body dissatisfaction and interoceptive awareness. Those engaging in self-harm behavior and suicide attempts exhibited greater body dissatisfaction and greater interoceptive awareness than controls. These findings suggest that women with bulimia engaging in self-harm behavior, including suicide attempts, may be more attuned to their inner emotional states than controls. This raises the possibility that the negative, pessimistic, emotional state associated with high harm avoidance may be felt more acutely in women who engage in suicide attempts, or that high harm avoidance is reflective of a keen awareness of a negative emotional state. In turn, such an interpretation offers the intriguing possibility that comorbid alcohol dependence may function as a way to dull the effects of a heightened interoceptive awareness. In addition, the function of self-harm behavior may function as a means of distracting oneself from an acute awareness of emotional distress or, as Paul et al. (2002) suggest, to feel bodily instead of emotional pain.

A study by Corcos et al. (2002) confirmed the association of greater body dissatisfaction with suicide attempts in bulimia nervosa. Specifically, these investigators reported that participants engaging in suicide attempts had higher body dissatisfaction scores and more frequently reported viewing themselves as fat. It is likely that a heightened attention to negative thoughts and a pessimistic outlook associated with high harm avoidance affects one's perception of body image as well. This is particularly striking in light of the finding that women with bulimia who engaged in suicide attempts have significantly lower BMI and lower past weights. Again, a pattern of increasing body dissatisfaction in the face of lower BMI raises the question of a possible history of anorexia nervosa or severe behavioral restriction in women with bulimia who engage in suicide attempts. Depressive symptoms might also explain body dissatisfaction scores, and lower BMI and past lower weights, in women with bulimia who attempt suicide. A recent study of body dissatisfaction, bulimic symptoms, and depression found that body dissatisfaction was better explained by depression than by bulimic symptomatology (Keel, Mitchell, Davis, & Crow, 2001). In our study, self-harm and suicidal behaviors occurred in the presence of both depression and body dissatisfaction, and may have been a consequence of overall negative self-evaluation and cognitive distortion secondary to comorbid depression.

Self-Harm in Bulimia Nervosa

Clinical Features

We found self-harm behavior in bulimia nervosa to be associated with higher body mass index, higher past weight, and a past history of childhood sexual abuse. These results are largely consistent with the previous findings of an association of a history of childhood sexual abuse with self-harm (Favaro & Santonastaso, 1997; Paris & Zweig-Frank, 1996; Romans, Martin, Anderson, Herbison, & Mullen, 1995; Wonderlich, Myers, Norton, & Corby, 2002).

Several studies have found significant associations between childhood sexual abuse and self-harm (Paris & Zweig-Frank, 1996; Romans et al., 1995; Sansone & Levitt, 2002). Our findings suggest that a history of childhood sexual abuse may have a greater impact on self-harm than on suicide (Anderson & Bulik, 2002). The broad findings in the literature suggest that childhood sexual abuse appears to be a nonspecific risk factor for a range of psychiatric disorders (Kendler, Bulik, Silberg, Hettema, Myers, & Prescott, 2000; Wonderlich, Brewerton, Jocic, Dansky, & Abbott, 1997; Wonderlich,

Wilsnack, Wilsnack, & Harris, 1996) including major depression (Weiss, Longhurst, & Mazure, 1999), eating disorders (Bulik, Sullivan, & Rorty, 1989; Pope & Hudson, 1989; Zlotnick et al., 1996), and dissociative symptomatology (Kirby, Chu, & Dill, 1993). Kendler et al. (2000) found childhood sexual abuse to be most strongly associated with bulimia nervosa, and alcohol and other drug dependence.

There may be additional comorbid findings related to sexual abuse. Experiences of childhood sexual abuse have been found to negatively impact women's attitudes toward their bodies as indicated by measures of body dissatisfaction and cognitive-affective body image (Kearney-Cooke & Ackard, 2000; Wenninger & Heiman, 1998). Bulik et al. (1989) found that women with bulimia from families in which childhood sexual abuse occurred were more likely to have experienced a major depressive episode and to have a relative who had abused drugs. The pattern of comorbidity observed in bulimia nervosa and self-harm appears to have much in common with that observed in sequelae to childhood sexual abuse.

Most recently, Dohm, Striegel-Moore, Wilfley, Pike, Hook, and Fairburn (2002) found evidence that elevated rates of self-harm and substance abuse may not be uniquely related to bulimia nervosa per se, but to a characteristic shared by women with bulimia nervosa, such as a history of childhood sexual or physical abuse. This position is somewhat supported by our own finding that 84% of women with bulimia engaging in self-harm behavior also report a history of childhood sexual abuse. However, we also found a history of childhood sexual abuse to be quite prevalent (74%) in our control subjects with bulimia, suggesting a strong association between a history of childhood abuse, self-harm behavior, and bulimia nervosa.

We also found a trend toward a greater likelihood of laxative abuse, compared to those attempting suicide (Anderson & Bulik, 2002). Indeed, those engaging in self-harm behavior differed from control subjects with bulimia only in the greater frequency of laxative abuse. Previous studies have found that women with eating disorders who engage in vomiting and laxative use report a significantly higher frequency of self-injurious behaviors, and in women with bulimia, the self-injury was more likely to be a suicide attempt (Favaro & Santonastaso, 1996; Favaro & Santonastaso, 1997). Our findings are generally supportive of the association between purging and self-injurious behaviors. However, the only significant difference we found among groups was laxative abuse, which was significantly higher in individuals with self-harm behavior than either individuals with suicide attempts or controls, who did not differ. Although these findings do not support the specific association of laxative use with suicidality, they lend support to the broad conceptualization of laxative abuse as a self-punishing behavior and perhaps as another form of self-harm (Favaro & Santonastaso, 1996).

Axis I and II Comorbidity

While a broad pattern of psychiatric comorbidity is encountered in eating disorders, there appear to be specific associations of Axis I disorders with nonsuicidal self-harming behavior compared with controls. Specifically, we found self-harm behavior to be associated with comorbid major depression, drug dependence, and obsessive-compulsive disorder (Anderson & Bulik, 2002). The presence of affective disturbance in association with self-harm in bulimia nervosa (Favaro & Santonastaso, 1999) is consistent with the literature.

The strong association between drug dependence and self-harm observed in the present study is also consistent with previous findings in the literature (Casper & Lyubomirsky, 1997; Favaro & Santonastaso, 1997; Lacey, 1993; Welch & Fairburn, 1996). The constellation of greater drug dependence and laxative abuse in individuals with self-harm may suggest a stronger tendency toward abuse of any drugs in this group. Interestingly, Davis and Karvinin (2002) note an association of both addictive personality (characterized by impulsive, introverted, and anxious traits) and obsessive-compulsive disorder symptoms in intent to engage in self-harm behaviors. Broadly, self-harm behavior appears to be associated with (and may, in fact, constitute) behaviors designed to achieve anxiolytic relief, or are otherwise self-soothing and/or self-punishing.

The association of obsessive-compulsive behaviors with self-harm is intriguing in that self-harm behavior is often followed by an anxiolytic effect, which is similar to the function of compulsive behaviors in response to the obsession. This association may have implications for the efficacy of pharmacological treatments for obsessive-compulsive disorder in the treatment of self-harm behaviors.

Addictions, obsessive-compulsive symptoms, and self-harming behavior are each notable for their ability to release tension and, with the exception of obsessive-compulsive behaviors, may be self-harming. As Paul et al. (2002) observed, the function of self-injury is to reduce anger, self-punish, reduce tension, feel bodily instead of emotional pain, and end uncomfortable feelings. The association of disorders characterized by addictive, impulsive, obsessional, and compulsive traits appears to mirror an underlying psychological dynamic that is common to self-harm behavior, as opposed to constituting risk factors for self-harm in themselves.

With respect to personality disorder symptoms, we found a greater number in women with bulimia engaging in self-harm compared to control subjects with bulimia, but this increase did not reach significance. Among women with bulimia engaging in suicide attempts, the number of personality disorder symptoms differed significantly from controls for all three clusters. These findings are broadly consistent with the literature, although previous studies have reported significant associations with self-harm and personality disorder diagnoses (Dulit, Fyer, Leon, Brodsky, & Frances, 1994; Favaro & Santonastaso, 1997; Sansone, Gaither, & Songer, 2002; Schmidt & Telch, 1990; Yates, Sieleni, & Bowers, 1989). These differences may be related to our reduced power to detect differences based on a relatively small sample size. However, it is also possible that our findings could be accounted for by the exclusion of participants attempting suicide from the self-harm group.

Personality Characteristics

TCI Findings. In examining personality characteristics in self-harm behavior, we found the TCI personality dimension of *self-transcendence* to be significantly higher in individuals with self-harm than in individuals with suicide attempts or controls (Anderson & Bulik, 2002). In healthy individuals, self-transcendence is associated with qualities such as unpretentiousness, fulfillment, creativity, selflessness, and spirituality. In combination with lower scores on the other character dimensions such as self-directedness and cooperativeness, high self-transcendence is associated with proneness to psychosis and schizotypy. Previous studies have found high self-transcendence scores to be associated with depression (Hansenne et al., 1999), psychotic traits (Hansenne & Ansseau, 2001), dissociation (Grabe, Spitzer, & Juergen, 1999), and total Three Factor Eating Questionnaire scores and cognitive restraint (Gendall, Joyce, Sullivan, & Bulik, 1998). In the context of self-harm, it is possible that self-transcendence reflects dissociative aspects in which the individual's feeling of depersonalization and separateness creates a psychological distance between themselves and the act of self-harm. It may be, as well, that the act of self-harm occurs partly in response to feelings of dissociation and depersonalization. In this case, the act of self-harm may function to "bring them back" into a direct experience of the world via the sensual experience of self-inflicted injury. Gendall et al. (1998) observed that the characteristics of self-transcendence, such as the ability to disconnect from oneself and sustain suffering, may be advantageous to cognitively controlled individuals attempting to overcome the demands of hunger.

In an analysis of the self-transcendence subscales, we found a trend toward self-forgetfulness and transpersonal identification. The trend toward self-forgetfulness appears to be consonant with the feelings of dissociation and depersonalization discussed above. Transpersonal identification reflects a sense of spiritual or emotional connectedness with other people, animals, and nature, and a sense of unified connectedness in the world as a whole. This sense of involvement and connectedness may be partly reflective of adaptive attitudes and access to social support. While this may serve as a protective factor against suicide, the construct might also be tapping elements such as guilt and mortification associated with deeply held religious convictions. Indeed, another dimension of this subscale is that of altruistic self-sacrifice. Among individuals who engage in self-harm behavior, this construct might be associated with a willingness to self-punish as well as self-sacrifice.

Impulsivity/Compulsivity. Examining impulsivity and self-harming behavior in bulimia nervosa, we found self-harm behavior to fit the criteria established by Favaro and Santonastaso (2002) for impulsivity. As previously discussed, our follow-up analysis of impulsivity using the Barratt Impulsivity Scale found no significant association of impulsivity with self-harm, suicide attempts, or control subjects with bulimia. As such, measures of impulsivity per se may be of little utility in establishing risk factors for self-harm in bulimia nervosa. As previously noted, this may be in part a function of a broad association of bulimia nervosa with impulsivity that may mask impulsivity specifically associated with self-harm behavior.

Body Dissatisfaction/Interoceptive Awareness. As previously discussed, high scores in body dissatisfaction and interoceptive awareness characterized women with bulimia engaging in self-harm and suicide attempts compared to control subjects with bulimia. These findings suggest that women with bulimia engaging in self-harm behavior may actually be more acutely aware of their inner emotional state than control subjects with bulimia. As such, the experience of emotional pain may be more intense in women engaging in self-harm and suicide attempts, possibly providing greater impetus for displacing emotional pain into physical pain as suggested by Paul et al. (2002). With respect to body dissatisfaction, greater affective disturbance in women engaging in self-harming behavior, possibly exacerbated by a greater sensitivity to emotional pain, may account for cognitive distortion of body image resulting in a higher degree of reported body dissatisfaction.

Implications for Treatment

Although our research has been able to identify features that distinguish between individuals with bulimia who engage in self-harm behavior and those who attempt suicide, we do not wish to suggest that these features are predictive of risk for self-harm and suicide attempts. As mentioned previously, self-harm behavior can indeed turn lethal, and suicidal intent can vary across the course of illness. Characteristics shared by women with bulimia who engage in self-harm and suicide attempts include a history of childhood sexual abuse, affective disturbance, impulsivity, obsessive-compulsive features, body dissatisfaction, and interoceptive awareness. However, the salient distinguishing characteristics are as follows. Women with bulimia nervosa who attempt suicide may be broadly characterized by alcohol dependence, social phobia, impaired interpersonal functioning, and high harm avoidance. Women with bulimia engaging in nonsuicidal self-harm behavior may be characterized by both addictive behaviors (substance and laxative abuse), and higher self-transcendence. Higher self-transcendence may signal the utilization of dissociative defenses in response to a history of trauma and acute emotional pain.

The presence of an affective disturbance (Wonderlich, Myers, Norton, & Corby, 2002) and obsessive-compulsive characteristics in both self-harm and suicide attempts points to the role of serotonin dysregulation. As such, it is possible that current pharmacological treatments targeting serotonin dysregulation in depressive and obsessive-compulsive symptoms might be effective in the treatment of self-harm and suicidal behavior in bulimia nervosa. Other neurotransmitters may also be involved. For example, previous studies of self-harm behavior have noted their anxiolytic effects (Paul et al., 2002) and the possible association of this effect with endogenous opioid mechanisms (Davis & Karvinin, 2002). The involvement of endogenous opioid mechanisms has also been implicated in animal models of binge eating (Hagan, Holguin, Cabello, Hanscom, & Moss, 1997) and is well known to be involved in excessive exercise (which has also been found to be associated with intent to self-harm; Davis & Karvinin, 2002).

The attempt to self-sooth via binge eating and self-harm behavior and, arguably, drug and alcohol use, may suggest that the treatment of issues associated with underlying or past trauma (e.g., affective disturbance and childhood sexual abuse) may be critical to symptom remission and prevention of self-harm behavior and suicide attempts. Given the severity and early onset of abuse experiences, it is unlikely that short-term therapy models would be sufficient to address these issues fully. A combination of longer-term supportive therapy in individual or group therapy modalities designed to address the effects of past trauma, in combination with pharmacological treatment for depression and obsessive-compulsive features, might be indicated in patients presenting with features associated with self-harm and suicide attempts. In addition, focused behavioral and cognitive interventions designed to address comorbid alcohol and drug dependence appear to be strongly indicated, given the association of these disorders with self-harm, suicide attempts, and mortality (Keel et al., 2003).

In summary, the core characteristics associated with self-harm and suicide attempts in bulimia nervosa indicate a severity and complexity of presentation that requires targeted, focused therapeutic interventions designed to address specific patterns of comorbidity and interpersonal functioning. More effective treatment and prevention may be facilitated by the ability to understand factors that maintain self-harm behavior and lead to suicidal intent in women with bulimia via assessment of personality characteristics, drug and alcohol use, social support, and interpersonal functioning. Future research should seek to identify etiological factors related to self-harm and suicide attempts using prospective, longitudinal methodologies. Identifying risk factors for self-harm and suicide attempts would allow for the development of appropriate assessment, treatment, and prevention strategies.

References

Anderson, C. B., & Bulik, C. M. (2002). Self-harm and suicide attempts in bulimia nervosa. *Eating Disorders: The Journal of Treatment and Prevention, 10,* 227–243.

Barratt, E. S. (1985). Impulsiveness subtraits: Arousal and information processing. In J. T. Spence & C. E. Izzard (Eds.), *Motivation, emotion, & personality.* New York: Elsevier.

Bulik, C. M., Sullivan, P. F., & Joyce, P. R. (1999). Temperament, character and suicide attempts in anorexia nervosa, bulimia nervosa and major depression. *Acta Psychiatrica Scandinavica, 100,* 27–32.

Bulik, C. M., Sullivan, P. F., & Rorty, M. (1989). Childhood sexual abuse in women with bulimia. *Journal of Clinical Psychiatry, 50,* 460–464.

Casper, R. C., & Lyubomirsky, S. (1997). Individual psychopathology relative to reports of unwanted sexual experiences as predictor of a bulimic eating pattern. *International Journal of Eating Disorders, 21,* 229–236.

Chatterjee, S., Sunitha, T. A., Velayudhan, A., & Khanna, S. (1997). An investigation into the psychobiology of social phobia: Personality domains and serotonergic function. *Acta Psychiatrica Scandinavica, 95,* 544–550.

Cloninger, C. R. (1987). A systematic method for clinical description and classification of personality variants. *Archives of General Psychiatry, 44,* 573–588.

Corcos, M., Taieb, O., Benoit-Lamy, S., Paterniti, S., Jeammet, P., & Flament, M. F. (2002). Suicide attempts in women with bulimia nervosa: Frequency and characteristics. *Acta Psychiatrica Scandinavica, 106,* 381–386.

Davis, C., & Karvinin, K. (2002). Personality characteristics and intention to self-harm: A study of eating disordered patients. *Eating Disorders, 10,* 245–255.

Dohm, F. A., Striegel-Moore, R. H., Wilfley, D. E., Pike, K. M., Hook, J., & Fairburn, C. G. (2002). Self-harm and substance use in a community sample of Black and White women with binge eating disorder or bulimia nervosa. *International Journal of Eating Disorders, 32,* 389–400.

Dulit, R. A., Fyer, M. R., Leon, A. C., Brodsky, B. S., & Frances, A. J. (1994). Clinical correlates of self-mutilation in borderline personality disorder. *American Journal of Psychiatry, 151,* 1305–1311.

Eagles, J. M., Carson, D. P., Begg, A., & Naji, S. A. (2003). Suicide prevention: A study of patients' views. *British Journal of Psychiatry, 182,* 261–265.

Favaro, A., & Santonastaso, P. (1996). Purging behaviors, suicide attempts, and psychiatric symptoms in 398 eating disordered subjects. *International Journal of Eating Disorders, 20,* 99–103.

Favaro, A., & Santonastaso, P. (1997). Suicidality in eating disorders: Clinical and psychological correlates. *Acta Psychiatrica Scandinavica, 95,* 508–514.

Favaro, A., & Santonastaso, P. (1999). Different types of self-injurious behavior in bulimia nervosa. *Comprehensive Psychiatry, 40,* 57–60.

Favaro, A., & Santonastaso, P. (2002). The spectrum of self-injurious behavior in eating disorders. *Eating Disorders: The Journal of Treatment and Prevention, 10,* 215–225.

Gendall, K. A., Joyce, P. R., Sullivan, P. F., & Bulik, C. M. (1998). Personality and dimensions of dietary restraint. *International Journal of Eating Disorders, 24,* 371–379.

Grabe, H. J., Spitzer, C., & Juergen, F. H. (1999). Relationship of dissociation to temperament and character in men and women. *American Journal of Psychiatry, 156,* 1811–1813.

Hagan, M. M., Holguin, F. D., Cabello, C. E., Hanscom, D. R., & Moss, D. E. (1997). Combined naloxone and fluoxetine on deprivation-induced binge eating of palatable foods in rats. *Pharmacology Biochemistry and Behavior, 58,* 1103–1107.

Hansenne, M., & Ansseau, M. (2001). Contingent negative variation and personality in depression. *Neuropsychobiology, 44,* 7–12.

Hansenne, M., Reggers, J., Pinto, E., Kjiri, K., Ajamier, A., & Ansseau, M. (1999). Temperament and character inventory (TCI) and depression. *Journal of Psychiatric Research, 33,* 31–36.

Herzog, D. B., Greenwood, D. N., Dorer, D. J., Flores, A. T., Ekeblad, E. R., Richards, Blais, M. A., & Keller, M. B. (2000). Mortality in eating disorders: A descriptive study. *International Journal of Eating Disorders, 28,* 20–26.

Kearney-Cooke, A., & Ackard, D. M. (2000). The effects of sexual abuse on body image, self-image, and sexual activity of women. *Journal of Gender-Specific Medicine, 3,* 54–60.

Keel, P. K., Dorer, D. J., Eddy, K. T., Franko, D., Charatan, D. L., & Herzog, D. B. (2003). Predictors of mortality in eating disorders. *Archives of General Psychiatry, 60,* 179–183.

Keel, P. K., & Mitchell, J. E. (1997). Outcome in bulimia nervosa. *American Journal of Psychiatry, 154,* 313–321.

Keel, P. K., Mitchell, J. E., Davis, T. L., & Crow, S. J. (2001). Relationship between depression and body dissatisfaction in women diagnosed with bulimia nervosa. *International Journal of Eating Disorders, 30,* 48–56.

Kendler, K. S., Bulik, C. M., Silberg, J., Hettema, J. M., Myers, J., & Prescott, C. A. (2000). Childhood sexual abuse and adult psychiatric and substance use disorders in women: An epidemiological and cotwin control analysis. *Archives of General Psychiatry, 57,* 953–959.

Kim, S. W., & Hoover, K. M. (1996). Tridimensional personality questionnaire: Assessment in patients with social phobia and a control group. *Psychological Reports, 78,* 43–49.

Kirby, J. S., Chu, J. A., & Dill, D. L. (1993). Correlates of dissociative symptomatology in patients with physical and sexual abuse histories. *Comprehensive Psychiatry, 34,* 258–263.

Lacey, J. H. (1993). Self-damaging and addictive behaviour in bulimia nervosa: A catchment area study. *British Journal of Psychiatry, 163,* 190–194.

Mitchell, J. E., Pyle, R. L., Eckert, E. D., Hatsukami, D., & Soll, E. (1990). Bulimia nervosa in overweight individuals. *Journal of Nervous and Mental Disease, 178,* 324–327.

Murphy, G. E. (1988). Suicide and substance abuse. *Archives of General Psychiatry, 45,* 593–594.

Murphy, G. E., & Wetzel, R. D. (1990). The lifetime risk of suicide in alcoholism. *Archives of General Psychiatry, 47,* 383–392.

Paris, J., & Zweig-Frank, H. (1996). Deliberate self-harm and childhood sexual abuse. *American Journal of Psychiatry, 153,* 1237–1238.

Paul, T., Schroeter, K., Dahme, B., & Nutzinger, D. O. (2002). Self-injurious behavior in women with eating disorders. *American Journal of Psychiatry, 159,* 408–411.

Penas-Lledo, E., Vaz, F. J., Ramos, M. I., & Waller, G. (2002). Impulsive behaviors in bulimic patients: Relation to general psychopathology. *International Journal of Eating Disorders, 32,* 98–102.

Pope, H. G., & Hudson, J. I. (1989). Are eating disorders associated with borderline personality disorder? A critical review. *International Journal of Eating Disorders, 8,* 1–9.

Romans, S. E., Martin, J. L., Anderson, J. C., Herbison, G. P., & Mullen, P. E. (1995). Sexual abuse in childhood and deliberate self-harm. *American Journal of Psychiatry, 152,* 1336–1342.

Roy, A., & Linnoila, M. (1986). Alcoholism and suicide. *Suicide and Life-Threatening Behavior, 16,* 244–273.

Sansone, R. A., Gaither, G. A., & Songer, D. A. (2002). Self-harm behaviors across the life cycle: A pilot study of inpatients with borderline personality disorder. *Comprehensive Psychiatry, 43,* 215–218.

Sansone, R. A., & Levitt, J. L. (2002). Self-harm behaviors among those with eating disorders: An overview. *Eating Disorders: The Journal of Treatment and Prevention, 10,* 205–213.

Schmidt, N. B., & Telch, M. J. (1990). Prevalence of personality disorders among bulimics, non-bulimic binge eaters, and normal controls. *Journal of Psychopathology and Behavioral Assessment, 12,* 169–185.

Simeon, D., Stein, D. J., & Hollander, E. (1995). Depersonalization disorder and self-injurious behavior. *Journal of Clinical Psychiatry, 56 (Suppl. 4),* 36–39.

Svrakic, D. M., Whitehead, C., Przybeck, T. R., & Cloninger, C. R. (1993). Differential diagnosis of personality disorders by the seven-factor model of temperament and character. *Archives of General Psychiatry, 50,* 991–999.

van der Kolk, B. A., Perry, J. C., & Herman, J. L. (1991). Childhood origins of self-destructive behavior. *American Journal of Psychiatry, 148,* 1665–1671.

Weiss, E. L., Longhurst, J. G., & Mazure, C. M. (1999). Childhood sexual abuse as a risk factor for depression in women: Psychosocial and neurobiological correlates. *American Journal of Psychiatry, 156,* 816–828.

Welch, S. L., & Fairburn, C. G. (1996). Impulsivity or comorbidity in bulimia nervosa: A controlled study of deliberate self-harm and alcohol and drug misuse in a community sample. *British Journal of Psychiatry, 169,* 451–458.

Wenninger, K., & Heiman, J. R. (1998). Relating body image to psychological and sexual functioning in child sexual abuse survivors. *Journal of Traumatic Stress, 11,* 543–562.

Wonderlich, S., Myers, T., Norton, M., & Corby, R. (2002). Self-harm and bulimia nervosa: A complex connection. *Eating Disorders: The Journal of Treatment and Prevention, 10,* 257–267.

Wonderlich, S. A., Brewerton, T. D., Jocic, Z., Dansky, B. S., & Abbott, D. W. (1997). Relationship of childhood sexual abuse and eating disorders. *Journal of the American Academy of Child and Adolescent Psychiatry, 36,* 1107–1115.

Wonderlich, S. A., Wilsnack, R. W., Wilsnack, S. C., & Harris, T. R. (1996). Childhood sexual abuse and bulimic behavior in a nationally representative sample. *American Journal of Public Health, 86,* 1082–1086.

Yates, W. R., Sieleni, B., & Bowers, W. A. (1989). Clinical correlates of personality disorder in bulimia nervosa. *International Journal of Eating Disorders, 8,* 473–477.

Zlotnick, C., Hohlstein, L. A., Shea, M. T., Pearlstein, T., Recupero, P., & Bidadi, K. (1996). The relationship between sexual abuse and eating pathology. *International Journal of Eating Disorders, 20,* 129–134.

CHAPTER 5

Borderline Personality Disorder: Self-Harm and Eating Disorders

RANDY A. SANSONE, LORI A. SANSONE, AND JOHN L. LEVITT

Introduction

In this chapter, we provide an overview of borderline personality disorder (BPD) and discuss the relationship between BPD, self-harm behavior, and eating disorders. BPD is a disorder characterized by ongoing self-regulation difficulties (e.g., eating disorders) and chronic self-destructive behavior (e.g., self-harm). Epidemiological studies indicate that up to one-third of patients who engage in binging/purging have comorbid BPD. The etiology of BPD appears to be associated with early developmental trauma, although this does not exclude other possible contributory variables. With regard to diagnosis, reasonably clear *DSM* criteria exist, but we recommend using the Gunderson criteria, which can be organized around an acronym for easy recall. From a dynamic perspective, in those with BPD, the eating disorder symptoms appear to have dual meaning—complex relationships with food, body, and weight issues, as well as overt self-harm behavior (i.e., self-injury equivalents). Treatment for these issues is an integrated and long-term process.

In our opinion, one of the most fascinating psychiatric interfaces with eating disorders is BPD. This Axis II disorder is characterized by an intact social façade coupled with self-regulation difficulties and chronic self-destructive behavior. Although the explicit etiology of BPD remains unknown, empirical data suggest that an early history of abuse is often a common contributory variable, and various forms of abuse have been implicated. Present in up to one-third of patients with eating disorders, comorbid BPD alters the functional significance of the eating disorder symptoms. In this chapter, we discuss these various issues and overview the integration of eating-disorder and BPD treatment, with an emphasis upon the management of self-harm behavior (SHB).

Definition of BPD

Classified as a personality disorder in *DSM-IV* (American Psychiatric Association, 1994), BPD is characterized by longstanding and enduring pathological patterns of cognition, affect, and behavior that often date back to childhood. BPD is most distinguished by chronic self-regulation difficulties and longstanding self-harm behavior. Self-regulation difficulties may manifest in many behavioral areas including difficulties modulating eating behavior (e.g., anorexia or bulimia nervosa, binge eating disorder, obesity), substances (e.g., prescription and/or illicit substance abuse), mood (e.g., chronically dysphoric or labile mood), money (e.g., bankrupt-cies, difficulty managing credit cards, gambling problems), sexual behavior (e.g., promiscuity), and interpersonal boundaries in relationships with others. Chronic SHB may manifest in a panoramic and seemingly endless number of ways including self-mutilation (e.g., cutting, burning, hitting, biting, slapping oneself), multiple suicide attempts, engagement in abusive relationships, and high-risk hobbies (e.g., bungee jumping) or behaviors (e.g., frequenting dangerous bars, jogging in city parks at night). Despite the internal chaos manifested by pervasive self-regulation difficulties and SHB, borderline individuals display an amazingly intact social façade for intermittent periods of time. Because of this seeming paradox (i.e., internal chaos versus a transiently intact social façade), individuals suffering from BPD have been the subject of many movies including *Leave Her to Heaven* (1946), *Play Misty for Me* (1971), *Looking for Mr. Goodbar* (1977), *The Rose* (1979), *Fatal Attraction* (1987), *Misery* (1990), *Single White Female* (1992), and *The Crush* (1993).

Epidemiology

Prevalence of BPD in the General Population

According to *DSM-IV* (American Psychiatric Association, 1994), the prevalence of BPD among the general population is approximately 2%. Stone suggests a higher prevalence at 10% (Stone, 1986). However, to date, no large epidemiological studies, such as the National Comorbidity Survey, have explored the prevalence of Axis II disorders in the general population.

BPD and Gender Differences

While *DSM-IV* indicates a greater prevalence of BPD among females compared with males, this conclusion may not be accurate. Investigators have found differences in personality stylings according to gender (Zanarini et al., 1998a), with females appearing more histrionic and males appearing more narcissistic and/or antisocial. Because of this, it may be that males are misdiagnosed with narcissistic or antisocial personality. As a clinical caveat, males with antisocial features can be subdivided according to interpersonal attachment style. Those with low interpersonal attachment are likely to be genuine antisocial personalities, while those with high interpersonal attachment are likely to suffer from BPD.

In addition to gender differences in BPD, Zlotnick, Rothschild, and Zimmerman (2002) found that associated Axis I disorders displayed gender patterns as well. In this regard, men with BPD were more likely to be diagnosed with substance abuse and intermittent explosive disorder, while women with BPD were more often diagnosed with eating disorders.

BPD and Cultural Influences

Paris (1996) suggests that BPD is more prevalent in Westernized cultures. However, cultural influences may temper symptom presentation, thus affecting diagnosis and perceived prevalence rates. For example, compared with patients in the United States, Moriya, Myake, Minakawa, Ikuta, and Nishizino-Maher (1993) found a lower prevalence of substance abuse and more frequent masochistic relationships with parents among Japanese subjects with BPD, while Ikuta and colleagues (1994) found few symptom differences. In this regard, we suspect that cultural influences genuinely temper the types of symptoms that emerge in individuals with BPD, which could have implications for measures of and diagnostic approaches to BPD that have been developed in the United States.

Prevalence of BPD among Those with Eating Disorders

In studies concurrently assessing for multiple Axis II diagnoses, the majority of researchers report that BPD is the predominant personality disorder among those with binging/purging eating disorders (Dennis & Sansone, 1997). The prevalence of BPD among binging/purging bulimics and anorexics appears to be around one-third (Dennis & Sansone, 1997). As expected, inpatient populations demonstrate a higher prevalence of comorbid BPD than outpatient populations (Dennis & Sansone, 1997). In contrast, among restrictors with anorexia nervosa, the most common personality pathologies are the Cluster C disorders, which include obsessive-compulsive personality disorder (Dennis & Sansone, 1997).

With regard to obesity, most studies indicate that a minority of subjects suffers from BPD (Sansone & Sansone, in 2003; Sansone, Sansone, & Morris, 1996; Sansone, Wiederman, & Sansone, 2000), with higher prevalence rates among those seeking psychological treatment (Sansone et al., 1996) and/or suffering from binge-eating disorder (Sansone et al., 2000). As for binge eating disorder, prevalence rates of BPD have varied from 6 to 30% (Sansone et al., 2000). In a recent study, Azuma and colleagues (2000) found that, on Rorschach testing, obese individuals with binge eating disorder had lower scores on reality testing and more characteristics of BPD than those without binge eating behavior, which supports earlier conclusions.

Prevalence of Eating Disorders among Those with BPD

BPD is characteristically associated with multiple Axis I diagnoses (Zanarini et al., 1998b; Zimmerman & Mattia, 1999). In a large cohort of patients with BPD, Zanarini and colleagues (1998b) reported the lifetime prevalence for eating disorders as 53%. Zimmerman and Mattia reported similar findings.

Prevalence of BPD among Those with Eating Disorders and Comorbid Substance Abuse

A number of studies have explored the relationship between substance abuse and eating disorders (Sansone, Fine, & Nunn, 1994). Suzuki, Hihuchi, Yamada, Misutani, and Kono (1993) found a higher prevalence of BPD among subjects with both substance abuse and eating disorders (62%), compared with alcoholics without an eating disorder. Sansone and colleagues (1994) found that women with eating disorders *and* substance abuse were far more likely to have borderline personality symptomatology, as well as a higher number of SHBs, compared with either subjects with eating disorders only or those with substance abuse only. Collectively, these preceding studies suggest that Axis I symptoms characterized by impulsivity (e.g., binge eating, purging behavior, substance abuse, SHB) predict a greater likelihood of a comorbid Axis II diagnosis of BPD.

Etiology of Borderline Personality

The explicit etiology of BPD remains unknown. However, repetitive trauma (e.g., sexual, emotional, physical abuse; witnessing of violence) by a caretaker during early development has been associated with BPD in numerous studies (Sansone & Sansone, 2000). In support of these findings, in a sample of patients with BPD, Zanarini and colleagues (1997) empirically confirmed the presence of early developmental trauma in 85%. Likewise, using three different diagnostic approaches to BPD, we found that those with histories of childhood abuse had a significantly greater number of confirmations on BPD measures than participants without a history of abuse (Sansone, Gaither, & Songer, 2002). If studies confirm a causal, or partially causal, relationship between childhood trauma and BPD, clinicians might more accurately conceptualize BPD as an *early developmental trauma syndrome*, rather than a genuine personality disorder. Indeed, some clinicians are lobbying to rename the disorder. However, not all studies support the childhood-abuse hypothesis (Sansone & Sansone, 2000).

There may be other contributory variables to BPD as well, including a predisposing or vulnerable temperament (Zanarini & Frankenburg, 1997), traumatic triggering events (Zanarini & Frankenburg, 1997), inconsistent treatment by a caretaker (Zanarini, Ruser, Frankenburg, Hennen, & Gunderson, 2000), and a negative family environment (Gunderson & Lyoo, 1997) characterized by "biparental failure" (Zanarini et al., 2000). Compared with other psychiatric disorders, a genetic predisposition to BPD remains controversial (Torgerson, 1994, 2000) in that clear and convincing evidence is lacking.

Some studies suggest various biological abnormalities in patients with BPD. These include hypometabolism in portions of the cerebral cortex (De la Fuente et al., 1997), abnormal neurochemical levels in cerebral spinal fluid (Chotai, Kullgren, & Asberg, 1998), abnormal electroencephalogram studies (De la Fuente, Tugendhaft, & Mavroudakis, 1998), low serum cholesterol levels (New et al., 1999), and specific relationships with serotonin and arginine vasopressin levels in cerebrospinal fluid (Cocarro, Berman, Kavoussi, & Hauger, 1996; Coccaro, Kavoussi, Hauger, Cooper, & Ferris, 1998). As caveats, the findings of these studies are limited by very small sample sizes. In addition, it is unknown whether these biological findings are geniune causal factors for BPD or relate to the outcomes of early developmental trauma (Coupland, 2000).

To summarize, at the present time, the likely etiology of BPD appears to be repetitive trauma in early development coupled with a lack of parental support (i.e., "biparental failure"; Zanarini et al., 2000), although various other factors may temper the degree or severity of the disorder.

If the childhood trauma theory is accurate, how does early developmental trauma relate to SHB in adulthood? We explored this issue in a sample of 147 women in a primary care setting (Wiederman, Sansone, & Sansone, 1999), and found that sexual abuse, physical abuse, and witnessing violence in childhood were related to an increased likelihood of bodily self-injury in adulthood. Emotional abuse was not. These findings suggest that the direct experience or observation of body violation in childhood may developmentally precede subsequent bodily self-injury in some individuals in adulthood. Indeed, the violation of body boundaries in childhood, either directly (e.g., physical and/or sexual abuse) or indirectly (e.g., witnessing of violence), may lower the threshold for subsequent bodily self-harm through a devaluing or dehumanization of one's own body. Likewise, dissociation, a psychological response to trauma in childhood, may result in the disconnection of psychological self from bodily self (i.e., "you can hurt my body, but not me"), lowering the threshold for self-directed SHB. Thus, the backdrop of childhood trauma might explain the seeming acceptance and tolerability of SHB among adolescents and adults with eating disorders and BPD.

The Diagnostic Approach to BPD

DSM-IV and the Gunderson Criteria

While *DSM-IV* (American Psychiatric Association, 1994) provides reasonably clear and specific criteria for the diagnosis of BPD (see Table 5.1), they can be difficult to recall. In the clinical setting, we suggest the use of the Gunderson criteria (Kolb & Gunderson, 1980), which were originally introduced as a semi-structured interview, the Diagnostic Interview for Borderlines, to diagnose subjects with BPD in research settings. These criteria can be organized around the acronym P-I-S-I-A and are shown in Table 5.2.

TABLE 5.1 The Criteria for Borderline Personality Disorder as Listed in the *Diagnostic and Statistical Manual of Mental Disorders* (4th ed.; American Psychiatric Association, 1994) Reprinted with permission.

Frantic efforts to avoid real or imagined abandonment
A pattern of unstable and intense interpersonal relationships characterized by alternating between extremes of idealization and devaluation
Identity disturbance: markedly and persistently unstable self-image or sense of self
Impulsivity in at least two areas that are potentially self-damaging (e.g., spending, sex, substance abuse, reckless driving, binge eating)
Recurrent suicidal behavior, gestures, or threats, or self-mutilating behavior
Affective instability due to a marked reactivity of mood (e.g., intense episodic dysphoria, irritability, or anxiety usually lasting a few hours and only rarely more than a few days)
Chronic feelings of emptiness
Inappropriate, intense anger or difficulty controlling anger (e.g., frequent displays of temper, constant anger, recurrent physical fights)
Transient, stress-related paranoid ideation or severe dissociative symptoms

TABLE 5.2 Adaptation of the Gunderson Criteria for Borderline Personality Disorder*
Reprinted with permission.

P	**Psychotic/quasi-psychotic episodes:** transient, fleeting, brief episodes that tend to be persistent over the patient's lifetime (i.e., the particular phenomenon recurs); may include Depersonalization Derealization Dissociation Rage reactions Paranoia (patient recognizes the illogical nature of their suspiciousness) Fleeting or isolated hallucinations or delusions Unusual reactions to drugs
I	**Impulsivity:** longstanding behaviors that may be stable over time, coexist with other behaviors, or replace each other over time (i.e., substitution) **Self-regulation** difficulties (e.g., eating disorders such as anorexia and bulimia nervosa, binge eating disorder, obesity; drug/alcohol/prescription abuse; money management difficulties such as bankruptcies, credit card difficulties, uncontrolled gambling; promiscuity; mood regulation difficulties) **Self-destructive behaviors** (e.g., self-mutilation such as hitting, cutting, burning, or biting oneself; suicide attempts; sadomasochistic relationships; high-risk hobbies such as parachuting or racing; high-risk behaviors such as frequenting dangerous bars or jogging in parks at night)
S	**Social adaptation:** superficially intact social veneer; if the individual demonstrates high achievement, performance is usually inconsistent and erratic
I	**Interpersonal relationships:** chaotic and unsatisfying relationships with others; the relationship style is characterized by "dichotomous relatedness," wherein social relationships tend to be very superficial, and transient and personal relationships tend to be extremely intense, manipulative, and dependent; intense fears of being alone; rage with the primary caretaker
A	**Affect:** chronically dysphoric or labile; since adolescence, the majority of the mood experience has been dysphoric with the predominant affects being anxiety, anger, depression, and/or emptiness

* Kolb, J. E., & Gunderson, J. G. 1980. Diagnosing borderline patients with a semi-structured interview. *Archives of General Psychiatry, 37*, 37–41. Adapted with permission.
Note: In using the above criteria, the patient must meet criteria in each category (i.e., the patient must have one type of longstanding quasi-psychotic phenomenon, both longstanding self-regulation difficulties and self-destructive behavior, a superficially intact veneer, chronically unsatisfying relationships with others, and chronic mood disturbance with either persistent dysphoria or mood lability.

The Self-Harm Inventory

In addition, clinicians may consider the use of self-report measures such as the Self-Harm Inventory (SHI; Sansone, Wiederman, & Sansone, 1998), a 22-item, self-report measure that assesses SHB as well as indicates a possible diagnosis of BPD (see the chapter on assessment). In comparison studies with the Diagnostic Interview for Borderlines (Kolb & Gunderson, 1980), the SHI demonstrated a diagnostic accuracy of 84%, yet takes minimal time to administer. While other measures are available for the diagnosis of BPD, most are designed for research settings and have specific limitations (e.g., fee for use; training required for administration; too lengthy, impersonal, or structured for the clinical setting).

Polymorphic Symptom Presentation

From a phenomenological perspective, BPD appears to have a seemingly endless array of clinical manifestations, but there are valid explanations for this. First, there are endless behavioral permutations of self-regulation difficulties and SHB (i.e., polymorphic symptom presentation). Second, individuals with BPD exist along a functional continuum, from low-functioning to high-functioning, with marked variability in presentation at the ends of the continuum. For example, low-functioning individuals may exhibit graphic SHB (e.g., obvious scars), multiple and recurrent quasi-psychotic episodes, dramatic mood lability, and exceedingly unstable interpersonal relationships. In contrast, high-functioning individuals may exhibit a binging/purging eating disorder, abuse of alcohol and alprazolam, several "soft" suicide attempts, and a longstanding marital relationship to a financially successful but emotionally abusive partner. Both individuals on this continuum fulfill criteria, but in very contrasting ways. In our experience, the majority of individuals with eating disorders and comorbid BPD appear to reside in the middle to upper levels of this functional continuum.

Another element of variability among individuals with BPD is the various comorbid personality stylings, which introduces the topic of psychostructural theory (Chatham, 1985; Kernberg, 1985; Stone, 1980). According to psychostructural theory, there are only a handful of distinct levels of psychological functioning, which the psychostructuralists describe as the "core wiring" of an individual. For most theorists, these levels include narcissistic, borderline, and psychotic levels of functioning. According to the theory, these core wirings are negotiated through various personality stylings, many of which are represented by the DSM Axis II disorders. For example, a borderline individual could have comorbid obsessive-compulsive, histrionic, antisocial, or dependent personality features. The relationship between the core psychostructure and the personality styling might be conceptualized as a coated chocolate candy in which the borderline core is coated with a personality styling (see Figure 5.1). The advantage of the psychostructural approach is that it facilitates a more descriptive sense of the patient. In addition, these personality stylings appear to have prognostic

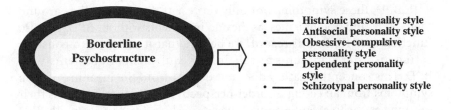

Fig. 5.1 The relationship between a borderline psychostructure and several personality stylings

significance (Stone, 1990), with antisocial overlays predicting poorer prognoses, compared with obsessive-compulsive overlays, which are common among those with eating disorders and BPD.

Multi-Impulsive Personality Disorder

In 1986, Lacey and Evans introduced the concept of "multi-impulsive personality disorder," a personality disorder that they defined by multiple impulsive behaviors. In 1994, Fichter, Quadflieg, and Rief introduced the concept of "multi-impulsive bulimia," which they defined as the combination of bulimic symptoms and minimally three of the following impulsive characteristics: suicide attempts, severe "autoregression," shoplifting, alcohol abuse, drug abuse, and sexual promiscuity. According to *DSM-IV*, the criteria for borderline personality include binge eating, recurrent suicidal behaviors, transient stress-induced dissociative symptoms, substance abuse, and impulsivity with sex. The only potential differences between these two criteria sets are "autoregression" (transient stress-induced symptoms?) and shoplifting (not explicitly stated in the *DSM*). While the explicit relationship between BPD and multi-impulsivity bulimia is unknown, they appear to be related constructs (Wonderlich, Myers, Norton, & Crosby, 2002). Empirical studies support this impression. Matsunaga and colleagues (2000b) found that patients with multi-impulsive bulimia had a high prevalence of BPD, and Miller (2000) found that multi-impulsive bulimia accounted for nearly one-third of their study sample and was associated with a poor prognosis (similar observations are noted with BPD). In our opinion, multi-impulsive bulimia is most likely another variation or subpopulation of patients with the combination of BPD and bulimia nervosa.

Functional Meaning of Symptoms

In our opinion, eating disorder symptoms appear to have functional differences in patients with BPD versus those without BPD. For patients with BPD, these symptoms not only represent distorted beliefs around food, body, and weight issues, as they do in patients without BPD, but also function as SHB. In this regard, we believe that it is logical to construe eating disorder symptoms as self-injury equivalents in patients with BPD. This conceptualization does not detract from the meaning of such symptoms from an eating disorder perspective, but rather *augments* their meaning as a whole. For example, substance abuse for a patient with BPD clearly fulfills the function of substance abuse as in patients without BPD (i.e., escapism, avoidance, acting out). In addition, however, it functions as a self-injury equivalent in these patients through self-sabotage (e.g., poor academic and/or job performance, erratic behavior in relationships). Therefore, we conceptualize eating disorder symptoms in the patient with BPD as part eating disorder and part SHB, but neither alone.

Treatment Strategy

The treatment of individuals with both BPD and eating disorders is a long-term, integrated, and multidimensional process. We have described the actual treatment process, and its stages, elsewhere (Dennis & Sansone, 1990; Dennis & Sansone, 1997; Sansone & Johnson, 1995). In our experience, most of these patients seem to benefit from a treatment perspective that predominantly focuses on BPD, with a secondary emphasis on eating disorder issues. We base this upon the importance of stabilizing the treatment relationship in terms of transference issues, reasonably containing multiple SHBs at the outset of treatment, and recognizing the deeper issues around self-regulation and early developmental trauma with regard to dysfunctional eating behaviors. The eating disorder is approached from a cognitive (e.g., working on dysfunctional beliefs), behavioral (e.g., food records), and educational approach (e.g., nutritional education), but symptoms are framed as part of a larger spectrum of SHB.

In working with these complex patients, one needs to be alert to: (a) the engulfing and intense transference issues; (b) the "two steps forward, one step backward" nature of the treatment; (c) the crucial role of emotionally neutral limit-setting by the therapist (essential for the facilitation of self-regulation); (d) the need for combination treatment approaches (e.g., pharmacotherapy and psychotherapy); (e) the long-term nature of the treatment (e.g., years); (f) the potential development of very unexpected and intense counter-transference reactions; (g) the increased risk of suicide among these patients; and (h) the need for a consistent treatment structure (e.g., same time, same place, same office staff). At the outset of treatment, it is essential that high-lethal behaviors be contained (Sansone & Johnson, 1995), and that low-lethal behaviors be confronted only if they interfere with treatment. We also caution the rapid integration of multiple treatment providers prior to stabilization of the therapy relationship because of the toxic effects of splitting. Finally, and most importantly, we believe that this type of treatment directly and actively involves the therapist as an emotional participant. This process can be exceedingly demanding, and therapists may need team support in maintaining their stamina with more difficult cases.

One interesting question is whether personality disorder features remit with eating disorder treatment. According to Matsunaga and colleagues (2000a), recovery may have an attenuating effect, but personality disorder symptoms often persist, as one might expect. This finding is consistent with our clinical experience. For those patients with both BPD and an eating disorder, the fundamental goals of treatment are to advance them along the functional continuum and to contain the more toxic effects of symptoms. In essence, treatment ameliorates symptoms but may not fully eradicate them.

Conclusion

A substantial minority of patients with eating disorder has comorbid BPD. This disorder appears to have trauma-related etiological underpinnings. Diagnosis can be difficult due to the potential for polymorphic presentations. With regard to treatment, the eating disorder symptoms may be seen as both related to food/body/weight issues and self-injury equivalents. We recommend that the treatment focus predominantly on BPD and secondarily on the eating disorder symptoms. Treatment is long-term, and while eating disorder symptoms may ameliorate, the symptoms of personality disorder often continue. Further research is needed to determine the long-term outcome of patients suffering from both an eating disorder and BPD, particularly in terms of their functionality, social adjustment, and the presence or not of symptom substitution.

References

American Psychiatric Association. (1994). *Diagnostic and statistical manual of mental disorders* (4th ed.). Washington, DC: Author.

Azuma, Y., Kodama, K., Noda, S., Sato, R., Okada, S., Yamanouchi, N., et al. (2000). Personality traits of simple obese patients with binge eating disorder. *Clinical Psychiatry, 42,* 605–610.

Chatham, P. M. (1985). *Treatment of the borderline personality.* New York: Jason Aronson.

Chotai, J., Kullgren, G., & Asberg, M. (1998). CSF monoamine metabolites in relation to the Diagnostic Interview for Borderline patients (DIB). *Neuropsychobiology, 38,* 207–212.

Coccaro, E. F., Berman, M. E., Kavoussi, R. J., & Hauger, R. L. (1996). Relationship of prolactin response to d-fenfluramine to behavioral and questionnaire assessments of aggression in personality-disordered men. *Biological Psychiatry, 40,* 157–164.

Coccaro, E. F., Kavoussi, R. J., Hauger, R. L., Cooper, T. B., & Ferris, C. F. (1998). Cerebrospinal fluid vasopressin levels: Correlates with aggression and serotonin function in personality-disordered subjects. *Archives of General Psychiatry, 55,* 708–714.

Coupland, N. J. (2000). Brain mechanisms and neurotransmitters. In D. Nutt, J. R. T. Davidson, & J. Zohar (Eds.), *Post-traumatic stress disorder: Diagnosis, management and treatment.* London: Martin Dunitz.

De la Fuente, J. M., Goldman, S., Stanus, E., Vizuete, C., Morlan, I., Bobes, J., et al. (1997). Brain glucose metabolism in borderline personality disorder. *Journal of Psychiatric Research, 31,* 531–541.

De la Fuente, J. M., Tugendhaft, P., & Mavroudakis, N. (1998). Electroencephalographic abnormalities in borderline personality disorder. *Psychiatry Research, 77,* 131–138.

Dennis, A. B., & Sansone, R. A. (1990). The clinical stages of treatment for the eating disorder patient with borderline personality disorder. In C. Johnson (Ed.), *Psychodynamic treatment for anorexia and bulimia nervosa* (pp. 128–164). New York: Guilford.

Dennis, A. B., & Sansone, R. A. (1997). Treatment of patients with personality disorders. In D. M. Garner & P. E. Garfinkel (Eds.), *Handbook of treatment for eating disorders* (2nd ed., pp. 437–449). New York: Guilford.

Fichter, M. M., Quadflieg., N., & Rief, W. (1994). Course of multi-impulsive bulimia. *Psychological Medicine, 24,* 591–604.

Gunderson, J. G., & Lyoo, I. K. (1997). Family problems and relationships for adults with borderline personality disorder. *Harvard Review of Psychiatry, 4,* 272–278.

Ikuta, N., Zanarini, M. C., Minakawa, K., Miyake, Y., Moriya, N., & Nishizono-Maher, A. (1994). Comparison of American and Japanese outpatients with borderline personality disorder. *Comprehensive Psychiatry, 35,* 382–385.

Kernberg, O. F. (1985). *Borderline conditions and pathological narcissism* (2nd ed.). Northvale, NJ: Jason Aronson.

Kolb, J. E., & Gunderson, J. G. (1980). Diagnosing borderline patients with a semistructured interview. *Archives of General Psychiatry, 37,* 37–41.

Lacey, J. H., & Evans, C. D. (1986). The impulsivist: A multi-impulsive personality disorder. *British Journal of Addiction, 81,* 641–649.

Matsunaga, H., Kaye, W. H., McConaha, C., Plotnicov, K., Pollice, C., & Rao, R. (2000a). Personality disorders among subjects recovered from eating disorders. *International Journal of Eating Disorders, 27,* 353–357.

Matsunaga, H., Kiriike, N., Iwasaki, Y., Miyata, A., Matsui, T., Nagata, T., et al. (2000b). Multi-impulsivity among bulimic patients in Japan. *International Journal of Eating Disorders, 27,* 348–352.

Miller, K. B. (2000). The long-term course of bulimia nervosa: Relapse, recovery and comorbidity over time. *Dissertation Abstracts International, 61,* 542.

Moriya, N., Miyake, Y., Minakawa, K., Ikuta, N., & Nishizono-Maher, A. (1993). Diagnosis and clinical features of borderline personality disorder in the East and West: A preliminary report. *Comprehensive Psychiatry, 34,* 418–423.

New, A. S., Sevin, E. M., Mitropoulou, V., Reynolds, D., Novotny, S. L., Callahan, A., et al. (1999). Serum cholesterol and impulsivity in personality disorders. *Psychiatry Research, 85,* 145–150.

Paris, J. (1996). Cultural factors in the emergence of borderline pathology. *Psychiatry, 59,* 185–192.

Sansone, R. A., Fine, M. A., & Nunn, J. L. (1994). A comparison of borderline personality symptomatology and self-destructive behavior in women with eating, substance abuse, and both eating and substance abuse disorders. *Journal of Personality Disorders, 8,* 219–228.

Sansone, R. A., Gaither, G. A., & Songer, D. A. (2002). The relationships among childhood abuse, borderline personality, and self-harm behavior in psychiatric inpatients. *Violence and Victims, 17,* 49–55.

Sansone, R. A., & Johnson, C. L. (1995). Treating the eating disorder patient with borderline personality: Theory and technique. In J. Barber & P. Crits-Christoph (Eds.), *Dynamic therapies for psychiatric disorders (Axis I)* (pp. 230–266). New York: Basic Books.

Sansone, R. A., & Sansone, L. A. (2000). Borderline personality disorder: The enigma. *Primary Care Reports, 6,* 219–226.

Sansone, R. A., & Sansone, L. A. (2003). Obesity and borderline personality: An integrated research perspective. In F. Columbus (Ed.), *Progress in eating disorders research.* Huntingon, New York: Nova Science Publishers, pp. 195–208.

Sansone, R. A., Sansone, L. A., & Morris, D. W. (1996). Prevalence of borderline personality symptoms in two groups of obese subjects. *American Journal of Psychiatry, 153,* 117–118.

Sansone, R. A., Wiederman, M. W., & Sansone, L. A. (1998). The Self-Harm Inventory (SHI): Development of a scale for identifying self-destructive behaviors and borderline personality disorder. *Journal of Clinical Psychology, 54,* 973–983.

Sansone, R. A., Wiederman, M. W., & Sansone, L. A. (2000). The prevalence of borderline personality disorder among individuals with obesity. A critical review of the literature. *Eating Behaviors, 1,* 93–104.

Stone, M. H. (1980). *The borderline syndromes: Constitution, adaptation and personality.* New York: McGraw-Hill.

Stone, M. H. (1986). Borderline personality disorder. In R. Michels & J. O. Cavenar (Eds.), *Psychiatry* (2nd ed., pp. 1–15). Philadelphia: Lippincott.

Stone, M. H. (1990). *The fate of borderline patients.* New York: Guilford.

Suzuki, K., Higuchi, S., Yamada, K., Misutani, Y., & Kono, H. (1993). Young female alcoholics with and without eating disorders: A comparative study in Japan. *American Journal of Psychiatry, 150,* 1053–1058.

Torgersen, S. (1994). Genetics in borderline conditions. *Acta Psychiatrica Scandinavica, 379,* 19S–25S.

Torgersen, S. (2000). Genetics of patients with borderline personality disorder. *Psychiatric Clinics of North America, 23,* 1–9.

Wiederman, M. W., Sansone, R. A., & Sansone, L. A. (1999). Bodily self-harm and its relationship to childhood abuse among women in a primary care setting. *Violence against Women, 5,* 155–163.

Wonderlich, S., Myers, T., Norton, M., & Crosby, R. (2002). Self-harm and bulimia nervosa: A complex connection. *Eating Disorders, 10,* 257–267.

Zanarini, M. C., & Frankenburg, F. R. (1997). Pathways to the development of borderline personality disorder. *Journal of Personality Disorders, 11,* 93–104.

Zanarini, M. C., Frankenburg, F. R., Dubo, E. D., Sickel, A. E., Trikha, A., Levin, A., et al. (1998a). Axis II comorbidity of borderline personality disorder. *Comprehensive Psychiatry, 39,* 296–302.

Zanarini, M. C., Frankenburg, F. R., Dubo, E. D., Sickel, A. E., Trikha, A., Levin, A., et al. (1998b). Axis I comorbidity of borderline personality disorder. *American Journal of Psychiatry, 155,* 1733–1739.

Zanarini, M. C., Frankenburg, F. R., Reich, D. B., Marino, M. F., Lewis, R. E., Williams, A. A., et al. (2000). Biparental failure in the childhood experiences of borderline patients. *Journal of Personality Disorders, 14,* 264–273.

Zanarini, M. C., Ruser, T. F., Frankenburg, F. R., Hennen, J., & Gunderson, J. G. (2000). Risk factors associated with the dissociative experiences of borderline patients. *Journal of Nervous and Mental Disease, 188,* 26–30.

Zanarini, M. C., Williams, A. A., Lewis, R. E., Reich, R. B., Vera, S. C., Marino, M. F., et al. (1997). Reported pathological childhood experiences associated with the development of borderline personality disorder. *American Journal of Psychiatry, 154,* 1101–1106.

Zimmerman, M., & Mattia, J. I. (1999). Axis I diagnostic comorbidity and borderline personality disorder. *Comprehensive Psychiatry, 40,* 245–252.

Zlotnick, C., Rothschild, L., & Zimmerman, M. (2002). The role of gender in the clinical presentation of patients with borderline personality disorder. *Journal of Personality Disorders, 16,* 277–282.

CHAPTER 6

Feminist Perspectives on Self-Harm Behavior and Eating Disorders

BETH HARTMAN MCGILLEY

Younger women … may experience a greater disparity between new social opportunities for equity that have not been matched with equity in the body domain. This discrepancy may relate to the prevalence of potentially harmful bodily mediated behaviors such as eating disorders, smoking, self-harm or high risk sexual behavior in young women.

Niva Piran, 2001

Introduction

Researchers and clinicians in the eating disorder (ED) and trauma fields have recently synergized efforts to further understand the phenomenon of self-harm behavior (SHB). In the aftermath of trauma or in relationship to borderline personality disorder (BPD), theories regarding the etiology and function of SHB have received considerable attention (Herman, 1993; Paris, 1992; van der Kolk, 1987; van der Kolk, Hostetler, Herron, & Fisler, 1994; van der Kolk, Perry, & Herman, 1991). However, the specific relationship between ED and SHB, especially in the absence of a traumatic history or BPD, requires further clarification (Paul, Schroeter, Dahme, & Nutzinger, 2002). A theoretical perspective that can illuminate the possibilities beyond simple diagnostic classifications is required. A feminist formulation, by design, attempts to incorporate diverse perspectives and to locate the crux of understanding in the sociopolitical structure within which the phenomenon is occurring.

Feminist literature is replete with discussions regarding the body as a source of trauma, degradation, objectification, and commodification, and is thus a rich resource for integrating and expanding upon the understanding of SHB in the context of ED. In her seminal work with young women, Piran (2001) critically examines the "plight of female" bodies in a patriarchal context, and advocates for the restorative and transformative applications of feminist interventions.

> Feminism, I believe, has a special role in supporting young women's voicing of problematic experiences in the body domain, contextualizing it socially and politically, reinforcing peer- and multi-generational connections in exploring these experiences, and using these newly forged connections for the sake of social transformation and change. (Piran, 2001, p. 172)

In this chapter, a brief review of SHB and its dynamics will be followed by a description of core, organizing feminist constructs essential to honoring this perspective. These principles will then be integrated into a feminist understanding of the relationship between SHB and ED. In keeping with feminist tradition, which authorizes and enlists the "experience of the oppressed in their own voices" (Brabeck & Brown, 1997, p. 32), this chapter will close with a poignant depiction of one patient's healing journey through her journaling and poetry.

The Definition of SHB

SHB was first documented in the psychiatric literature in the nineteenth century (Bergman, 1846). In recent decades, extensive research has investigated the relationship between SHB and a history of trauma (Briere & Zaidi, 1989; Herman, 1993; Romans, Martin, Anderson, Herbison, & Mullen, 1995; van der Kolk & Fisler, 1994; van der Kolk et al., 1991; Walsh & Rosen, 1988), borderline personality disorder (Russ, Shearin, Clarkin, Harrison, & Hull, 1993; Sansone, Sansone, & Fine, 1995; Shearer, 1994; van der Kolk et al., 1991; Zweig-Frank, Paris, & Guzder, 1994), substance abuse (Dohm et al., 2002; Favaro & Santonastaso, 2000; Harrison, Fulkerson, & Beebe, 1997; Wonderlich et al., 2001) and ED (Dohm et al., 2002; Favaro & Santonastaso, 2000; Favazza, DeRosear, & Conterio, 1989; Lacey, 1993; Paul, Schroeter, Dahme, & Nutzinger, 2002; Winchel & Stanley, 1991; Wonderlich et al., 2001; Yager, Landsverk, Edelstein, & Jarvik, 1988).

Definitions of SHB converge on the core concept that the individual is acting deliberately with the intention to alter bodily tissue or integrity—without regard to health or safety, and without suicidal intent (Walsh & Rosen, 1988). This type of SHB, often referred to as "delicate self-cutting," is to be distinguished from dramatic or "coarse" self-injury (e.g., eye enucleation or genital amputation), which has historically been more associated with males or psychotic patients. However, in contemporary clinical settings, such distinctions may not provide clear differences between sexes or diagnostic categories (Conterio & Lader, 1998).

Although substance abuse and ED symptoms are inherently self-damaging and are often included in broad definitions of SHB, in this context they will be distinguished from the more direct methods of self-mutilation discussed in the literature. Specifically, here SHB includes cutting; burning; hitting; biting; head banging; excessive scratching; hair pulling; interfering with wound care; breaking bones; chewing lips, cheeks, tongue or fingers; ingesting or inserting toxic or sharp objects; excessive sun burning; and unnecessary surgeries. Most that engage in self-harm are female, use multiple methods, do so spontaneously, and begin this behavior in early adolescence (Conterio & Lader, 1998; Favazza & Conterio, 1989; Phillips & Muzaffer, 1961). Considered a pervasive problem in the United States, SHB cuts across geographic, cultural, age, class, and psychiatric boundaries. Estimates of prevalence in the general population are as high as 1,400 out of every 100,000 people (Conterio & Lader, 1998). Cutting and burning are the most common behaviors, and arms and legs the most frequent sites of injury.

Behavioral overlaps between ED and SHB have been examined within each respective patient population. Estimates of ED among self-injuring patients range from 60 to 100% (Favazza & Rosenthal, 1993; Sachsse, 1989). Conversely, a recent study controlling for suicidal behavior and BPD found a 35% lifetime occurrence of self-injury in patients with ED (Paul et al., 2002). Given the high comorbidity of early developmental trauma in both populations, it is not surprising to find such alarming rates of overlap between these populations. In support of this, Paul and colleagues (2002) found significantly higher rates of traumatic events (as well as more severe eating disorder pathology) in patients with ED who engaged in self-harm versus those who did not.

Dynamic Perspectives on SHB

Prominent theories of SHB, derived largely from studies of trauma survivors, suggest that the individual is variously attempting to "numb out," "act in," or "come to" as a result of intolerable internal feeling states.

Favazza (1989) describes habitual self-mutilation as "a purposeful ... act of self-help which enables the subject to re-establish contact with the world." Lacking capacities to self-soothe or self-regulate, self-injurers appear to self-medicate by virtue of the dissociative, transcendent qualities inherent in self-injurious behavior. Psychic relief from feelings of depersonalization, emptiness, shame, rage, tension, and emotional pain is mitigated through the physical pain that inevitably registers. Though often exquisitely unbearable in its own right, physical pain is preferred over the mental anguish it was otherwise intended to assuage.

Critical to current theories of SHB is the apparently unanimous perspective that the behavior is intended to be self-saving rather than self-destructive, and, as such, is to be distinguished from acts with clear suicidal intent. Conterio and Lader (1998) emphasize the ill-directed nurturing intentions of the self-injurer:

> Strange as it may seem to the uninitiated, self-injury represents a frantic attempt by someone with low coping skills to mother herself... bodily care has been transformed into bodily harm ... the razor blade becomes the wounding care-giver ... a cold but available substitute for the embrace, kiss or loving touch she truly desires. (p. 20)

Recent neurobiological research on post-traumatic stress disorder offers compelling explanations for both the predisposing biological vulnerability of certain individuals to the deleterious effects of trauma as well as the immediate and long-term structural, neurochemical, and psychophysiological sequelae following trauma (van der Kolk, 1988; van der Kolk, Greenberg, Orr, & Pittman, 1989; van der Kolk, McFarlane, & Weisaeth, 1996). Lastly, Miller (1994), a specialist in SHB, has expanded upon these perspectives by describing a crucial function of SHB in abuse survivors—the physical and psychological reenactment of childhood trauma. She defines this phenomenon as "Trauma Reenactment Syndrome" (TRS), and includes ED and substance abuse symptoms in her definition of SHB.

While these theories offer compelling and practical perspectives on the adaptive and functional underpinnings of SHB, they tend to ignore the backdrop within which these behaviors are expressed. Conceptually, they lack the cultural and sociopolitical context in which SHB has become endemic, especially among our youth (Conterio & Lader, 1998). Feminist theory, which is rooted in the conceptualizations of patriarchal culture as power driven, male dominated, and objectifying of females, offers this perspective. Within a feminist formulation, symptoms are contextualized and reframed such that self-inflicted body violations could be experienced by and within the individual as acts, however misdirected, of corporeal "liberation" or rebellion, on both the intrapsychic and sociopolitical level. Following a brief review of core, organizing feminist theoretical constructs, these concepts will be applied to an understanding of SHB in the context of ED.

Feminist Theoretical Constructs

At its most elemental level, feminism is concerned with engendering social and political transformation through active implementation of feminist consciousness. Lerner (1993) articulates feminist consciousness as "the awareness of women that they belong to a subordinate group; that they have suffered wrongs as a group; that their condition of subordination is not natural, but is societally determined" (p. 14). Feminism recognizes *all* women, regardless of class, ethnicity, appearance, age, orientation, income, or religious affiliation, as victims of oppression. Simultaneously, feminism honors distinctions in power between women not afforded to those who are privileged within current patriarchal systems (e.g., white, younger, heterosexual, educated, thin women). Feminism seeks to illuminate and transform the cultural practices that serve to marginalize those outside of the patriarchal nexus. Thus, in locating the genesis of social inequities and oppression in patriarchy (not men), feminism argues that women's authority is specifically delineated outside the boundaries of organized hegemonic power. Feminist ED theorists further argue that women's bodies are subjugated to relentless constrictions, overtly and insidiously designed to circumvent their social, economic, and political status (Bordo, 1993; Fallon, Katzman, & Wooley, 1994; Wolf, 1991).

Feminist perspectives are inherently directed at empowering those otherwise silenced, and creating a new "authoritative knowledge" that transcends the mainstream ideology. This reconfiguration of who holds or defines "truth" embraces the diversity, experience, and "lived data" of the oppressed, in addition to traditional quantitative, scientific sources of information. Lerman (1986) accentuates the centrality of this concept, suggesting that feminist theory must "arise from and be true to the data of lived, clinical experience" (Brabeck & Brown, 1997, p. 17). Additionally, a "multiplicity of subjectivities" is endorsed by feminist theorists, contrary to the notion that any one particular perspective is "the objective view" (Brabeck & Brown, 1997). The language one uses to inform a feminist perspective is also a matter of concern. In order to de-silence and re-voice those who are marginalized, feminism values "native emotional language... without relying on patriarchal terms, consciousness or understandings" (Brabeck & Brown, 1997, p. 26).

Other feminist principles relevant to this discussion include: (a) eradicating false dichotomies; (b) reconceptualizing power; (c) renaming; and (d) "the personal is political" (Van Den Bergh & Cooper, 1986). Eliminating false dichotomies relates to expanding one's view from simple, discrete entities (e.g., mind/body) to appreciating the diversity and interrelatedness of phenomena. For example, Bordo (1993) thoroughly examines the demoralizing and gendered implications of mind/body dualism. Historically, when the dualities of mind/body and men/women dueled for superior distinction, the male/mind was clearly the victor. Woman, and the body, thus forge a doomed combination. "For if, whatever the specific historical content of the duality, *the body* is the negative term, and if woman *is* the body, then women *are* that negativity, whatever it may be…" (Bordo, 1993, p. 5).

Reconceptualizing power has to do with shifting from a "power over" model in which power is equated with control over others, to a "power with" model in which rights, responsibilities, and access to resources are more equitably shared. Renaming implies a valuing of diversity in language, behavior, and success, contrary to patriarchal imperatives for conformity and compliance with the status quo or abiding norms. Lastly, the "personal is political" essentializes the sociopolitical context within which people make meaning of their lives—i.e., within a contemporary Western context or a patriarchy. Stated otherwise, the personal is political means "that experiences in one's personal life can be seen as the individualized outcome of societal inequalities" (Van Den Bergh, 1991, p. 6), and as political acts.

Translating these feminist constructs into the psychological realm requires repositioning and reformulating notions such as "disease," "healthy," and "pain," and incorporating them within the individual's experience. "Viewing life through the oppositional gaze of the oppressed" (Brabeck & Brown, 1997, p.28) shifts the interpretation of psychiatric symptoms from one of dysfunction to one that translates their meaning into acts of survival, if not resistance. "The psychopathologies that develop within a culture, far from being anomalies or aberrations, (are) characteristic expressions of that culture…indeed, the crystallization of much that is wrong with it" (Bordo, 1993, p. 141). Eating disordered and self-mutilating practices would thus be considered self-salvaging efforts within a pathological culture—i.e., reflections of the resilience of the human spirit faced with the vagaries of physical, social, and interpersonal violence (Bordo, 1993; Brabeck & Brown, 1997; Weitz, 1998).

ED and SHB: A Feminist Integration

> To preserve personal beauty, woman's glory! The limbs and faculties are cramped with worse than Chinese bands ... Taught from their infancy that beauty is woman's scepter, the mind shapes itself to the body, and, roaming round its gilt cage, only seeks to adorn its prison.

> Wollstonecraft, 1792

Feminist scholars have made critical contributions to the understanding of ED (Bloom, Gitter, Gutwill, Kogel, & Zaphiropoulos, 1994; Fallon, Katzman, & Wooley, 1994) and addictions (Van Den Bergh, 1991). Feminist formulations of SHB more broadly defined, however, are notably rare (Miller, 1994). A literature search combining the topics of ED and SHB with feminist theory failed to identify a single specific article. Thus, this appears to be the first published effort to incorporate feminist theory on ED with the burgeoning literature on women who also engage in self-harm. In welcoming multiple perspectives, this conceptualization is offered as edifying rather than explanatory in its intent.

As previously noted, lending a feminist perspective to the relationship between ED and SHB involves an extrapolation of extant biopsychosocial models into one that contextualizes these behaviors within a sociopolitical system wherein women's lives and bodies are subjugated to and objectified by patriarchal dictates (see Figure 6.1). With regard to ED, feminist authors point to contributory agents such as the contradictory role demands in personal and professional realms, capitalistic investment in the commodification of girl's and women's bodies, and multimedia propaganda promoting dieting and the "tyranny of slenderness." Piran's (2001) work with girls further distinguishes the role of social power, beyond the influence of media-generated appearance mandates, in the development of ED. In one young woman's words, "you need to have power to accept yourself" (Piran, 2001, p. 173).

Katzman & Lee (1997) bridge feminist and cross-cultural scholarship to offer a perspective on ED that challenges Western biomedical models emphasizing fear of fatness as a primary diagnostic feature. Reinterpreting the meaning of food refusal within a broader frame, their feminist/transcultural interpretation recognizes "not only the gendered nature of eating disorders but their embodiment of power differentials as well" (Katzman & Lee, 1997, p. 385). They offer an illuminating example of a Chinese, non–fat phobic individual with anorexia with a history of trauma who described her symptoms as "symbolizing a loss of voice in a social world perceived to be solely oppressive" (Lee, 1995).

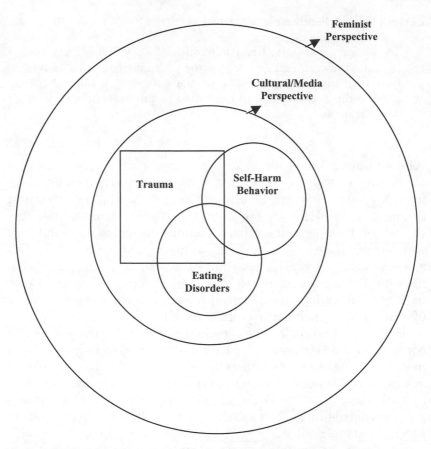

Fig. 6.1 Feminist perspectives on self-harm behavior and eating disorders.

Bordo (1993) examines this perspective at length in her essay, *Anorexia Nervosa*, noting that the "social manipulation of the female body (has) emerged as an absolutely central strategy in the maintenance of power relations between the sexes over the past hundred years" (p. 143). If, then, we are to similarly contextualize our understanding of SHB, we must first locate the SHB population within a societal realm that views the body as an instrument of power, and then cultivates, disciplines, and sanctions bodily practices to serve the dominant social, political, and economic forces at play (Bartky, 1998; Bordo, 1993; Foucault, 1977; Foucault, 1979).

How this power is enforced and why women have been seduced into experiencing these disciplinary practices (e.g., excessive dieting, exercising, cosmetic surgery) as empowering versus destructive is further clarified by the work of Michel Foucault (1977, 1979). Foucault (1979) extended the feminist view of the body as the focal point for struggles over the shape of power (Bordo, 1993; Johnson, 1989). In contrast to the nature of modern power or autocratic sociopolitical systems, Foucault (1979) views contemporary power as nonauthoritarian and as a dynamic process, systematically operating on everyone. While feminist scholars describe patriarchy as a power-over model, Foucault (1979) understands power as operating "from below." Maintained not by coercion or restraint from a specific authority, power is enforced by individuals policing themselves—self-correcting to meet accepted norms and values. This reconceptualization has profound implications for understanding the female body vis-à-vis the "body politic." Within this model, "there is no need for arms, physical violence, material constraints. Just a gaze. An inspecting gaze which each individual... [interiorizes] to the point that he is his own overseer...exercising this surveillance over and against himself" (Foucault, 1977, p.155).

In tragic irony, it was the ingenious architecture of a prison design that provided Foucault with a metaphorical monument to enliven this perspective. The Panopticon, a model prison designed by Bentham, is a circular structure in which the windowed guard tower is situated in the center, opening out to the enclosing periphery of similarly windowed cells, instilling the inmates with the experience of being constantly visible to the guards. Perception, then, becomes the eye of the beholder—one is in the grips of the gaze whether or not actually within eyeshot of the "guard." For the female body, within the patriarchal prison, the effect is synergetic and catabolic. The prison and the prisoner meld seamlessly—the body thus hostage to a condition of virtual, chronic self arrest. "No matter where they live or in what time, there are cages waiting always; too-small lives into which women can be lured or pushed" (Estes, 1995, p. 215).

This concept of the Panopticon and the paralytic potential of the "gaze" inform a feminist perspective on how and why women operate "as if" under constant scrutiny, embattled within and between themselves, their bodies host and hostage to self-harming dynamics. The prison, as described above, is patriarchal culture, perpetuating an oppressive, violating disregard for women's bodies. The guard tower is manifested by the male gaze, under which women ambivalently, and too often destructively, seek sanction, solace, or surrender. Women with ED and SHB could be understood within this paradigm as the ultimate bait for such entrapment. If "genes load the gun and culture pulls the trigger" (Bulik, 1996), and culture, patriarchally organized, is inherently pathologizing and violating of females, then ED and SHB could be construed as inevitable manifestations of traumatic embodiment within a particularly vulnerable group.

As noted above, SHB as post-traumatic symptoms have been conceptualized as survival skills adapted in the service of self-regulating, reorienting, or dissociating from intolerable affective states. ED symptoms serve similar functions. Starving, binging, purging, and ritualistic exercise variously organize, ignite, and consume the sufferer's energies and drives. In the context of a "deadly and misogynist culture" (Gutwill & Gitter, 1994, p.186), a feminist formulation would posit that ED and SHB are essentially post-traumatic adaptations through which the body, site of both oppressor and oppressed, attempts to voice the unspeakable, escape the gaze, resist the opposition, and/or seek redemption. Sundered from claiming their native tongue, accepting their natural body, and directing their vital energy, women with ED and SHB violently implode and act out their indignation. "Self-mutilation can be seen as a concrete interpretation of our culture's injunction to young women to carve themselves into culturally acceptable pieces" (Pipher, 1994, p.157).

That "woman's body is the woman" (Bierce, 1911), and that most women then experience the body as a prison versus a sanctuary, is far from a contemporary formulation. From foot binding to corsets, to ED and SHB, across cultures and through time, women's bodies have borne the emblem of patriarchal power constraints. The brutal irony regarding the Panopticon, alluded to above, is extraordinarily relevant to this discussion.

While women clearly outnumber men in the self-harming community, of those males who do self-harm, the highest prevalence is among prisoners. Favazza (1996) describes prisons as "hotbeds of self-mutilation" and the understanding of this epidemic is hauntingly similar to the feminist paradigm offered above. Conterio and Lader (1998) suggest, "prison, in some ways, seems to stand out as the physical embodiment of the feelings commonly expressed by our female patients, who say they feel 'trapped' and unsafe to express their anger" (p. 131). The potent, piercing glare of the gaze appears to effectively operate both as artifice and artifact—women and prisoners, alike, seeking a modicum of control, through their bodies, over the powers holding them captive.

To suggest that patriarchal culture is inherently traumatizing and sufficient, if not necessary, to turn a woman against her own body is by no means intended to equate this form of social/symbolic assault with actual forms of physical violence. It is, instead, an effort to illuminate the dangerously synergistic impact of being raised female in a body-objectifying culture in which later violations such as sexual abuse only serve to further ravage the individual's psychic integrity and physical sanctity. Gutwill & Gitter (1994) discuss these homologous forms of female violation in their feminist examination of the relationship between ED and sexual abuse. They underscore the relevance of both sources of trauma—the personal and the political, if you will—noting that "the beauty myth, especially as it expresses itself in a fat-phobic diet ethos, is a homologous form of violation against women that resonates with the assaults to self deriving from sexual abuse" (Gutwill & Gitter, 1994, p.186).

In closing, and in keeping with feminist tradition, the voices of the oppressed must be authorized as legitimate, and their bodies given license to speak into the silenced domains where their truth and power ache for release. The words of a recovering anorexic and multiple-trauma survivor who self-harmed tells the story too often true, and too rarely told. Feminist concerns noted above regarding issues of familial, social, and physical violation; mind/body dualism; renaming; and the body as an instrument of power are poignantly revealed and articulated through her experience. Three excerpts from her journal, depicting various stages in her recovery process, reveal the horror, the courage, and the redemption of a child betrayed, her body reclaimed, and her life restored.

Recipe for a Perfect Family

Take four divorces,
mix well with two alcoholics,
throw in a dash of drug abuse.
Stir in one cup of incest.
Beat until blue.
Place under rug and bake on low for 28 years.

Reconciling Recovery

I feel caught in a trap between my mind and my body. I can't claim ownership to my body and my mind is constantly betraying me. To heal, I must attend to my body. I don't feel my body deserves the attention. I don't want to feed it what it desires. I want it to starve, to go without. I want it to pay for the damage it has done to my mind … to starve until it has no choice but to disappear. It's like I want to live but I want my body to die. I have become engaged in a battle—whichever side wins I fear I'll still lose. How can I feel safe in knowing which voice to listen to? The one that says: Yes! Open your eyes, experience life as it is! Or, the one that says: Climb a little deeper inside yourself, for it is a safer darkness.

Resurrection

The darkness has passed
And I no longer hate
Come on me
Let's celebrate!

The incest victim has gone away
She has discovered a better day!
The alcoholic is sober,
She cries no more.
The world awaits outside her door!
The lesbian decides
What's past is okay.
The anorexic has learned to play!
The drug addict finally is tired
Of living like this,
Being constantly wired!
The bulimic as she runs for the stool
passes a mirror
and thinks her body is cool!
The self-mutilator
Puts down the blade
And doesn't destroy
What the good Lord made!
The suicide
Tosses away her pills
And takes her first steps
In climbing life's hills.
The darkness has passed
And I no longer hate!
COME ON ME!
LET'S CELEBRATE!

Conclusion

Feminist formulations are intended to be evolving and edifying, providing "another mother tongue" with which to awaken consciousness and speak to matters of oppression and injustice. ED and SHB, "complex crystallizations of culture" (Bordo, 1993), and still largely the symptomatic province of girls and women, represent female loss of voice, internalization of violating portrayals of their bodies, and misdirected but stalwart efforts to reconcile power imbalances in the body politic. As Brabeck and Brown (1997) note, "dis-ease may be indicative of health and the capacity to resist patriarchy, even at a cost" (p.28). This cost is a cultural tax that is ruinous in its toll, and dangerously deep-rooted in the patriarchal landscape.

If the body, for women, is to remain the battlefield upon which power is relegated and negotiated, contemporary allegiance to a docile and disciplined body (Foucault, 1979) must be understood as ill-guided, duplicitous, and co-opted efforts to embody power. Feminist conscious-ness invites one to be "response-able to self and others, attend to one's own and collective well-being; it is unnumbing and reintegrating of all experiences and leads to social transformation" (Brabeck & Brown, 1997, p. 32). Such higher order change would eliminate the "need" for girls and women to exercise their indignity and resistance through self-destructive practices, authorize their bodies as sites of knowledge and power (Piran, 2001), and transform their energy into valuable cultural and sociopolitical resources. Woman, thus whole and unscathed, would possess the coveted gaze, operate as seer instead as seen, host of her own dominion, safe haven to her "incorporated" life.

References

Bierce, A. (1911). *The devil's dictionary* (6th ed.). New York: Oxford University Press.

Bartky, S. (1998). Foucault, femininity and the modernization of patriarchal power. In R. Weitz (Ed.), *The politics of women's bodies* (pp. 25–45). New York: Oxford University Press.

Bergman, G. (1846). Ein Fall von religioser Monomanie [A case of religious monomania]. *Allegemeine Zeitschrift Psychiatrie, 3,* 365–380.

Bloom, C., Gitter, A., Gutwill, S., Kogel, L., & Zaphiropoulos, L. (1994). *Eating problems: A feminist psychoanalytic treatment model.* New York: Basic Books.

Bordo, S. (1993). *Unbearable weight: Feminism, Western culture & the body.* Berkeley: University of California Press.

Brabeck, M., & Brown, L. (1997). Feminist theory and psychological practice. In J. Worell, & N. Johnson (Eds.), *Shaping the future of feminist psychology* (pp. 15–35). Washington, DC: APA.

Briere, J., & Zaidi, L. (1989). Sexual abuse histories and sequelae in female psychiatric emergency room patients. *American Journal of Psychiatry, 146,* 1602–1606.

Bulik, C. (1996). The new biology of eating disorders: New findings and new directions. Paper presented at the Eating Disorders Research Society, Pittsburgh, PA.

Conterio, K., & Lader, W. (1998). *Bodily harm: The breakthrough treatment program for self-injurers.* New York: Hyperion.

Dohm, F., Striegel-Moore, R., Wilfley, D., Pike, K., Hook, J., & Fairburn, C. (2002). Self-harm and substance abuse in a community sample of black and white women with binge eating dis-order or bulimia. *International Journal of Eating Disorders, 32,* 389–400.

Estes, C. P. (1995). *Women who run with the wolves.* New York: Ballantine Books.

Fallon, P., Katzman, M., & Wooley, S. (Eds.). (1994). *Feminist perspectives on eating disorders.* New York: Guilford Press.

Favaro, A., & Santonastaso, P. (2000). Self-injurious behaviors in anorexia nervosa. *Journal of Nervous & Mental Disease, 188,* 537–542.

Favazza, A. (1989). Why patients mutilate themselves. *Hospital and Community Psychiatry, 40,* 137–145.

Favazza, A. (1996). *Bodies under siege* (2nd ed.). Baltimore: John Hopkins University Press.

Favazza A., & Conterio, K. (1989). Female habitual self-mutilators. *Acta Psychiatrica Scandinavica, 79,* 283–289.

Favazza, A., DeRosear, D., & Conterio, K. (1989). Self-mutilation and eating disorders. *Suicide and Life-Threatening Behavior, 19,* 352–361.

Favazza, A., & Rosenthal, R. (1993). Diagnostic issues in self-mutilation. *Hospital & Community Psychiatry, 44,* 134–140.

Foucault, M. (1977). The eye of power. In C. Gordon (Ed.), *Power/knowledge: Selected interviews and other writings.* New York: Pantheon.

Foucault, M. (1979). *Discipline and punish: The birth of the prison* (A. Sheridan, Trans.). New York: Vintage.

Gutwill, S., & Gitter, A. (1994). Eating problems and sexual abuse: Theoretical considerations. In C. Bloom et al. (Eds.), *Eating problems: A feminist psychoanalytic treatment model* (pp. 184–204). New York: Basic Books.

Harrison, P., Fulkerson, J., & Beebe, T. (1997). Multiple substance use among adolescent physical and sexual abuse victims. *Child Abuse and Neglect, 21,* 529–539.

Herman, J. 1993. *Trauma and Recovery.* New York: Basic Books.

Johnson, D. (1989). The body: Which one? Whose? *Whole Earth Review* (Summer), 4–8.

Katzman, M., & Lee, S. (1997). Beyond body image: The integration of feminist and transcultural theories in the understanding of self starvation. *International Journal of Eating Disorders, 22,* 385–394.

Lacey, J. (1993). Self-damaging and addictive behavior in bulimia nervosa. *British Journal of Psychiatry, 163,* 190–194.

Lee, S. (1995). Self-starvation in context: Towards a culturally sensitive understanding of anorexia nervosa. *Social Science & Medicine, 41,* 25–36.

Lerman, H. (1986). *A mote in Freud's eye: From psychoanalysis to the psychology of women.* New York: Springer.

Lerner, G. (1993). *The creation of feminist consciousness.* New York: Oxford University Press.

Miller, D. (1994). *Women who hurt themselves: A book of hope and understanding.* New York: Basic Books.

Paris, J. (Ed.). (1992). *Borderline personality disorder: Etiology and treatment.* Washington, DC: American Psychiatric Press.

Paul, T., Schroeter, K., Dahme, B., & Nutzinger, D. (2002). Self-injurious behavior in women with eating disorders. *American Journal of Psychiatry, 159,* 408–411.

Phillips, R., & Muzaffer, A. (1961). Some aspects of self-mutilation in the general population of a large psychiatric hospital. *Psychiatric Quarterly, 35,* 421–423.

Pipher, M. (1994). *Reviving Ophelia: Saving the selves of adolescent girls.* New York: G. P. Putnam & Sons.

Piran, N. (2001). Reinhabiting the body. *Feminism & Psychology, 11,* 172–176.

Romans, S., Martin, J., Anderson, J., Herbison, G., & Mullen, P. (1995). Sexual abuse in childhood and deliberate self-harm. *American Journal of Psychiatry, 152,* 1336–1342.

Russ, M., Shearin, E., Clarkin, J., Harrison, K., & Hull, T. (1993). Subtypes of self-injurious patients with borderline personality disorder. *American Journal of Psychiatry, 150,* 1869–1871.

Sachsse, U. (1989). Blut tut gut: Genese, Psychodynamik und Psychotherapie offener Selbstbeschädigungen der Haut. In M. Hirsch (Ed.), *Der eigene Körper als Object* (pp. XXX). Berlin: Springer.

Sansone, R., Sansone, L., & Fine, M. (1995). The relationship of obesity to borderline personality symptomatology, self-harm behaviors, and sexual abuse in female subjects in a primary-care setting. *Journal of Personality Disorders, 9,* 254–265.

Shearer, S. (1994). Phenomenology of self-injury among inpatient women with borderline personality disorder. *Journal of Nervous & Mental Disease, 182,* 524–526.

Van Den Bergh, N. (Ed.). (1991). *Feminist perspectives on addictions.* New York: Springer.

Van Den Bergh, N., & Cooper, L. (1986). *Feminist visions for social work.* Silver Springs, MD: NASW.

van der Kolk, B. (Ed.). (1987). *Psychological trauma.* Washington, DC: American Psychiatric Press.

van der Kolk, B. (1988) The traumatic spectrum: The interaction of biological and social events in the genesis of the trauma response. *Journal of Traumatic Stress, 1,* 273–290.

van der Kolk, B, & Fisler, R. (1994). Childhood abuse and neglect and loss of self-regulation. *Bulletin of the Menninger Clinic, 58,* 145–168.

van der Kolk, B., Greenberg, M., Orr, S., & Pittman, R. (1989). Endogenous opioids and stress induced analgesia in posttraumatic stress disorder. *Psychopharmacology Bulletin, 25,* 108–119.

van der Kolk, B., Hostetler, A., Herron, N., & Fisler, R. (1994). Trauma and the development of borderline personality disorder. *Psychiatric Clinics of North America, 17,* 715–730.

van der Kolk, B., McFarlane, A., & Weisaeth, L. (Eds.). (1996). *Traumatic stress: The effects of overwhelming experience on mind, body and society.* New York: Guilford Press.

van der Kolk, B., Perry, J., & Herman, J. (1991). Childhood origins of self-destructive behavior. *American Journal of Psychiatry, 148,* 1665–1671.

Walsh, B., & Rosen, P. (1988). *Self-mutilation: Theory, research and treatment.* New York: Guilford Press.

Weitz, R. (Ed.). (1998). *The politics of women's bodies.* New York: Oxford University Press.

Winchel, R., & Stanley, M. (1991). Self-injurious behavior: A review of the behavior and biology of self-mutilation. *American Journal of Psychiatry, 148,* 306–317.

Wolf, N. (1991). *The beauty myth.* New York: William Morrow.

Wollstonecraft, M. (1792). A vindication of the rights of women. In A. Rossi (Ed.), *The feminist papers* (pp. 55–57). Boston: Northeastern University Press, 1988.

Wonderlich, S., Crosby, R., Mitchell, J., Thompson, K., Redlin, J., Demuth, G., Snyth, J., & Haseltine, B. (2001). Eating disturbance and sexual trauma in childhood and adulthood. *International Journal of Eating Disorders, 30,* 401–412.

Yager, J., Landsverk, J., Edelstein, C., & Jarvik, M. (1988). A 20-month follow-up study of 628 women with eating disorders. *International Journal of Eating Disorders, 7,* 503–513.

Zweig-Frank, H., Paris, J., & Guzder, J. (1994). Psychological risk factors for dissociation and self-mutilation in female patients with borderline personality disorder. *Canadian Journal of Psychiatry, 39,* 259–264.

Assessment

CHAPTER 7

Assessment Tools: Eating Disorder Symptoms and Self-Harm Behavior

RANDY A. SANSONE AND LORI A. SANSONE

Introduction

A substantial minority of patients with eating disorders report self-harm behavior (SHB). While many clinicians inquire about such behaviors during clinical evaluation, assessment tools potentially offer a more systematic and consistent means of obtaining clinical information. In this chapter, we review several assessment tools that are promoted specifically for the evaluation of eating disorders or SHB. Through this review, we find that the current eating disorder assessments do not contain any items related to SHB. While several of the self-harm measures contain eating disorder items, there are not a sufficient number to confirm an eating disorder diagnosis. In summary, there are no currently available assessment tools that simultaneously facilitate the diagnosis of an eating disorder *and* elicit information about various forms of SHB. Due to the high prevalence of comorbidity, clinicians may wish to elect two assessment measures for both eating disorders and SHB. We make specific recommendations for assessment tools in this chapter.

SHB (e.g., suicide attempts, cutting oneself, burning oneself) appears to affect a substantial number of individuals suffering from eating disorders. In an overview of the literature, Sansone and Levitt (2002) found that the prevalence of suicide attempts was surprisingly high (e.g., 16% among outpatients with anorexia nervosa, 23% among outpatients with bulimia,

39% among inpatients with bulimia, 54% among individuals with bulimia and with alcohol abuse). In addition to suicide attempts, self-injury occurred in about one-fourth of outpatients with anorexia nervosa, and 25% of outpatients and inpatients with bulimia nervosa. Despite the frequency of SHB among individuals with eating disorders, few measures exist to assess it. In addition, given the prevalence of SHB, it seems clinically logical to explore for these behaviors at the time of the initial eating-disorder assessment. While these behaviors may be explored informally during the clinician's interview with the patient, we wished to review available assessment tools as adjunctive options in assessment.

In this chapter, we first review the number of self-harm items among several assessment tools currently used in the field of eating disorders. Next, we review several self-harm measures and for each measure describe the number of eating-disorder items as well as overt self-harm items (i.e., behavior intentionally and actively directed at self) and high-lethal items (i.e., behaviors associated with the risk of death, such as attempted suicide). We have only included for review in this chapter those measures that we were able to obtain for examination. Several additional measures were noted in the literature, but we were either unable to locate the authors (e.g., the Eating Habits Questionnaire, Coker & Roger, 1990; the Eating Disorder Belief Questionnaire, Cooper, Cohen-Tovee, Todd, Wells, & Tovee, 1997) or the questionnaire was at a pilot stage of development (Shearer, 1994). In addition, we tend to provide more detail on the self-harm rather than on the eating disorder measures, as they are likely to be less familiar to the eating disorder clinician.

Assessment Tools for Eating Disorders

A number of assessment tools are now available for the evaluation of individuals with eating disorders. We present, in alphabetical order, several of these and describe the measure as well as specifically note the presence of any overt self-harm or high-lethal items. By overt self-harm, we refer to behaviors that are actively, intentionally, and directly undertaken to hurt oneself. Behaviors such as laxative abuse could be interpreted as self-harming, but we specifically eliminated the element of interpretation and did not include these types of behaviors. Note that a high-lethal item was counted both as an overt self-harm behavior and as a high-lethal item.

Binge Eating Scale

The Binge Eating Scale (Gormally, Black, Daston, & Rardin, 1982) is a 16-item self-report measure with Likert-style response options that explores binge eating and purging behavior. On the actual measure, the scale is entitled "Eating Habits Checklist." There are no self-harm or high-lethal items in the scale.

The Binge Scale

The Binge Scale (Hawkins & Clement, 1980) is a 19-item self-report measure with Likert-style response options that explores binge-eating and purging behavior. There are no self-harm or high-lethal items in the scale.

Bulimia Test-Revised (BULIT-R)

The BULIT-R (Thelen, Farmer, Wonderlich, & Smith, 1991) is a 39-item, six-page self-report measure with Likert-style response options that explores binge-eating and purging behavior. There are no self-harm or high-lethal items in the scale.

Eating Attitudes Test-26 (EAT-26)

Derived from the 40-item parent measure, the Eating Attitudes Test (Garner & Garfinkel, 1979), the EAT-26 (Garner, Olmstead, Bohr, & Garfinkel, 1982) is a shorter, 26-item self-report inventory with Likert-style response options that explores general eating pathology. While this inventory has no self-harm or high-lethal items, five additional yes/no questions were added for the National Eating Disorders Screening Program, one of which inquired about past suicide attempts.

Eating Disorder Diagnostic Scale

The Eating Disorder Diagnostic Scale (Stice, Telch, & Rizvi, 2000) is a 22-item self-report inventory with various response formats (i.e., Likert-style, yes/no, and write-in response options) that explores eating disorder pathology including binge eating disorder. This one-page inventory is entitled "Eating Screen," and there are no self-harm or high-lethal items.

Eating Disorder Examination (EDE)

The Eating Disorder Examination (Fairburn & Cooper, 1993) is a semi-structured interview that focuses on eating disorder symptoms over the past 28 days. Response options are graded in severity from 0 to 6. There is also a self-report version, the Eating Disorder Examination Self-Report Questionnaire Version (EDE-Q) that has reported adequate psychometric properties (Luce & Crowther, 1999). The EDE does not have any items that relate to either self-harm or high-lethal behavior.

Eating Disorder Family History Interview

The Eating Disorder Family History Interview (Strober, 1993) is a 13-page semi-structured interview that explores eating pathology. This assessment tool concludes with a *DSM-III-R* diagnostic confirmation that includes the criteria for binge eating disorder. While more of a clinical assessment tool than a psychological measure, the Eating Disorder Family History Interview has no self-harm or high-lethal items.

Eating Disorders Inventory-2 (EDI-2)

The second generation of the Eating Disorders Inventory (Garner, Olmsted, & Polivy, 1983), the EDI-2 (Garner, 1991), is a 91-item, two-page (front and back) self-report measure that explores general eating pathology. The 91 Likert-style response items are preceded by a series of fill-in and yes/no questions. The EDI-2 has no self-harm or high-lethal items.

Exercise Orientation Questionnaire

The Exercise Orientation Questionnaire (Yates, Edman, Crago, Crowell, & Zimmerman, 1999) is a 27-item, one-page self-report measure with Likert-style response options that explores beliefs and attitudes about exercise. This measure has no self-harm or high-lethal items.

McKnight Risk Factors Survey-IV (MRFS-IV)

The MRFS-IV (Shisslak et al., 1999) is a 103-item self-report survey with a variety of response formats (e.g., Likert-style, yes/no, multiple-choice options) that explores multiple clinical areas associated with eating pathology, including depression as well as perfectionism. This measure assesses the potential risk and protective factors for preadolescent and adolescent girls with regard to the eventual development of an eating disorder. This measure has no self-harm or high-lethal items.

Revised Restraint Scale

The Revised Restraint Scale (Herman & Polivy, 1980) is a one-page, 10-item self-report inventory with multiple response options that measures restrained eating or dieting behavior. None of the items relates to self-harm or high-lethal behaviors.

Yale-Brown-Cornell Eating Disorder Scale (YBC-EDS)

The YBC-EDS (Mazure, Halmi, Sunday, Romano, & Einhorn, 1994) is an 82-item semi-structured interview that explores general eating pathology.

Among the items, 62 are clinical symptoms rated as "current" or "past," and the remainder has Likert-style response options. This eight-page measure focuses on eating preoccupation and rituals associated with eating pathology. There are no self-harm or high-lethal items.

Summary

None of the preceding eating disorder measures, inventories, or interviews has any questions or items that relate to self-harm or high-lethal behavior. Given the prevalence of such behaviors among populations with eating disorders (Sansone & Levitt, 2002), this observation is somewhat surprising. However, the developers of these various eating disorder measures likely perceived self-harm items as related to comorbid disorders such as depression or borderline personality disorder, and therefore did not include them in measures of eating pathology.

Assessment Tools for Self-Harm Behavior

While there are a variety of measures for eating pathology and its various facets (e.g., exercise orientation, body-image issues, predisposition to an eating disorder, perfectionism), there are relatively few for the assessment of SHB. We present the available measures that we were able to locate for review in alphabetical order. Measures or tools with the terms "borderline, borderline personality" or "borderline personality disorder" were excluded from this summary. These measures are summarized in Table 7.1.

TABLE 7.1 Assessment Tools for Self-Harm Behavior: A Comparative Summary

Measure	First Author (Publication Year)	Eating Disorder Items	Overt Self-Harm Items	High-Lethal Items
CSDS	Kelley (1985)	X		
HASS-II	Friedman (1989)		X	X
Impulsive and Self-Harm Questionnaire	Rossotto (1997)	X	X	X
Self-Harm Behavior Survey	Favazza (1986)	X	X	
SHI	Sansone (1998)	X	X	X
SIB-Q	Schroeder (1997)		X	
SIQ	Vanderlinden (1997)	X	X	
Self-Injury Survey	Simpson (1994)	X	X	X
Timed Self-Injurious Behavior Scale	Brasic (1997)		X	

Note: CSDS = Chronic Self-Destructiveness Scale; HASS = Harkavy Asnis Suicide Survey; SHI = Self-Harm Inventory; SIB-Q = Self-Injurious Behavior Questionnaire; SIQ = Self-Injury Questionnaire.

Chronic Self-Destructiveness Scale (CSDS)

The CSDS (Kelley et al., 1985) is a 73-item, two-page (one printed side) inventory with Likert-style response options that explores high-risk behaviors that are typically reflective of impulsivity (e.g., "Riding fast in a car is thrilling, I have done dangerous things just for the thrill of it"). Unlike most of the other self-harm measures, there are several health-related items such as, "I have a complete physical examination once a year, I always do what my doctor or dentist recommends," and "I have my eyes examined at least once a year." The inventory is entitled, "Personal Preferences Scale." The scoring key is gender-specific, and the measure has some reverse-score items. The resulting score is the "self-destructiveness score." There are five eating-related items (i.e., "I take care to eat a balanced diet, I eat too much, I often skip meals, I often use non-prescription medicines [aspirin, laxatives, etc.]," and "I like to exercise"). Surprisingly, there are no overt self-harm or high-lethal items.

Harkavy Asnis Suicide Survey II (HASS-II)

The HASS-II (Friedman & Asnis, 1989) is a 21-item, one-page self-report survey with Likert-style response options that measures, over the respondent's lifetime, suicidal preoccupation and behavior. There are no eating disorder items within the measure. The inquiry about suicide attempts represents both an overt self-harm as well as a high-lethal item. Other forms of self-harm behavior are not explored.

Impulsive and Self-Harm Questionnaire

The Impulsive and Self-Harm Questionnaire (Rossotto, 1997) is a 14-item, one-page self-report survey with Likert-style response options that explores a variety of impulsive and self-destructive behaviors. This measure was developed for a dissertation and has had limited clinical exposure. There are two eating disorder items (i.e., "stolen food, eating food before paying for it") as well as five overt self-harm items (i.e., "suicide attempts, suicide gestures, self-mutilated, hurt yourself regularly, accident prone") and one high-lethal item (i.e., suicide attempts).

Self-Harm Behavior Survey

The Self-Harm Behavior Survey (Favazza, 1986; Favazza & Conterio, 1988) is a 174+-item, multi-page self-report survey with a variety of response options and broad array of questions. The survey content includes a demographic inquiry, family history of mental illness, religious background, family relationships, SHB, personal feelings about self-harm events, scar history, function of SHB, eating disorder symptoms, psychotropic medication history, and hospitalization history secondary to self-mutilation. There are 5 eating disorder items (i.e., questions regarding current versus past eating disorder symptoms, previous diagnosis by a health professional, specific eating-disorder diagnosis, age of onset of symptoms, hospitalization history) and 11 overt self-harm items (e.g., scratched or cut wrists, cut other body areas, carved words or symbols on skin, burned skin, pulled out hair, broken bones, infected self), but no high-lethal items.

Self-Harm Inventory (SHI)

The SHI (Sansone, Wiederman, & Sansone, 1998a; see Figure 7.1) is a 22-item, yes/no, one-page self-report questionnaire that explores respondents' histories of self-harm. Each item in the inventory is preceded by the phrase, "Have you ever intentionally, or on purpose..." Among the items, there are 14 overt self-harm behaviors (e.g., "cut yourself, burned yourself, hit yourself, scratched yourself, prevented wounds from healing"), three eating-disorder items (i.e., "exercised an injury on purpose, starved yourself to hurt yourself, abused laxatives to hurt yourself"), and two high-lethal items (i.e., "overdosed, attempted suicide"). All endorsements are pathological so that the SHI score is simply the sum of "yes" responses. Unlike the other self-harm measures described in this chapter, the SHI score empirically relates to a *DSM* diagnosis of borderline personality. Indeed, in comparison with the Diagnostic Interview for Borderlines (Kolb & Gunderson, 1980), the SHI demonstrated an accuracy of 84% in diagnosing borderline personality disorder, at a cut-off score of 5 (Sansone, Wiederman, & Sansone, 1998a).

Self-Injurious Behavior Questionnaire (SIB-Q)

The SIB-Q (Schroeder, Rojahn, & Reese, 1997) is a clinician-rated 25-item scale with Likert-style response options that measures self-injurious behavior among those with mental retardation. Examples of items are "physical aggression towards others, destructive to property or objects," and "tantrums." Three items deal with behavior frequency and severity, and the need for restraints. There are no traditional eating-disorder items, although there is one item for Pica. There are two overt SHBs (i.e., self-inflicted wounds, self-inflicted bruises) but no high-lethal items.

FIGURE 7.1

Self-Harm Inventory

Instructions: Please answer the following questions by checking either, "Yes" or "No." Check "yes" *only* to those items that you have done intentionally, or *on purpose*, to hurt yourself.

Yes	No	Have you ever intentionally, or on purpose
—	—	1. Overdosed? (If yes, number of times ____)
—	—	2. Cut yourself on purpose? (If yes, number of times ____)
—	—	3. Burned yourself on purpose? (If yes, number of times ____)
—	—	4. Hit youself? (If yes, number of times ____)
—	—	5. Banged your head on purpose? (If yes, number of times ____)
—	—	6. Abused alcohol?
—	—	7. Driven recklessly on purpose? (If yes, number of times ____)
—	—	8. Scratched yourself on purpose? (If yes, number of times ____)
—	—	9. Prevented wounds from healing?
—	—	10. Made medical situations worse, on purpose (e.g., skipped medication)?
—	—	11. Been promiscuous (i.e., had many sexual partners)? (If yes, how many? ____)
—	—	12. Set yourself up in a relationship to be rejected?
—	—	13. Abused prescription medication?
—	—	14. Distanced yourself from God as punishment?
—	—	15. Engaged in emotionally abusive relationships? (If yes, number of relationship? ____)
—	—	16. Engaged in sexually abusive relationships? (If yes, number of relationships? ____)
—	—	17. Lost a job on purpose? (If yes, number of times ____)
—	—	18. Attempted suicide? (If yes, number of times ____)
—	—	19. Exercised an injury on purpose?
—	—	20. Tortured yourself with self-defeating thoughts?
—	—	21. Starved yourself to hurt yourself?
—	—	22. Abused laxatives to hurt yourself? (If yes, number of times ____)

Have you engaged in any other self-destructive behaviors not asked about in this inventory? If so, please describe below. © Sansone, Sansone, & Wiederman

Self-Injury Questionnaire (SIQ)

The SIQ (Vanderlinden & Vandereycken, 1997) is a 54-item self-report questionnaire with various response options including Likert-style and multiple-choice options. Among the Likert-response items, there are four overt self-harm behaviors (i.e., opening wounds, scratching scabs or lumps, cutting or hurting self, tormenting self physically to punish self). There are five other non–Likert-style overt self-harm items (i.e., pulling out hair, scratching self, bruising self intentionally, cutting self, burning self) that have three adjunctive questions each related to them. There is one item for eating disorder symptoms ("eating sweets") and no high-lethal items.

Self-Injury Survey

The Self-Injury Survey (Simpson, Zlotnick, Begin, Costello, & Pearlstein, 1994) is a four-page self-report measure with 31 self-harm items, a write-in listing of suicide attempts, and a check-off list of reasons for self-injury, types of past intervention, and damage effects. Five items explore eating disorder behaviors (i.e., consumed large amounts of food in one sitting, severely restricted food, made self vomit, used laxatives or diuretics to control weight, exercised to exhaustion). Thirteen items relate to overt SHB and two (i.e., overdosed, attempted suicide) are high-lethal.

Timed Self-Injurious Behavior Scale

The Timed Self-Injurious Behavior Scale (Brasic et al., 1997) is a 16-item clinician-rated scale that rates the frequency of self-injurious behaviors at 6 consecutive time intervals, each 10 minutes apart. This scale was developed for use among those with mental retardation. There are no eating disorder items. There are 16 overt self-harm items and no high-lethal items.

Summary

Several of the available assessment tools for SHB are either designed for populations of patients unrelated to eating disorders (e.g., mental retardation, such as the SIB-Q and the Timed Self-Injurious Behavior Scale) and/or very specific subpopulations (e.g., HASS-II for suicidal ideation and behavior).

Regarding item content for the nine described measures, the majority (6/9) has eating disorder items, but not a sufficient number within any measure to confirm a diagnosis. Most (8/9) have overt self-harm items. Oddly, however, only a minority (4/9) of the self-harm measures has high-lethal items (i.e., suicide attempts, overdosed). Because of the prevalence of suicide attempts in various eating disorder populations, it seems prudent to have high-lethal items in an ideal scale.

In identifying measures that have all three types of items (i.e., eating disorder, overt self-harm, high-lethal behaviors), there are only three measures—the Impulsive and Self-Harm Questionnaire (Rossotto, 1997), the SHI (Sansone, Wiederman, & Sansone, 1998a), and the Self-Injury Survey (Simpson et al., 1994). The Impulsive and Self-Harm Questionnaire has only been reported in one study (Rossotto, 1997). In contrast, the SHI

(Sansone, Fine, & Nunn, 1994; Sansone, Sansone, & Fine, 1995; Sansone, Sansone, & Morris, 1996; Sansone, Wiederman, & Sansone, 1998b) and the Self-Injury Survey (Zlotnick, Donaldson, Spirito, & Pearlstein, 1997; Zlotnick, Mattia, & Zimmerman, 1999; Zlotnick et al., 1996) have been reported in several studies. As an additional clinical feature, the SHI is the only self-harm measure, to our knowledge, to diagnose borderline personality symptomatology, a common comorbid condition among those with eating disorders (Dennis & Sansone, 1997).

Recommendations

Given that none of the available eating disorder measures assess for SHB in any meaningful way, the practicing clinician is left without a global assessment tool. Given this limitation, clinicians who prefer to use measures of eating disorder pathology should elect ones that fit their clinical situation in terms of convenience, cost, number of patients seen, and desired detail. With regard to SHB, two measures, the SHI and the Self-Injury Survey, have empirical track records and include both eating disorder and self-harm items. However, the SHI has the additional advantage of detecting borderline personality symptomatology, a frequent comorbid psychiatric condition among those with eating disorders. Because of this, the SHI may be more ideally suited for eating disorder assessment, although the Self-Injury Survey offers more detail.

Conclusion

Despite the prevalence of SHB among those suffering from eating disorders, none of the eating disorder assessment tools we describe has items that assess such behavior. We suspect that this finding relates to the principle focus of these measures—eating disorder pathology—and that SHB is viewed as related to a comorbid psychiatric disorder. Despite a limited number of available self-harm measures, three have a combination of eating disorder, overt self-harm, and high-lethal items. While none is capable of diagnosing an eating disorder, each offers a reasonable panorama of SHB, and one predicts for borderline personality symptomatology. In summary, for the present the clinician is left with using two assessment tools—one for eating disorder symptoms and one for SHB. However, future investigators may develop a combined measure that will offer far broader patient assessment than the tools currently available.

References

Brasic, J. B., Barnett, J. Y., Ahn, S. C., Nadrich, R. H., Will, M. V., & Clair, A. (1997). Clinical assessment of self-injurious behavior. *Psychological Reports, 80,* 155–160.

Coker, S., & Roger, D. (1990). The construction and preliminary validation of a scale for measuring eating disorders. *Journal of Psychosomatic Research, 34,* 223–231.

Cooper, M., Cohen-Tovee, E., Todd, G., Wells, A., & Tovee, M. (1997). The Eating Disorder Belief Questionnaire: Preliminary development. *Behaviour Research & Therapy, 35,* 382–388.

Dennis, A. B., & Sansone, R. A. (1997). Treatment of patients with personality disorders. In D. M. Garner & P. E. Garfinkel (Eds.), *Handbook of treatment for eating disorders* (2nd ed.) (pp. 437–449). New York: Guilford.

Fairburn, C. G., & Cooper, Z. (1993). The Eating Disorder Examination (12th ed.). In C. G. Fairburn and W. G. Wilson (Eds.), *Binge eating: Nature, assessment, and treatment* (pp. 317–360). New York: Guilford Press.

Favazza, A. (1986). Self-Harm Behavior Survey. Columbia, MI: Author.

Favazza, A., & Conterio, K. (1988). The plight of chronic self-mutilators. *Community Mental Health Journal, 24,* 22–30.

Friedman, J. M. H., & Asnis, G. M. (1989). Assessment of suicidal behavior: A new instrument. *Psychiatric Annals, 19,* 382–387.

Garner, D. M. (1991). Eating Disorder Inventory-2. Odessa, Florida: Psychological Assessment Resources, Inc.

Garner, D. M., & Garfinkel, P. E. (1979). The Eating Attitudes Test: An index of the symptoms of anorexia nervosa. *Psychological Medicine, 12,* 871–878.

Garner, D. M., Olmstead, M. P., Bohr, Y., & Garfinkel, P. E. (1982). The Eating Attitudes Test: Psychometric features and clinical correlates. *Psychological Medicine,* Monograph Supplement 14, 1–34.

Garner, D. M., Olmstead, M. P., & Polivy, J. (1983). Development and validation of a multidimensional eating disorder inventory for anorexia nervosa and bulimia. *International Journal of Eating Disorders, 2,* 15–34.

Gormally, J., Black, S., Daston, S., & Rardin, D. (1982). The assessment of binge eating severity among obese persons. *Addictive Behaviors, 7,* 47–55.

Hawkins, R. C., & Clement, P. F. (1980). Development and construct validation of a self-report measure of binge eating tendencies. *Addictive Behaviors, 5,* 219–226.

Herman, C. P., & Polivy, J. (1980). Experimental and clinical aspects of restrained eating. In A. Stunkard (Ed.), *Obesity: Basic mechanisms and treatment* (pp. 208–225). Philadelphia: W. B. Saunders.

Kelley, K., Byrne, D., Przybyla, D. P. J., Eberly, C. C., Eberly, B. W., Greendlinger, V., et al. (1985). Chronic self-destructiveness: Conceptualization, measurement, and initial validation of the construct. *Motivation and Emotion, 9,* 135–151.

Kolb, J. E., & Gunderson, J. G. (1980). Diagnosing borderline patients with a semi-structured interview. *Archives of General Psychiatry, 37,* 37–41.

Luce, K. H., & Crowther, J. H. (1999). The reliability of the Eating Disorder Examination— Self-Report Questionnaire Version (EDE-Q). *International Journal of Eating Disorders, 25,* 349–351.

Mazure, C. M., Halmi, K. A., Sunday, S. R., Romano, S. J., & Einhorn, A. M. (1994). The Yale-Brown-Cornell Eating Disorder Scale: Development, use, reliability and validity. *Journal of Psychiatric Research, 28,* 425–445.

Rossotto, E. (1997). Bulimia nervosa with and without substance use disorders: A comparative study. *Dissertation Abstracts International: Section B, 58,* 4469.

Sansone, R. A., Fine, M. A., & Nunn, J. L. (1994). A comparison of borderline personality symptomatology and self-destructive behavior in women with eating, substance abuse, and both eating and substance abuse disorders. *Journal of Personality Disorders, 8,* 219–228.

Sansone, R. A., & Levitt, J. L. (2002). Self-harm behaviors among those with eating disorders: An overview. *Eating Disorders, 10,* 205–213.

Sansone, R. A., Sansone, L. A., & Fine, M. A. (1995). The relationship of obesity to borderline personality symptomatology, self-harm behaviors, and sexual abuse in female subjects in a primary care setting. *Journal of Personality Disorders, 9,* 254–265.

Sansone, R. A., Sansone, L. A., & Morris, D. W. (1996). Prevalence of borderline personality symptoms in two groups of obese subjects. *American Journal of Psychiatry, 153,* 117–118.

Sansone, R. A., Wiederman, M. W., & Sansone, L. A. (1998a). The Self-Harm Inventory (SHI): Development of a scale for identifying self-destructive behaviors and borderline personality disorder. *Journal of Clinical Psychology, 54,* 973–983.

Sansone, R. A., Wiederman, M. W., & Sansone, L. A. (1998b). Borderline personality symptomatology, experience of multiple types of trauma, and health care utilization among women in a primary care setting. *Journal of Clinical Psychiatry, 59,* 108–111.

Schroeder, S. R., Rojahn, J., & Reese, R. M. (1997). Brief report: Reliability and validity of instruments for assessing psychotropic medication effects on self-injurious behavior in mental retardation. *Journal of Autism and Developmental Disorders, 27,* 89–103.

Shearer, S. L. (1994). Phenomenology of self-injury among inpatient women with borderline personality disorder. *Journal of Nervous and Mental Disease, 182,* 524–526.

Shisslak, C. M., Renger R., Sharpe, T., Crago, M., McKnight, K. M., Gray, N., Bryson, S., Estes, L. S., Parnhy, O. G., Killen, J., & Taylor, C. B. (1999). Development and evaluation of the McKnight Risk Factor Survey for assessing potential risk and protective factors for disordered eating in preadolescent and adolescent girls. *International Journal of Eating Disorders, 25,* 195–214.

Simpson, E., Zlotnick, C., Begin, A., Costello, E., & Pearlstein, T. (1994). Self-Injury Survey. Providence, RI: Authors.

Stice, E., Telch, C. F., & Rizvi, S. L. (2000). Development and validation of the Eating Disorder Diagnostic Scale: A brief self-report measure of anorexia, bulimia, and binge-eating disorder. *Psychological Assessment, 12,* 123–131.

Strober, M. (1993). Eating Disorders Family History Interview. Los Angeles: Author.

Thelen, M. H., Farmer, J., Wonderlich, S., & Smith, M. (1991). A revision of the Bulimia Test: The BULIT-R. *Psychological Assessment, 3,* 199–124.

Vanderlinden, J., & Vandereycken, W. (1997). *Trauma, dissociation, and impulse dyscontrol in eating disorders* (pp. 193–198). Philadelphia: Brunner/Mazel.

Yates, A., Edman, J. D., Crago, M., Crowell, D., & Zimmerman, R. (1999). Measurement of exercise orientation in normal subjects: Gender and age differences. *Personality and Individual Differences, 27,* 199–209.

Zlotnick, C., Donaldson, D., Spirito, A., & Pearlstein, T. (1997). Affect regulation and suicide attempts in adolescent inpatients. *Journal of the American Academy of Child and Adolescent Psychiatry, 36,* 793–798.

Zlotnick, C., Mattia, J. I., & Zimmerman, M. (1999). Clinical correlates of self-mutilation in a sample of general psychiatric patients. *Journal of Nervous and Mental Disease, 187,* 296–301.

Zlotnick, C., Shea, M. T., Begin, A., Pearlstein, T., Simpson, E., & Costello, D. (1996). The relationship between dissociative symptoms, alexithymia, impulsivity, sexual abuse, and self-mutilation. *Comprehensive Psychiatry, 37,* 12–16.

CHAPTER 8

An Assessment Tool for Self-Injury: The Self-Injury Self-Report Inventory (SISRI)

K. R. JUZWIN

Introduction

Recently, there has been an increase in the number of workshops on the identification and assessment of self-injury (SI), especially as it relates to eating disorders (ED) and other compulsive-spectrum problems (e.g., substance abuse) as well as to abuse and trauma such as post-traumatic stress disorder (PTSD) (e.g., Levitt 2000a, 2000b). Through these workshops, a number of professionals expressed interest in obtaining additional knowledge about the identification and assessment of SI. Many professionals reported difficulty in finding tools and techniques to efficiently and consistently assess the various facets of SI. In response to this and other factors, an instrument was developed for assessing SI that is especially appropriate for use with patients with ED. In this chapter, the issue of assessment and identification of SI behaviors using the Self-Injury Self-Report Inventory (SISRI) will be discussed.

Assessment of Self-Injury

In order to assess the domains of SI, it is important to clarify what is referred to in this broad category of behaviors. In the context of this discussion, SI refers to all behaviors that bring intentional harm to one's "self." That is, SI refers to the deliberate or intentional harming of one's body in order to achieve some psychological goal. SI involves a range of behaviors, from low-level to very damaging behaviors.

Patients report a number of psychological functions of SI including staying (psychologically) "alive," increasing one's ability to function in daily activities, or giving themselves a feeling of power and control. Many patients report that SI behaviors help them to numb out, decrease internal sensory or affective awareness (i.e., feelings), remove or distract themselves from their life situations, stop emotional pain, hurt themselves before anyone else can hurt them, or punish themselves for a supposed wrongdoing.

Patients generally report that the intent of SI is not for the purpose of ending life (i.e., a bona fide suicidal gesture or attempt). Most acknowledge that if death were to occur, it was not the primary goal of their behavior. SI is, in many patients' minds, a distinctly different type of behavior compared with a suicide effort. In keeping with this concept, some authors conceptualize ED as another form of SI. From our point of view, both may be viewed as compulsive behaviors that have distinct meaning(s) for patients.

Many of the community-based clinicians who attend our workshops identify SI behaviors as a symptom area they feel unprepared to manage, especially when it is the presenting problem. Many misinterpret such behavior as suicidal. When associated with a comorbid ED presentation, clinicians may struggle with how to assess the patient's clinical picture. Indeed, while most report that they feel able to treat the majority of Axis I disorders, they acknowledge considerable difficulty with the treatment of ED and self-destructive behavior. Part of this dilemma is that their patients generally do not report SI unless directly asked about it, or until later as the therapeutic relationship develops. Many clinicians appear surprised when their patients reveal more and more self-destructive symptoms and behaviors as therapy progresses. In response, clinicians have consistently requested a tool that would help them, at the outset of treatment, to consistently and efficiently assess the presence and type(s) of SI behaviors.

Assessment and Levels of Care

Throughout treatment, continuously assessing patients for the appropriate level of care is very important. Indeed, therapists need to be able to make important therapeutic decisions that directly relate to the treatment environment. Given the constraints of managed care, and the shift toward very short inpatient hospitalizations, the emphasis of treatment has shifted from inpatient and residential care to shortened outpatient treatment programs, such as partial hospitalization and outpatient therapy.

In addition, while intervention for the initial acute symptoms of the patient is important, being able to evaluate the broader clinical picture is equally relevant. For most patients, the clinician's assessment needs to look beyond the initial presenting symptoms of the current episode. Many psychiatric illnesses have presenting symptoms that, when acute, are relatively clear to define. However, many patients use self-destructive or SI behaviors that may not be reported or focused upon at the time of initial presentation. For example, a patient who presents with prominent anxiety or mood symptoms might not normally be asked about SI behaviors. Realistically, for many patients presenting with histories of depression and other mood disorders, transient psychoses, dissociation, ED, anxiety disorders, or substance abuse problems, the global clinical picture is not easily clarified. It is important to understand the patient's broad symptom constellation in order both to better identify what is actually happening and to develop an appropriate intervention plan.

Assessment Tools for SI and Eating Disorders

Sansone and Levitt (2002) reviewed the current literature on the relationship between ED and self-harm behavior. Their review suggests that patients with comorbid ED and self-harm behavior tend to have greater severity of psychiatric illness, early histories of abuse, dissociation, impulsivity, and possibly personality disorders. In their analysis, the authors found a prevalence rate of approximately 25% for SI among outpatients with anorexia or bulimia nervosa. Further, the prevalence rates for suicide attempts among outpatients with anorexia nervosa was 16%, that for outpatients with bulimia nervosa was 23%, and that for inpatients with bulimia nervosa 39%. When alcohol abuse and bulimia nervosa were considered together, the prevalence rate for suicide attempts rose to 54% (Sansone & Levitt, 2002).

Sansone and Sansone (2002) underscore the importance of simultaneously assessing for SI behaviors, particularly suicide attempts, when assessing those with ED. Indeed, because of the general prevalence of SI and suicidal behaviors in ED populations, assessing these behaviors as part of the self-destructive spectrum is critical. The converse appears to be valid, as well—among self-injurers, there appears to be a much higher frequency of current or past ED symptoms (Sansone & Levitt, 2002). For example, Conterio and Lader (1998) report that 61% of self-injurers in their program sample indicated a current or past ED. Further examination of this relationship indicates that the presence of SI behavior may often begin after the development of the ED.

A number of authors have developed tools to help in the assessment of ED as well as self-destructive behavior. These instruments, both self-report and interview, aid the clinician in assessing complex symptomatic patterns. In a review of 15 ED instruments, Sansone and Sansone (2002) found that none specifically looked at self-destructive behavior. One instrument alone possessed an item that queried for past suicide attempts. Of the nine self-harm instruments reviewed, six queried for ED symptoms, eight for overt self-harm behavior, and four for high-lethal behaviors. None of these instruments adequately assesses the combination of ED and SI symptomatology. One instrument (i.e., the Self-Harm Inventory, SHI; Sansone, Wiederman, & Sansone, 1998) was designed to evaluate ED and SI behaviors in association with the presence of borderline personality disorder.

Saxe, Chawla, and van der Kolk (2002) used the Dissociative Experiences Scale (DES) and the Dissociative Interview Schedule (DIS) to assess self-destructive behavior in patients with dissociative disorders, depression, and borderline personality disorder. In this study, 86% of patients with dissociative disorders were found to engage in self-destructive behavior. While these results yielded a strong relationship between the degree of dissociation and the degree of self-destructiveness, the results did not show similar findings between self-destructiveness and borderline personality. Further, findings indicated a weak relationship between depression and self-destructiveness. In this study, those who dissociated reported a history of chronic childhood trauma as well as SI that began in early adolescence. Clearly, an instrument that helps the clinician screen for the presence and the types of SI behaviors would be clinically useful at all levels of treatment.

History and Development of the Self-Injury Self-Report Inventory

Our freestanding hospital is located in a suburb of a large metropolitan area and serves a broad range of social, economic, ethic, and religious groups. We provide both inpatient and outpatient services for psychiatric disorders across all age groups. Funding sources also vary, including both managed care and public assistance. Within this program, we operate a SI program.

The development of the SI program was based, in part, on the work of Levitt (2000a, 2000b). Levitt found that many patients with ED seeking treatment were disorganized, complex, and multi-compulsively symptomatic (Levitt, 1998). For these patients, effective treatment needed to address a spectrum of behaviors, not just those presenting at intake (Levitt & Sansone, 2003). Using the SHI in a sample of patients with ED from the Eating Disorders Program, Levitt found that of the 13 patients surveyed, 85% reported a history of SI (Levitt & Sansone, 2002). It soon became clear that specialized assessment, training, and treatment programming for SI was necessary. As a result, a specialized SI treatment program was developed at the hospital. In structure and philosophy, it is very similar to the ED program (for a general description, see Levitt & Sansone, 2003).

The SISRI (Table 8.1) was developed as a method to assess current and past SI symptomatology, including severity and frequency, the pervasiveness of patterns, and the patient's perspective of the general "purpose" of these behaviors. The SISRI is a self-report measure that can be given to a patient at any time in the treatment, including at the outset as a screening tool or after the likely presence, or history, of SI has been detected. The SISRI data can then be reviewed as part of a broader assessment/interview process with the patient, specifically to clarify the endorsed items.

The items of the SISRI were developed by identifying important symptoms and patterns of self-destructive behaviors reported in the literature, and from clinical interviews and interactions through our own clinical experience. The SISRI was initially designed to augment a general biopsychosocial questionnaire given to all patients in the hospital and the semistructured interview that occurs during the general admission process to the hospital. We have also used the SISRI as a screening tool in order to identify patients who are appropriate for SI program services. Written at about a fourth-grade reading level, the majority of adolescents and adults are comfortable reading it.

The questions in the SISRI tend to cluster into the following categories: SI, ED, high-risk behaviors, and substance abuse patterns. Several questions briefly survey for a possible history of abuse or trauma. One question screens for a history of suicide attempts. The SISRI also contains items that inquire about the patient's perceptions of the purpose or function of SI behaviors as well as the impact of these behaviors on their daily life. Lastly, several questions assess the patient's motivation for changing their use of SI behaviors. The development of these latter items came primarily from clinical observations and experience in working with these patients.

As with any clinical instrument, the usefulness of the SISRI derives from the information obtained and its integration into treatment by the clinician.

We have experimented with the SISRI among patients attending the SI treatment program. In our groups and programs for SI, most of our participants are women (about 75%), which is consistent with the literature (e.g., Conterio & Lader, 1998). As an overview, the population attending this treatment program consists of, in descending order, adolescent females, adult women, adolescent males, and adult males. The average age of our group attendees tends to range between 13 and 19 years, although we have had some participants in their 60s.

TABLE 8.1 Self-Injury Self-Report Inventory*

Instructions: Please answer the questions by checking either "YES" or "NO" to each question. Check "YES" for those items that you have done intentionally or on purpose to injure yourself. Each question has two parts, the first column asks about CURRENT behaviors (within the past 6 months) or problems, and the second column asks about any past behaviors or problems. Please explain all YES answers.

	Within the Past 6 Months Have You:		In the Past:		Have You Ever Intentionally, (If Yes, Describe Briefly)	What Age Did You Start?	Estimate How Many Times?	When Was the Last Time?	Did You Get Treatment? What Type? When?
1.	YES	NO	yes	no	Cut yourself enough to tear the skin and/or bleed?				
2.	YES	NO	yes	no	Scratched, rubbed, bruised or pinched at your skin?				
3.	YES	NO	yes	no	Burned yourself?				
4.	YES	NO	yes	No	Tattooed or pierced yourself? Where? Did you use anything to numb yourself?				
	YES	NO	yes	no					
5.	YES	NO	yes	no	Pulled out hair, eyelashes or eyebrows?				
6.	YES	NO	yes	no	Drawn blood from yourself?				
7.	YES	NO	yes	no	Have you/do you dissociate (feel unreal or detached) when you self-injure?				
8.	YES	NO	yes	no	Is your self-injury planned or ritualized?				
	YES	NO	yes	no	Is your self-injury impulsive?				

9.	YES	NO	yes	no	Banged your head or any of your limbs against something with the intent to injure the limb or yourself? Hit yourself?				
10.	YES	NO	yes	no	Prevented injuries or wounds from healing?				
11.	YES	NO	yes	no	Fallen down stairs, banged against items, etc, to bruise or hurt yourself?				
12.	YES	NO	yes	no	Broken your own limbs?				
13.	YES	NO	yes	no	Gouged at your eyes, ears or other bodily parts?				
14.	YES	NO	yes	no	Mutilated your genitals or anus?				
15.	YES	NO	yes	no	Engaged in fighting or other aggressive activities with the intention to get hurt?				
	YES	NO	yes	no	Were drugs or alcohol used?				
16.	YES	NO	yes	no	Ingested/swallowed items with the intention to hurt yourself (without the intention of dying)?				
17.	YES	NO	yes	no	Over-exercised to hurt yourself or manage your weight?				
18.	YES	NO	yes	no	Starved to hurt yourself or manage your weight?				
19.	YES	NO	yes	no	Purged to hurt yourself or manage your weight?				

TABLE 8.1 (Continued)

	Within the Past 6 Months Have You:		In the Past:	Have You Ever Intentionally, (If Yes, Describe Briefly)	What Age Did You Start?	Estimate How Many Times?	When Was the Last Time?	Did You Get Treatment? What Type? When?
20.	YES	NO	yes / no	Used laxatives to hurt yourself or manage your weight?				
21.	YES	NO	yes / no	Engaged in specific rituals to punish/harm yourself?				
22.	YES	NO	yes / no	Acted out sexually to punish yourself or re-enact abuse?				
23.	YES	NO	yes / no	Hurt yourself before someone else hurt you?				
24.	YES	NO	yes / no	Used drugs or alcohol to numb out, escape or bring harm to yourself?				
25.	YES	NO	yes / no	Not followed medical advice on purpose to hurt yourself?				
26.	YES	NO	yes / no	Caused or made medical conditions worse so they would need medical attention or cause serious harm?				
27.	YES	NO	yes / no	Have you ever attempted suicide? When, how?				
28.	YES	NO	yes / no	Have you ever been sexually abused?				
29.	YES	NO	yes / no	Have you ever been physically abused?				

	YES	NO	yes	no	
30.					Have you ever been emotionally abused?
31.					What are the reasons that you hurt yourself?
32.					Do these behaviors interfere with your daily life or relationships? If YES, how?
33.					Do you think self-injury is a problem for you? If YES, how?
34.					Do you want to stop or decrease these behaviors? If YES, how?

Assessment Summary and Recommendations:

Patient Signature: _____   Date: _____   Staff Signature: _____

Date: _____

*Juzwin, K. R., Alexian Brothers Behavioral Health Hospital, Rolling Meadows, Illinois.

Using the SISRI, we collected data from a small sample of patients ($N = 29$) in the SI treatment program. The majority reported using some form of SI since the age of eight years. Approximately 93% of the sample endorsed cutting themselves, 38% burning themselves, 17% ingesting substances, and 17% injecting themselves or bloodletting. In addition, 48% endorsed a current or past history of anorexia nervosa, 31% a current or past history of bulimia nervosa, and 38% problems with substance abuse. Regarding abuse, 65% reported a history of sexual abuse, 62% physical abuse, and 76% emotional abuse. When exploring the function of SI, a large proportion of respondents reported that self-destructive behavior provided a mechanism to help them manage the real and perceived problems that they encountered in their current lives. Many indicated that they were not ready, or were unable, to stop any of their SI behaviors.

Clinical Utilization of the SISRI

The data generated by the SISRI is designed to help clarify a patient's past and current symptomotology (e.g., severity, frequency, and purpose) so that appropriate and effective treatment decisions can be made. In this regard, the clinician reviewing the SISRI data generally considers the following information:

1. *Types of self-injurious behaviors used.* Critical areas to consider include how many types of injury are being acknowledged, whether the individual is exploiting one or many parts of the body, and whether or not a tool is being used.
2. *Intention.* Is the SI ritualized, or seemingly spontaneous or impulsive? What is the perceived outcome by the patient?
3. *Status of the self-injurious behavior.* Is the SI perceived as a primary problem, secondary, or comorbid to other psychiatric difficulties? What other behaviors or symptoms exist and to what extent? What purpose do these behaviors serve the patient? How do the SI behaviors interact with other symptoms?
4. *Current versus past use of behaviors.* What is the present SI pattern, how long has it been going on, and how has the pattern changed over time? What happened to deter SI behaviors or did they undergo substitution to another compulsive type of behavior (e.g., ED, chemical abuse)?
5. *Frequency.* How often are the behaviors used, in what context, and in reaction to what situations, events, etc.?
6. *Severity.* How severe have the injuries been? Did the individual receive treatment, and, if so what kind? Should they have received

treatment? What kinds of scars exist and/or what kinds of other physical damage have been caused by SI?

7. *Onset.* When did the SI start, what was (were) the precipitating factor(s), and how did the patient learn about SI?

8. *Chronicity.* To what degree does the patient's life center around, or controlled by, the use of SI behaviors?

9. *Pattern.* What is the relationship between SI and other compulsive behavior(s) (e.g., ED)?

10. *Previous treatment.* Has the patient had treatment before, for what, when, and with what outcome?

11. *Patterns and comorbidity.* Are there other coping behaviors used to help the individual function (e.g., dissociative symptoms, ED)? Do the self-injurious behaviors exist in the context of an acute psychiatric episode?

12. *Purpose that SI serves for the individual.* What purpose or meaning does SI provide to the individual?

13. *Impact on life.* How does the behavior impact their life? Is the behavior used to attain or avoid certain responsibilities, relationships, etc.? How do they respond to the consequences of using SI (e.g., how does it affect their ability to go to work, relationships, health, and so forth)?

Our initial approach to the SISRI data is to determine the degree of SI severity for the purposes of deciding appropriate level of care. Our treatment options include referral to specific skill-based groups, partial hospital treatment, inpatient treatment, complex multi-program assignment, or specific types of outpatient services. Items on the treatment-entry SISRI that warrant the most immediate clinical concern are those that involve repetitive SI with the goal of harming oneself, and involve damage to the skin or tissue in any form.

The information obtained from the SISRI may directly guide further assessment and patient disposition, as well as enhance other aspects of treatment. For example, when a patient completes the inventory, the staff reviews the information with the patient in order to clarify and gather more extensive information on any endorsed items. If one item or more among questions 1 through 16 are endorsed, this triggers further evaluation for special SI treatment. Items endorsing any form of SI are considered in the context of severity, frequency, and duration. These items are then considered in the context of the individual's responses to items 30 through 34 (i.e., reasons for hurting oneself or interference with daily functioning). Similarly, endorsed ED behaviors are referred for more extensive ED assessment. Likewise, a patient who endorses substance abuse items receives a more extensive chemical dependency assessment. In addition, SISRI items present a general framework for understanding the patient's current SI, the role the SI plays in their life, and their motivation for change. The SISRI provides information that allows the clinical team an opportunity to efficiently obtain a quick overview of the patient's SI functioning. In addition, the data obtained can be used directly with the patient so that they can begin to understand their own SI patterns.

There are two general approaches for using the data collected from the SISRI. First, as illustrated above, a patient's responses may be analyzed and, as a result, a specific treatment plan may then be developed. For example, a patient who endorsed past but not current SI would *not* be referred for special SI program services. For those individuals who endorsed only a past history (beyond 6 months), assessment would focus more on understanding how the patient moved past SI as a mechanism of self-regulation and how he/she is managing in the present. This information would be presented in the patient's staffing or as part of a general outpatient treatment plan. If the patient is endorsing current SI behaviors or issues, then further assessment and referral to specific SI groups or programming would be made. As a caveat, we have not developed any statistically based thresholds for the SISRI as benchmarks for determining levels of care. This dimension is currently being explored as data is being collected.

The second approach to using the information from the SISRI is to examine the data obtained from the group as a whole and to use it to evaluate program services. This improves our ability to provide specific treatment programming to meet the needs of the treatment population. For example, the data obtained from the above sample ($N = 29$) indicated somewhat low motivation to abstain from SI and some degree of hopelessness regarding change. Consequently, for that group, we increased the emphasis upon exploring alternatives to using SI, emphasizing skills, and stressing and looking at the positive advantages for not relying on SI behaviors (i.e., hope).

Limitations and Conclusion

The use of a self-report instrument such as the SISRI always carries with it a number of limitations. Since it is a self-report measure, the patient's motivation, honesty, insight, current mental state, degree of openness, and ability to answer questions may limit the reliability of the information reported. Many of our patients have refused to fill out the inventory for various reasons, and consequently the assessment process was limited. Other patients found the amount of direct inquiry about so many SI behaviors to be somewhat provocative. That is, they reacted to being asked questions about their SI. The SISRI is also limited in its exposure with various age groups. We have not, for example, used this inventory with children or most pre-teens.

In using the SISRI, some items are more frequently endorsed than others. We suspect that that is due to the relevance of those particular questions for the population of patients that we typically encounter. In future revisions of the instrument, a number of items may be reconsidered. This is particularly true for those areas that ask the patient to report on the impact of SI on their life and willingness to change.

Because of the initial design and purpose of the inventory, there are presently no clear thresholds or formulas to determine level-of-care decisions. The reviewing clinician must rely on their training and experience to integrate the information obtained in the inventory. Therefore, it is important for clinicians who are using the SISRI to have specialized training in SI, ED, and the other behaviors and symptoms surveyed on the SISRI.

Finally, a significant limitation of the SISRI is that it has never been compared to other instruments, such as the SHI (Sansone et al., 1998). Though the SISRI appears to have face validity, the SISRI lacks statistical validity. The SISRI does, however, provide a consistent method for collecting information about SI, is easy to use, and may be used in a variety of clinical settings.

Assessment of SI behavior is an important component to thoroughly assessing and treating many types of patients, especially those with ED. Having an understanding of the range of SI symptoms and their history is a vital component of providing effective treatment. This SISRI was designed to augment this understanding.

References

Conterio, K., & Lader, W. (1998). Bodily harm: The breakthrough treatment program for self-injurers. New York: Hyperion.

Levitt, J. L. (1998). The disorganized client: New management strategies. *Paradigm, 2,* 20.

Levitt, J. L. (2000a). Nature and treatment of the symptomatically complex eating disordered clients: Trauma, self-injury, and dual diagnosis. Invited workshop given at Pinecrest Christian Hospital, Professional Lecture Series, Grand Rapids, MI, March.

Levitt, J. L. (2000b). Surviving the storm: Treating the complex eating disordered client. Institute presented at the International Association of Eating Disorder Professionals, Annual Conference, Orlando, FL, August.

Levitt, J. L., & Sansone, R. A. (2002). Searching for the answers: Eating disorders and self-harm. *Eating Disorders: The Journal of Treatment and Prevention, 10,* 189–191.

Levitt, J. L., & Sansone, R. A. (2003). The treatment of eating disorder clients in a community-based partial hospitalization program. *Journal of Mental Health Counseling, 25,* 140–151.

Sansone, R. A., & Levitt, J. L. (2002). Self-harm behaviors among those with eating disorders: An overview. *Eating Disorders, 10,* 205–213.

Sansone, R. A., & Sansone, L. A. (2002). Assessment tools for self-harm behavior among those with eating disorders. *Eating Disorders, 10,* 193–203.

Sansone, R. A., Wiederman, M. W., & Sansone, L. A. (1998). The Self-Harm Inventory (SHI): Development of a scale for identifying self-destructive behaviors and borderline personality disorder. *Journal of Clinical Psychology, 54,* 973–983.

Saxe, G. N., Chawla, N., & Van der Kolk, B. (2002). Self-destructive behavior in patients with dissociative disorders. *Suicide & Life-Threatening Behavior, 32,* 313–320.

Treatment

An Overview of Psychotherapy Strategies for the Management of Self-Harm Behavior

RANDY A. SANSONE, JOHN L. LEVITT, AND LORI A. SANSONE

Introduction

The psychotherapy approaches to the management of self-harm behavior (SHB) among individuals with eating disorders are quite varied. Empirical data are scant, and most of the techniques for SHB described in the literature evolve from two populations—individuals with borderline personality and those with mental retardation. In this chapter, we summarize these various psychotherapy techniques. As with all treatment interventions, the integration of these techniques is highly individualized and the patient's motivation for recovery is critical. Because SHB is semi-chronic in many cases, these interventions should be conceived as part of an ongoing treatment structure that may also include other interventions such as medications (this material is covered in another chapter) and/or brief psychiatric hospitalization.

SHB among those with eating disorders is a common comorbid phenomenon. However, the explicit relationship between eating disorders and SHB is unclear. At times, SHB may manifest as overt behavior (e.g., self-cutting); in other instances, the eating disorder symptoms, themselves, may function as self-injury equivalents. From our clinical experience, individuals with longstanding SHB appear to require a longitudinal treatment approach. For many clinicians, this approach consists of a combination of techniques designed to reduce the frequency of such behaviors, explore their possible deeper meaning(s), and assist the patient to psychologically reframe the behaviors as ego-dystonic. In this chapter, we review the various general psychotherapy strategies for the management of these behaviors. Like any therapeutic intervention, psychotherapy treatment must be individualized and, regardless of strategy, efficacious treatment requires a motivated patient. Most importantly, we emphasize those strategies that are relevant in working with patients with *both* eating disorder and self-harm symptoms. As a caveat, there is little empirical evidence regarding the efficacy of these treatments, although many authors, including ourselves, have found these approaches clinically useful.

Cognitive Restructuring

In our work with patients with eating disorders, we have found that many harbor faulty cognitive beliefs that subtly promote SHB. These illogical beliefs may have developed from dysfunctional family backgrounds (i.e., learned behavior) and/or have been constructed by the patient through a variety of negative, or difficult, life experiences (i.e., early abuse, developmental transitions). Regardless, the resulting cognitive structure, which is often beyond the patient's immediate awareness, establishes a conducive backdrop for SHB.

An example of a common cognitive distortion is, "Self-harm behavior is acceptable." This belief may parallel a family environment in which other members routinely participate in various self-harm, self-defeating, or high-risk behaviors. "What I do isn't any worse than the rest of my family—my mother abuses prescription drugs, my father is an alcoholic, and my sister has had multiple suicide attempts."

Another example of a common faulty cognition is, "I deserve to be punished." This conclusion is frequently entangled with the patient's exceedingly low self-esteem, lack of personal value, and very negative self-image. As a final example of common cognitive distortions, some patients believe that SHB is a necessary and legitimate means of communicating needs or resolving intolerable feelings—"Cutting myself is necessary to convince others that I really hurt or to bring me relief from emotional pain."

The basic therapeutic strategy in this approach is to be aware that these cognitions exist, to actively elicit them, to explore how they legitimize SHB, and to have the patient challenge and restructure them. For example, in response to, "I deserve to be punished," the therapist might respond, "I think that this is a misguided thought—you don't deserve this kind of maltreatment, nor does anyone else." From this juncture, the therapist might explore the rationales for this conclusion, challenge those rationales in a logical and intellectualized manner, and encourage the patient to reexamine the conclusions. This technique is very similar in style to the cognitive approaches that are utilized to confront faulty thinking around food, body, and weight issues, and is empirically reported as effective with both suicidal behavior and eating disorder symptoms (Perris & Herlofson, 1993).

Dynamic Intervention

According to Gunderson (1984; 2001), there are a number of strategic intrapsychic and interpersonal functions that are achieved by SHB. For example, SHB may be used to regulate, or distract oneself from, intolerable affects (e.g., overwhelming feelings of anger, anxiety, emptiness) that cannot be psychologically managed by the patient. In addition, SHB may function as a means of atonement (i.e., to punish oneself for a perceived failing or negative outcome—"He didn't show up for our date, so I cut myself"). For some psychosis-prone patients with the borderline personality symptomatology, SHB may alleviate impending psychotic fragmentation.

At times, SHB may function as a means of reinforcing an identity for those individuals without a solid sense of self. In this regard, the identity is organized around themes of self-destruction (i.e., "rebel without a cause"). This function is readily apparent in the group treatment setting, wherein some patients with eating disorders actively compete with each other regarding who has exhibited the worst behavior (e.g., "How many times have you been in the intensive care unit for low potassium?" "How many times have you had a hyperalimentation line put in?"). For these individuals, being the worst is at least perceived as being something, rather than the intense distress of perhaps being nothing.

Finally, Gunderson (1984) emphasizes that SHB may function to elicit caring responses from others. In this way, SHB enables one to bypass the normal processes of interpersonal communication and vulnerability that accompany the negotiation of needs with others. Given its dramatic nature, SHB acutely elicits powerful emotional and caretaking responses from others (e.g., "You cut yourself—we need to get that taken care of immediately!").

Given that any or all of the preceding dynamics may be present, the therapist must scrutinize each self-harming patient for the presence of these functions. It is critically important to appreciate that in patients without psychosis, pathological behavior has some *adaptive* value, and that this value must be acknowledged and validated by the therapist. When a specific adaptive function is encountered, the therapist might say, "I believe that you cut yourself because you genuinely struggle with your own anger, and this seems to be one way to control it." To further validate the function of the behavior, the therapist might continue, "I can really see how this would contain your anger." The therapist can then challenge this method of problem-solving. "But, we need to examine less costly ways for you to defuse your anger." In summary, this technique involves being alert for and exploring dynamics, identifying them with the patient, validating and interpreting the function of the dynamics, challenging the patient around the excessive emotional cost of this behavior, and guiding the patient to contemplate less costly alternatives.

Interpersonal Restructuring

In our opinion, one of the most important contributions by Gunderson (1984) to the field of borderline personality is his description of the technique of interpersonal restructuring. This intervention is based upon the assumption that one significant role of SHB among patients is the elicitation of caring responses from others. Intervention is designed to restructure the meaning and function of SHB in the therapy relationship—a challenging task—with the expectation that this will generalize to other social relationships.

The Gunderson approach to interpersonal restructuring is engaged at the outset of every self-harm threat or crisis. The basic principles during the acute crisis phase are: (a) explore what the patient is really asking for or needing in the therapeutic relationship; (b) clarify that SHB has an effect on the treatment relationship by heightening the anxiety of the therapist, thereby impeding his/her effectiveness in the treatment process; and (c) regardless of what intervention is decided upon, the therapist's response to the patient is governed by legal and ethical concerns—that therapists choose to show caring to patients in healthier ways than rescuing them.

As a working clinical example, imagine a 1:00 a.m. telephone call. The patient states, "I hope that I am not disturbing you, but I had an academic question. How much Zoloft do I need to take to kill myself?" Using the Gunderson approach, the therapist might respond, "I need to understand what you are *really* wanting or needing from me right now." With some prodding, the patient admits that the previous session left her feeling very angry with the therapist. During the telephone conversation, she episodically returns to self-harm threats. The therapist might respond, "You know, when you make threats to harm yourself, it really heightens my anxiety, which makes me less effective as a therapist for you. I don't know how we will resolve this crisis, tonight—whether we will talk this out next week or send you to the emergency room. But, I need to let you know that whatever we do is based upon my legal and ethical obligations to you—that therapists choose to show caring in healthier ways than rescuing patients."

During the post-crisis phase, Gunderson recommends that therapists: (a) explore the patient's reaction to the intervention; (b) reinforce the mutual need to understand the patient's SHB; and (c) acknowledge satisfaction at having been available for the crisis, but clarify that the therapist is *not* always available. For the preceding example, these techniques might unfold during the next appointment during the following week. The therapist might say, "How did you feel about how I managed the situation last weekend?" The patient might respond, "I can tell you this—if you had called the police, I wouldn't have been there in my apartment when they arrived." The therapist might respond, "This incident underscores our need to keep focusing in your treatment on SHB. By the way, I was pleased that I could help you out last weekend, but please realize that I am not always available."

With regard to interpersonal restructuring, Gunderson emphasizes a consistent and repetitive verbal phraseology by the therapist. By using the same wording, the patient is able to inculcate the principles and internally use them to curb future SHB (this is somewhat akin to utilizing Alcoholics Anonymous clichés like, "one day at a time"). The therapist must anticipate the repeated use of interpersonal restructuring during the early phases of the treatment relationship. Once SHB is stabilized in the treatment relationship, this intervention will be less necessary.

Family Therapy

Family therapy can be an effective tool in the approach to SHB. Indeed, Lock, Le Grange, Agras, and Dare (2001) have developed a family therapy model based on clinical trials developed at Maudsley Hospital for treating adolescents with anorexia. The treatment team views SHB as part of an overall pattern of family communication. This enables the family therapist to examine self-harm patterns within the family, and their intended message and impact on family members. This model may be particularly effective for younger adolescents with low-level self-injury behaviors. For suicidal patients with anorexia, Achimovich (1985) reviews the literature on family therapy techniques.

Behavior Modification

Behavior modification entails identifying problematic behaviors and their frequency, and developing reinforcers and contingencies to extinguish negative behaviors and increase desired behaviors. In our experience with characterological patients with eating disorders, this approach has not worked particularly well for the treatment of SHB. For these dynamically complex patients, SHB is intimately intertwined with complex intrapsychic and interpersonal dynamics. To complicate matters, target behaviors for treatment can be quickly substituted for more covert behaviors (e.g., substituting cutting oneself with biting the inside of one's mouth), making effective monitoring of progress virtually impossible. We have also found that this behaviorally focused approach lacks the psychological intimacy that many of these patients yearn for. Because of these and other factors, behavior modification has not worked consistently well in our work with patients with eating disorders.

Substitution vs. Sublimation

The process of substitution entails exchanging high-damage behaviors for ones perceived to be less so. For example, instead of cutting oneself, the therapist contracts with the patient that he/she will substitute another behavior, like squeezing rubber balls. However, the strategic risk with the substitutive approach is that patients may use the new "therapeutic" substitute in an unexpected and equally damaging fashion. In one instance, we encountered a patient who was advised to snap rubber bands against her wrist, which resulted in extensive bruising. Another patient, who was burning herself, was advised to substitute the immersion of her face in ice water; she eventually appeared in the emergency room with cold injuries to her face. Because of these potential risks among self-harming patients, we do not encourage explicit substitution of behaviors.

We do, however, recommend sublimation, an approach that entails the redirection of unhealthy behaviors into healthier alternative behaviors. We have found this approach particularly helpful in somewhat higher functioning and/or creative patients. We typically suggest, for example, redirecting aggressive behaviors to expression on paper. Using journals or artwork, the patient learns how to manage as well as start to express overwhelming affects. We have found that many patients readily gravitate toward this type of personalized expression. As a caveat, the therapist must review these creative endeavors, but avoid allowing the materials to monopolize the session.

Contracting

In our opinion, contracting with patients is an essential but legally ambiguous issue. We recognize that from a legal perspective, contracts may have little substantiation in the courtroom. In the clinical setting, however, contracts have tremendous interpersonal value, particularly in learning how to develop a healthy and viable treatment relationship. Contracts may function to clarify the treatment structure, make expectations of therapist and patient explicit (e.g., "You need to call a support person before damaging yourself"), and/or specify the consequences of a patient's particular SHB. We advise that contracts, whether verbal or written, be undertaken by the therapist with absolute sincerity and candor, as they identify the roles and responsibilities of both the patient and the therapist. The therapist, therefore, must demonstrate a genuine belief in the value of the contracting process and should emphasize that the patient's functioning within the designated parameters of the contract enables continued treatment.

From a pragmatic standpoint, the contract functions to place the patient into a therapeutic bind. If the patient is able to reasonably meet the expectations of the contract, he/she secures the treatment relationship. If not, then the treatment must be reexamined and possibly redesigned or even abandoned. When the contract is being challenged, both the therapist and the patient must examine the reasons. For example, is the patient really *ready* for this type of treatment? Is this the *appropriate* treatment at this point in time? Repeatedly, the therapist should emphasize that the overall goal of the contract is to promote behavioral stability, which in turn promotes psychological work in the treatment relationship. Most importantly, the patient can utilize contracts as opportunities for learning about healthy relationships.

We have discussed possible formats for treatment-entry contracts elsewhere (Sansone, Fine, & Sansone, 1994), but wish to highlight one important dynamic in this type of negotiation. We believe that every form of psychotherapy has some risk of patient regression. Given this risk with treatment, at the outset, we contract with all self-harming patients who are seeking psychotherapy treatment around the issue of suicidal ideation. We clarify that if a patient is genuinely suicidal, the regression potential inherent in psychotherapy treatment might acutely precipitate such behavior and result in death. Based upon this concern, to enter into psychotherapy treatment, the patient must contract for *absolute* containment of suicidal impulses. If the patient is unable to do so, we supportively invite them to return for future evaluation when they are able to make this commitment. We then refer them to other forms of treatment that may be more suitable at this juncture (e.g., psychoeducational groups). We believe that this particular negotiation protects the patient as well as the treatment. As a secondary issue, this approach also screens out the rare individual, often with severe borderline personality symptomatology (i.e., the malignant borderline patient), who is committed to suicide and wishes to discharge the blame on an authority figure, the therapist.

We wish to emphasize that, in our contracting efforts, we do not require restraint of all SHB. To do so, we believe, it is initially impossible as well as risky—one might gain momentary stabilization at the risk of eventual and robust decompensation. However, we may contract for reductions (e.g., 80%) of low-lethal behaviors that specifically impair the treatment process or psychologically disturb the therapist. For example, we might contract for no smoking of marijuana three days before sessions because the cognitive abilities necessary for the treatment are affected. Likewise, we might temporarily ignore scratching oneself or low-lethal cutting behavior, unless such behavior is displayed in a way that disturbs the therapeutic relationship or directly affects the therapist (i.e., the patient who literally bleeds on the furniture). We acknowledge all of these concerns very openly with patients, explaining our need to protect the treatment as well as the patient.

If a patient is repeatedly unable to meet the demands of a contract, we supportively confront the patient's obstacles to treatment participation and reexplore their genuine *readiness* to undertake a psychotherapy treatment "*at this time.*" We state this in a manner to reduce stigmatization and "leave the door open" to future treatment. It is critical that the patient does *not* perceive the therapist as manipulative or controlling. To dispel such potential projections, it is critically important that the therapist is honest with the treatment agenda and maintains a sincere investment in the treatment process with the patient. Again, if termination and referral is indicated because of the patient's inability to meet the contract expectations at that time, other treatment options are considered, such as crisis management, supportive psychotherapy, and/or brief hospitalization.

Group Therapy

Given the proper selection of participants (Sansone et al., 1994), group intervention can be quite helpful as a component of a broader treatment process. However, several entry criteria must be considered. First, candidates must have reasonable social adaptability to effectively function within a group treatment setting. In this regard, some patients may not have the ability to function within a group because of their own specific psychopathology (e.g., severe comorbid obsessive-compulsive disorder, paranoid ideation), interpersonal sensitivity, and/or poor social or interpersonal skills. Second, a reasonable level of motivation is essential, as unmotivated participants may languish and impede the group's energy toward progress. Third, candidates must not be inexorably prone to competing with other patients around self-harm or eating disorder behaviors, which is counter to the group's focus. Fourth, graphic self-harmers should be carefully evaluated for group entry, as higher functioning members may not be tolerant of such behaviors from lower-functioning members; this issue needs to be actively dialogued with the candidate (i.e., the impact of SHB on other group members). Fifth, younger and/or naïve charactero-logical candidates may experience contagion phenomena in the group setting (i.e., the group functions as a catalyst for acquiring broader SHB). In this regard, we recall several patients who, while in a milieu-based program, acquired the art of purging from other patients with eating dis-order. Finally, the malignant borderline personality disorder patient (e.g., the severely aggressive, symptom absorbing) is *not*, in our opinion, a can-didate for group treatment.

The number of participants in a group treatment for self-harmers with eating disorders is also important. We have found that at least six to seven members are needed to enable an ongoing "rotating ego." Given this num-ber of participants, when several members are struggling, there are usually enough remaining members to psychologically buoy the group.

As therapists who have conducted such groups, we have used a combi-nation of dynamic techniques, contracting, interpersonal restructuring on a group level, and cognitive restructuring, as well as role playing, goal setting, and homework assignments, which often involve other group members. Note that, in parallel fashion, the group treatment contains the treatment components of the individual setting.

Group treatment has many potential advantages for patients. First, it can function to demystify SHB (i.e., cutting oneself is not unique beh-avior). Groups promote cohesion and support among members who, in this setting, have the potential to consolidate around a common goal (i.e., reducing SHB). Members can facilitate mutual problem solving within a unique milieu and member feedback has a unique authenticity (i.e., "I've been there!").

Crisis Intervention Plans

While perhaps not a true psychotherapy strategy, crisis intervention plans certainly play an invaluable role in a multi-setting treatment system (i.e., those with inpatient, outpatient, partial hospital services). These plans are basically roadmaps to guide other treatment providers in other settings of the treatment system should the patient require a higher level of care. Crisis intervention plans may be particularly useful for the patient who periodically requires brief inpatient hospitalization. Most typically, the outpatient therapist, who is likely to have the most extensive psychological contact with the patient, is the co-author with the patient of the crisis intervention plan.

Taking the patient's treatment history into account, the crisis intervention plan essentially details a suggested treatment approach in the event that the patient requires a higher level of care. Crisis intervention plans may clarify, for example, the use of specific medications (e.g., atypical antipsychotics, benzodiazepines, etc.), the role of seclusion and restraint, whether to contact the therapist at the time of admission, and the recommended number of days of treatment to promote stability and minimize regression. Given that each is unique, every patient requires a specific management approach if a higher level of care is indicated.

The following might be an example of a crisis intervention plan for an anticipated inpatient admission:

1. Please notify the therapist of the admission during working hours.
2. Avoid the use of seclusion, if at all possible; if necessary, leave the door open, if possible.
3. Avoid hospitalization length to exceed 4 days due to the known risk of regression.
4. Establish early contact with the outpatient group members, if possible.
5. Avoid antipsychotics, but if needed, please consider low-dose risperidone.
6. Please have the patient follow her outpatient menu plan while in the hospital.
7. Expressive therapies have been found to work well with the management of aggressive drives.

Crisis intervention plans are ideally designed to facilitate the patient's care in another setting. However, one particular dilemma for facilities may be where to locate these written plans and the process of transferring them from one setting to another (e.g., to an inpatient facility that is two miles from the outpatient site).

Formal Combination Approaches

Our observation is that most therapists in the field of SHB use a combination of techniques tailored to the patient and therapist, as well as the treatment setting. However, Linehan and colleagues were the first investigators to develop a manualized, formal, combination approach to SHB, which they labeled "Dialectical Behavior Therapy" (DBT; Linehan, Tutek, Heard, & Armstrong, 1994). DBT is a combination of both individual and group intervention with components of cognitive-behavioral treatment, psychoeducation, and dynamic intervention. The developers of DBT offer a training course, and there is a book (Linehan, 1993a) as well as a manual (Linehan, 1993b) describing the approach. At the present time, DBT is the only well-known, formalized combination approach for the treatment of SHB. This approach has been successful in women with binge-eating disorder (Safer, Telch, & Agras, 2001; Safer, Lively, Telch, & Agras, 2002) as well as in women suffering from multiple symptoms including eating disorders, chronic suicidal ideation, and SHB (Simpson et al., 1998).

Other Philosophies Relating to SHB

Before closing this chapter, we would like to mention several treatment philosophies that pertain to SHB and its management. Kernberg (1984) emphasizes the importance of identifying the secondary gains related to SHB. In addition, he broaches the delicate issue of educating the family about the patient's chronic risk when high-lethal behavior is present. Kernberg recommends repeatedly exploring in treatment the theme of SHB, and strongly advises therapists to avoid unusual treatment efforts (e.g., having psychotherapy sessions offsite). Kernberg advises therapists to view SHB as a contaminant to the treatment process and cautions allowing the treatment to deteriorate to addressing crises (i.e., "putting out fires").

Goldberg (1983) emphasizes setting limits on SHB (i.e., define the limits to which therapy can withstand SHB) and underscores its maladaptive function. He also believes that it is necessary to explain to the patient the consequences of continued behavior (e.g., changing therapists, changing treatment environments).

Levitt (1998; 2001a; 2001b) describes an approach to treating SHB in patients with eating disorder based upon the concept of self-regulation. In this regard, SHB and eating disorder symptoms are conceptualized as equivalents as well as self-protective in that they serve to regulate the patient. Stated another way, the symptoms allow the patient to maintain an "internal psychological steady-state" despite ongoing stressful life events. Therefore, symptoms evolve and are sustained in various interpersonal contexts. Levitt has developed a model-based approach to teach patients how to self-regulate more effectively without self-harm symptoms.

Viner (1985), who has extensive experience in inpatient settings, recommends that therapists not assume ultimate responsibility for the control of the patient's SHB. He emphasizes understanding the dynamics of such behavior, not controlling it. Viner states that, to maintain one's treatment, SHB needs to undergo a meaningful reduction. He also emphasizes that the staff cannot fully protect the patient and that meaningful treatment may entail the risk of suicide.

Other aspects to self-harm management have been described as well. For example, Guinjoan and colleagues (2001) describe the effective treatment of SHB using transitional objects to facilitate, contain, and structure the act or fantasy of self-harm. Miller (1996) describes the use of the trauma story, which focuses on the logic and interpersonal functions of self-harm, and Rice and Faulkner (1992) describe the role of self-harm in support and self-help groups.

Recommendations

Given the plethora of various techniques described for the management of SHB, it is evident that a single approach is not consistently effective. Indeed, this is similar per se to the treatment of eating disorders. Therefore, we actively encourage the use of multiple approaches and emphasize cognitive restructuring, dynamic approaches, interpersonal restructuring, and contracting as first lines of intervention. For higher functioning and/ or creative patients, sublimation may be utilized. Group therapy requires a sufficient number of qualified candidates and may be limited to large treatment settings and/or practices with a sizeable number of patients with eating disorders who engage in self-harm. Family therapy may be particularly helpful for young adolescents. Crisis intervention plans are best suited for patients who may periodically require access to higher levels of care. Finally, DBT may work best in larger treatment settings or facilities where the cost of training therapists in this technique can be absorbed. It is important that clinicians utilize strategies with which they are familiar and that are likely to apply to the treatment of eating disorder symptoms as well. In this way, the treatment of both SHB and eating disorders is coherent as well as consistent.

Conclusion

SHB is undoubtedly challenging to treat. A variety of techniques are available, and, given their number, it is evident that no single technique overshadows the others. Most therapists in the field of SHB use a variety of techniques in an individual case. Treatment requires a motivated patient and chronic SHB entails a longitudinal treatment approach.

References

Achimovich, L. (1985). Suicidal scripting in the families of anorectics. *Transactional Analysis Journal, 15,* 21–29.

Goldberg, R. L. (1983). Psychodynamics of limit setting with the borderline patient. *American Journal of Psychoanalysis, 43,* 71–75.

Guinjoan, S. M., Ross, D. R., Perinot, L., Maritato, V., Jorda-Fahrer, M., & Fahrer, R. D. (2001). The use of transitional objects in self-directed aggression by patients with borderline personality disorders, anorexia nervosa, or bulimia nervosa. *Journal of the American Academy of Psychoanalysis, 29,* 457–468.

Gunderson, J. G. (1984). *Borderline personality disorder.* Washington, DC: American Psychiatric Press.

Gunderson, J. G. (2001). *Borderline personality disorder. A clinical guide.* Washington, DC: American Psychiatric Publishing.

Kernberg, O. (1984). *Severe personality disorders: Psychotherapeutic strategies.* New Haven: Yale University Press.

Levitt, J. L. (1998). The disorganized client: New management strategies. *Paradigm, 2,* 20.

Levitt, J. L. (2001a). Complexity and therapist self-regulation: The challenge of eating disordered patients, Part I. Half-day pre-conference Institute presented at the International Association of Eating Disorder Professionals Annual Meeting, San Diego, August.

Levitt, J. L. (2001b). Complexity and therapist self-regulation: The challenge of eating disordered patients, Part II. Half-day pre-conference Institute presented at the International Association of Eating Disorder Professionals Annual Meeting, San Diego, August.

Linehan, M. M. (1993a). *Cognitive-behavioral treatment of borderline personality disorder.* New York: Guilford Press.

Linehan, M. M. (1993b). *Skills training manual for treating borderline personality disorder.* New York: Guilford.

Linehan, M. M., Tutek, D. A., Heard, H. L., & Armstrong, H. E. (1994). Interpersonal outcome of cognitive behavioral treatment for chronically suicidal borderline patients. *American Journal of Psychiatry, 151,* 1771–1776.

Lock, J., LeGrange, D., Agras, W. S., & Dare C. (2001). *Treatment manual for anorexia nervosa: A family-based approach.* New York: Guilford.

Miller, D. (1996). Challenging self-harm behavior through transformation of the trauma story. *Sexual Addiction & Compulsivity, 3,* 213–227.

Perris, C., & Herlofson, J. (1993). Cognitive therapy. In N. Sartorius & G. de Girolamo (Eds.), *Treatment of mental disorders: A review of effectiveness* (pp. 149–198). Washington, DC: American Psychiatric Press.

Rice, C., & Faulkner, J. (1992) Support and self-help groups. In H. Harper-Giuffre & K.R. MacKenzie (Eds.), *Group psychotherapy for eating disorders* (pp. 247–260). Washington, DC: American Psychiatric Press.

Safer, D. L., Lively, T. J., Telch, C. F., & Agras, W. S. (2002). Predictors of relapse following successful dialectical behavior therapy for binge eating disorder. *International Journal of Eating Disorders, 32,* 155–163.

Safer, D. L., Telch, C. F., & Agras, W. S. (2001). Dialectical behavior therapy adapted for bulimia: A case report. *International Journal of Eating Disorders, 30,* 101–106.

Sansone, R. A., Fine, M. A., & Sansone, L. A. (1994). An integrated psychotherapy approach to the management of self-destructive behavior in eating disorder patients with borderline personality disorder. *Eating Disorders, 2,* 251–260.

Simpson E. B., Pistorello, J., Begin, A., Costello, E., Levinson, J., Mulberry, S., Pearlstein, T., Rosen, K., & Stevens, M. (1998). Use of dialectical behavior therapy in a partial hospital program for women with borderline personality disorder. *Psychiatric Services, 49,* 669–673.

Viner, J. (1985). Milieu concepts for short-term hospital treatment of borderline patients. *Psychiatric Quarterly, 57,* 127–133.

CHAPTER **10**

Therapy-Related Assessment of Self-Harming Behavior in Patients with Eating Disorders: A Case Illustration

LAURENCE CLAES, WALTER VANDEREYCKEN,
AND HANS VERTOMMEN

Introduction

Understanding an individual's self-harming behaviors should be the basis for selecting person-specific therapeutic interventions. For that purpose, the assessment is aimed at (a) identifying specific self-harming behaviors and related symptoms as well as (b) analyzing the external (i.e., situational) and internal (i.e., cognitive and emotional) conditions that contribute directly to the instigation of the self-harming behaviors. In this chapter, we demonstrate the use of a new assessment procedure that may guide the selection of therapeutic interventions. Data collection and processing will be illustrated by means of an individual case study of a patient with eating disorder who has different types of self-harming behavior such as vomiting, alcohol abuse, cutting, and suicide attempts.

The literature stresses that a great deal of comorbidity in patients with eating disorder can be regarded as an expression of disturbed self-control (see Vanderlinden & Vandereycken, 1997). In most cases, the patient is no longer able to suppress a strong urge to perform undesired acts. Other signs of a similar failure in impulse control are stealing, self-inflicted injury, and sudden outbursts of anger. Along a similar line of reasoning, Lacey and Evans (1986) have proposed the term "multi-impulsive" bulimia, referring to those patients who not only binge, vomit, and purge, but who also have problems with alcohol abuse, drug abuse, kleptomania, self-mutilation, and promiscuous sexual activity.

However, Fahy and Eisler (1993) suggest that bulimia nervosa does not simply represent an extreme variant of an impulsiveness trait. More likely, differences in impulsiveness act as a pathoplastic factor influencing the expression of eating disorders such as anorexia or bulimia nervosa in at-risk populations. Furthermore, Fahy and Eisler argue that there is insufficient evidence to conceptualize these types of behavior as arising from an underlying disorder of impulse control. They propose that, in the absence of convincing evidence to the contrary, most so-called impulsive behavior arises from affective disturbances rather than a failure to consider the self-destructive consequences of the relevant actions. They suggest that closer scrutiny of the affective and cognitive disturbances associated with such behavior may point the way to more rational treatment interventions in these challenging patients.

In this chapter, we present a case study to illustrate how therapy-related assessment (i.e., assessment that gives useful indications for therapeutic interventions) can be performed. After presentation of the case history, we demonstrate how specific self-harming behaviors can be identified and how external (i.e., situational) as well as internal (i.e., cognitions, affects) triggers of self-destructive behavior can be assessed in a systematic way. We end with a presentation of selected therapeutic interventions based on the assessment results.

Case History

Suzy, a 23-year-old woman with bulimia, was referred to our inpatient unit by her psychotherapist. After several years of intensive inpatient and outpatient psychotherapy, no progress had taken place. Suzy was still binging and vomiting every day, and showed several other types of self-harming behavior such as drinking alcohol, cutting and scratching without suicidal intent, and suicide attempts. Her symptoms made it impossible for her to continue studying and her eating disorder also caused serious medical problems. Hospitalization seemed indicated to stop the vicious circle.

Suzy was born in a family with three children. Her parents had divorced when she was 4 years old. After the parents' separation, she stayed with her mother, whom she described as a lenient and emotionally unstable woman. The contacts with her father, a strict and authoritarian man, were limited to a few times a year. Both parents started a new relationship, and Suzy experienced some sexual harassment from her mother's boyfriend. Suzy's relationship with her younger brother was good, in contrast to the ambivalent relationship with her older sister. Sometimes she really admired her sister, but most of the time Suzy really envied her sister because of her attractive body shape and large group of friends.

Suzy reported the onset of her self-harming behavior around the age of 15. At that time, her mother was hospitalized for cancer treatment. Afraid of losing her mother, she started cutting herself to numb her feelings and also ceased eating in the hope that she would gradually die. After a period of strict dieting, she began to binge eat, which was accompanied by vomiting and increasing laxative abuse. Her condition deteriorated regardless of the outpatient therapy she engaged in. Due to a severe suicide attempt and deteriorating medical condition caused by extreme cutting and purging behaviors, she had to be admitted to an inpatient unit specializing in the treatment of eating disorders and related impulse control disorders.

During the first week of her inpatient treatment, we performed a psychodiagnostic evaluation to specifically identify self-harming behaviors and related symptoms. An analysis of the internal and external conditions that contributed to the instigation of self-harming was carried out in the following weeks using a special assessment method that we developed. We will present the results of Suzy's assessment and illustrate how these results were used as a guide for the choice of our therapeutic interventions.

Assessment of Self-Harming Behaviors and Related Problems

Suzy's disturbed eating behavior was analyzed by means of the *Eating Disorder Evaluation Scale* (EDES; Vandereycken, 1993), designed to judge the severity of an eating disorder, and the *Eating Disorder Inventory* (EDI; Garner, 1991), developed to measure attitudes and psychological features relevant to anorexia and bulimia nervosa. On the EDES, she scored in the pathological range, especially on the following subscales: anorexic preoccupation (e.g., food and weight preoccupation), bulimic behavior (e.g., daily binging, vomiting, and laxative abuse), and sexual problems (e.g., amenorrhea). Interpersonal problems were denied. These findings were confirmed by Suzy's responses on the EDI. On the EDI, Suzy scored very high on the following subscales: drive for thinness, bulimia, body dissatisfaction, ineffectiveness, and maturity fears.

In addition, using the *Self-Injury Questionnaire* (SIQ; Vanderlinden & Vandereycken, 1997), Suzy was asked if (and how) she had deliberately injured herself over the past year, how often this had happened, if she had felt some pain, and the kind of emotions experienced at the moment of self-injury. On the SIQ, Suzy described two types of self-injurious behaviors: scratching herself till she bled and cutting herself. The scratching behavior occurred more than 15 times a week, often triggered by a feeling of nervousness, but it was not painful. On the other hand, cutting herself happened up to five times a week, caused only slight pain, and was usually performed when she felt angry. The fact that Suzy did not feel much pain while cutting herself could possibly be explained by the fact that she was in a state of dissociation while cutting. In a recently published study on self-injury in patients with eating disorder (Claes, Vandereycken, & Vertommen, 2001), we found that the absence of pain while cutting is associated with higher levels of dissociation. This finding prompted us to administer the *Dissociation Questionnaire* (DIS-Q; Vanderlinden, Van Dyck, Vandereycken, Vertommen, & Verkes, 1993). Indeed, Suzy scored within the pathological range, especially on "absorption," "identity confusion," and "loss of control."

To assess the relationship between traumatic events and self-harm, we included the *Traumatic Experiences Questionnaire* (TEQ; Dutch version: Nijenhuis, van der Hart, & Vanderlinden, 1995). The TEQ assesses a variety of negative historical experiences: emotional neglect and abuse, physical abuse, sexual abuse (by family members and others), family problems (such as alcohol abuse, poverty, psychiatric problems of a family member), death or loss of a family member, bodily harm, severe pain, and war experiences. On the TEQ, Suzy reported many traumatic experiences that she did not report at the intake interview. These experiences included suffering emotional neglect and abuse in the family of origin, being sexually threatened by her mother's boyfriend, suffering severe stress due to father's alcohol abuse and mother's psychiatric problems, and experiencing life-threatening circumstances because of her low weight.

The results on the *Body Attitude Test* (BAT; Probst, Vandereycken, Van Coppenolle, & Vanderlinden, 1995), specially developed for female patients suffering from an eating disorder, confirmed the body dissatisfaction already revealed by the EDI. Suzy's total BAT score exceeded the average score found in a large group of patients with bulimia nervosa. The highest scores were found on the subscales "general body dissatisfaction," "negative appreciation of body size," and "lack of familiarity with one's own body" (often found in traumatized patients).

With respect to comorbidity, we also administered the following self-report instruments: (a) the *Munich Alcohol Test* (MALT; Dutch version: Walburg & Limbeek, 1985), assessing several aspects of alcohol abuse such as the admission of alcohol abuse, withdrawal symptoms, and psychological as well as social problems due to the abuse; (b) the *Symptoms Checklist 90* (SCL-90; Dutch version: Arrindell & Ettema, 1986), a well-known measure for the assessment of a wide array of psychiatric symptoms such as anxiety, depression, and hostility; and (c) the *ADP-IV* (Dutch version: Schotte, De Doncker, Vankerckhoven, Vertommen, & Cosyns, 1998), representing the criteria for the *DSM-IV* personality disorders. The MALT did not reveal a pathological score, and only three item scores were increased, suggesting some alcohol abuse without serious consequences. On the SCL-90, the total score was very high and comparable with scores found in a psychiatric population. The following subscales displayed very high scores: anxiety and somatic complaints (mostly due to her disturbed eating and purging behaviors), and depression with the crucial item of suicidal ideation strongly elevated. Suzy admitted that she thought a lot about killing herself, but she denied having genuine plans to do it. On the basis of the ADP-IV results, Suzy met all of the criteria for borderline personality disorder.

Assessment of the Internal and External Triggers of the Self-Harming Behavior

In a second assessment step, we tried to determine the external (i.e., situational) and internal (i.e., emotional and cognitive) conditions that contributed to the instigation of Suzy's self-harming behavior. The assessment procedure we used to detect and visualize Suzy's situation-behavior profile and the guiding cognitive/affective processes is extensively described by Claes, Van Mechelen, and Vertommen (2001). Here, we will restrict ourselves to a short description of this assessment procedure and focus on the results.

To retrieve the potentially relevant situational features of Suzy's self-harming behaviors as well as the guiding cognitive and affective processes of these behaviors, we resorted to the preceding assessment findings as well as her diary notes, in which she had identified situations, cognitions, and affects that instigated her self-injurious acts. On the basis of this information, four situational features seemed to be potentially relevant: (a) the degree in which she was hurt (strongly/slightly), (b) the valence of the person who had hurt her (positive/negative), (c) the status of this person (higher/the same), and (d) the way in which she was hurt (words/being ignored). Accordingly, we created 16 abstract situations ($2 \times 2 \times 2 \times 2$) based upon the following design: "Think of a situation in which you were [strongly/slightly] hurt by a person you [like/dislike], who has [a higher/the same] status than you, and who had hurt you by means of [words/ignoring you]." Then we asked Suzy to describe 16 real-life situations that corresponded to the abstract situational descriptions (see Appendix A). For example, S_3 (strongly-like-higher-words) was filled out by her as follows: "My sister said to me that I had not made enough efforts to get rid of my eating disorder"; and S_{16} (strongly-dislike-same-ignoring) referred to "A classmate did not pick me out to play in his team during a gym course, because I'm a bad player." As potential emotional triggers of Suzy's self-harming behaviors, we selected anxiety (A_1), anger at herself (A_2) and others (A_3), and sadness (A_4). As cognitive triggers, we chose ideas of self-punishment (C_1) instead of punishment of others (C_2), ideas of being abandoned (C_3), not knowing how to react in an appropriate way (C_4), and losing contact with reality (C_5). These emotional and cognitive triggers were selected on the basis of the preceding assessment findings, Suzy's diary notes, and our own research findings (Claes, Vandereycken & Vertommen, 2001).

To examine the link between the 16 situations, cognitive and affective variables, and the self-harming responses, we asked Suzy to indicate in each of the situations she had described (1 = yes, 0 = no) each of the self-harming behaviors and each of the affective and cognitive variables. This implied the collection of a zero/one ($16 \times 8 \times 4$) situation × cognitions/affects × behavior data matrix. To uncover Suzy's situation × response profile and the guiding cognitions and affect, the data matrix was subjected to a hierarchical classes analysis (De Boeck & Rosenberg, 1988) and the solution was graphically represented as shown in Table 10.1.

In the upper half of Table 10.1, one can find the situations (ordered in situation classes) that instigated particular cognitions, affects, and self-harming behaviors. To find out which behaviors and cognitive-affective processes were triggered by each class of situations, one follows the downward lines that link situation classes with behavior classes (in the lower half of Table 10.1). For example, as shown in Table 10.1, in the situations of Situation Class 1 (characterized by the common features, being strongly hurt by a disliked person with the same hierarchical position), Suzy injures herself (R_1 in Behavior Class D) because she experiences a mix of anxious and angry feelings (A_1, A_2, A_3) and she thinks she has to punish herself (C_1). At the same time, she has the idea of losing contact with reality (C_5) probably due to dissociative experiences (see the first part of her diagnostic assessment). Furthermore, she feels sad (A_4 in Situation Class F) because she does not know how to react in an appropriate way (C_4). In situations in which she is only slightly hurt by disliked people with a higher status (common features of situations of Situation Class 2), she starts binging and vomiting (R_4 in Situation Class E) because she also feels sad (A_4 in Situation Class F) and does not know how to react in an appropriate way (C_4). When strongly hurt by a person she likes (e.g., S_4, being ignored by her father), she not only injures herself (R_1 in Behavior Class D) and binges and vomits (R_4 in Behavior Class E), but also abuses alcohol (R_3 in Behavior

Class C), especially when feeling abandoned (C_3 in Behavior Class C). Guided by the results of this assessment procedure, we developed several therapeutic interventions as described in the following paragraph.

Assessment-Based Therapeutic Interventions

There are many strategies to improve a person's self-control. We refer, for example, to Linehan's Dialectical Behavior Therapy (DBT), which focuses on the emotional dysregulation of patients with borderline personality disorder. Linehan (1993) showed how her approach could be effective in reducing suicide attempts and self-injurious behaviors in these patients. Inspired by this work, as well by as our own clinical experiences (see Vanderlinden & Vandereycken, 1997), we used the following elements in our therapeutic approach with Suzy.

Suzy's treatment was started by discussing the results of her assessment (see above). Much attention was given to the situational, cognitive, and affective triggers that instigated her self-harming behaviors by making use of the graphical representation shown in Table 10.1. For example, we showed her that the self-injurious behaviors (R_1 in Class D) were always preceded by situations in which she was strongly hurt by another person (see Situation Classes 1, 4, 5) and that this type of situation triggered a lot of anxious and angry feelings (A_1, A_2, A_3), irrational thoughts (e.g., have to punish herself), and ideas of losing contact with reality (C_5).

Once we had identified the most important triggers, alternative and more effective coping behaviors were explored. For Suzy, this part of the treatment was quite difficult. Because of her long-lasting experience of being out of control, she found it hard to believe that she could learn to get better control over herself. Nevertheless, she was encouraged to make a list of possible alternatives and to practice them. For example, Suzy's alternative behavioral strategies when she felt strongly hurt were: "go to or call a friend; don't isolate myself in a room but stay with others; write down in my diary all my feelings and thoughts at that moment; and try other things such as painting, drawing, playing music or watching television." Furthermore, she selected different alternative strategies to help her to cope more effectively with emotional stimuli, because the assessment indicated that her self-injuring was frequently associated with feelings of anger and anxiety. The alternatives (e.g., firmly touching an object that symbolizes her "safe place," listening to her favorite music) were aimed at decreasing tension and distracting attention. These strategies were written down on a small piece of paper that Suzy always had to carry with her We further suggested that she read it over and over again, especially in confrontation with triggers that instigated her self-injurious behaviors.

TABLE 10.1 Graphical Representation of The Hierarchical Classes Model of Suzy's S-R Data

	Class 1	Class 2	Class 3	Class 4	Class 5	Class 6
Situation	S_{15}: strongly-dislike-same-words S_{16}: strongly-dislike-same-ignore	S_9: slightly-dislike-high-words S_{10}: slightly-dislike-high-ignore		S_{11}: strongly-dislike-high-words S_{12}: strongly-dislike-high-ignore	S_4: strongly-like-high-ignore	S_1: slightly-like-higher-words S_2: slightly-like-higher-ignore S_3: strongly-like-higher-words S_5: slightly-like-same-words S_6: slightly-like-same-ignore S_7: strongly-like-same-words S_8: strongly-like-same-ignore S_{13}: slightly-dislike-same-words S_{14}: slightly-dislike-same-ignore

	Class A	Class B	Class C	Class D	Class E	Class F	Class G
Behavior			R_3: alcohol abuse C_3: feel abandoned	R_1: self-mutilation A_1: anxious A_2: angry at oneself A_3: angry at others C_1: have to punish oneself C_5: lose contact with reality	R_4: bingeing/vomiting	A_4: sad C_4: don't know how to react appropriately	R_2: suicide attempt C_2: have to punish other person

Situational descriptions by Suzy

S_1: slightly-like-higher-words: My father became angry with me because I didn't go to his anniversary party due to the death of a friend who had just committed suicide.

S_2: slightly-like-higher-ignore: A particular person didn't say hello and looked sullen, when I said hello.

S_3: strongly-like-higher-words: My sister said to me that I had not made enough efforts to get rid of my eating disorder.

S_4: strongly-like-high-ignore: Since my ninth birthday, my father had not visited me until I was recently hospitalized.

S_5: slightly-like-same-words: One of the other patients in the hospital came into the kitchen while I was cooking and said that the kitchen smelled of garlic.

S_6: slightly-like-same-ignore: One of the other patients didn't answer me when I asked her how she had passed her weekend.

S_7: strongly-like-same-words: One of the other patients told me that I irritated her, because I was acting as if everything was all right, although I was feeling bad.

S_8: strongly-like-same-ignore: One of my friends has not phoned or written since I have been hospitalized.

S_9: slightly-dislike-high-words: One of the other patients continually criticized my eating behaviors while we were sitting at the table.

S_{10}: slightly-dislike-high-ignore: My sister's boyfriend didn't ask me to his birthday party some days ago.

S_{11}: strongly-dislike-high-words: My father's girlfriend laughed at me because I needed to eat a lot to gain some weight.

S_{12}: strongly-dislike-high-ignore: One of my teachers continually ignored me during class hours.

S_{13}: slightly-dislike-same-words: One of the other patients, I don't like, told me that I talked too much about food.

S_{14}: slightly-dislike-same-ignore: My father's girlfriend always ignores me when I visit him.

S_{15}: strongly-dislike-same-words: One of my classmates said he hoped that my mother would die, while she was hospitalized for a cancer treatment.

S_{16}: strongly-dislike-same-ignore: A classmate didn't pick me out to play on his team during a gym course, because I'm a bad player.

As soon as she made her list of possible alternatives, we proposed that Suzy expose herself gradually to the situations and emotional triggers that usually instigated her self-injurious behaviors. It was difficult to motivate Suzy for this very difficult phase in the treatment and we explained to her why gradual exposure, according to the principle of systematic desensitization, was necessary. The goal was to extinguish the self-harming reactions (i.e., negative feelings and behaviors) through habituation to threatening stimuli. Based on our assessment procedure (see Table 10.1), we could deduce that being strongly hurt by a liked person with a hierarchically higher position (Situation Class 5) was the most difficult situation (highest position in situational hierarchy), followed by situations in which Suzy was strongly hurt by a disliked, hierarchically higher person (middle position in hierarchy), and the most easy—but still difficult—situations were those in which she was strongly hurt by disliked persons with a similar hierarchical position. Following the same basic procedure, all major triggering situations were tackled in a hierarchical order. Suzy made the choice of each new step while the therapist watched the feasibility of the exposure program.

Because Suzy also showed dissociative reactions (see results of the DIS-Q, and C_5 in Behavioral Class D), she was also taught some strategies to reorient herself in the here-and-now (e.g., touching a familiar object or a symbol of safety; saying aloud where she is, what time it is, what she is actually doing). Cognitive reprocessing of her irrational ideas (e.g., C_1 in Behavior Class D, thinking that one has to punish oneself when hurt by another person) also formed an essential part of the treatment. Irrational thoughts were reprocessed and gradually replaced by more appropriate cognitions (e.g., "If strongly hurt by another person, I may become angry with him/her without having to punish myself"). Last but not least, Suzy participated in a social skills training program to learn how to react appropriately when hurt by other people. As shown in Table 10.1 (C_4 in Behavior Class F), Suzy admitted that she did not know how to react in an appropriate way in situations in which others hurt her.

At the end of her inpatient treatment, the rate of the self-injurious behaviors (e.g., cutting and scratching) as well as alcohol abuse was tremendously decreased thanks to the use of alternative behavioral strategies and the use of more rational thoughts when feeling bad and hurt by others. Her suicidal ideation had much improved, though still present at difficult moments, but her eating behavior was more difficult to get under control. At the onset of the therapy, Suzy was able to give up her purging behaviors (e.g., vomiting and laxative abuse). After serious weight gain, however, she resumed vomiting because she hated her "fat" body. This was confirmed by the results of the BAT at the end of the therapy (i.e., higher score on the body dissatisfaction scale compared to the score at the onset of therapy). Regardless of the extensive psycho-education about the medical risks of vomiting behavior (e.g., heart problems) and the search for alternative behaviors, she still vomited twice a week at the time of discharge. Of course, this behavior would become an important focus of further outpatient therapy after discharge from the hospital. We believe that one cannot expect such a complex group of eating disorder symptoms complex such as this to completely disappear in a short period of time.

Discussion

At the onset of this article, we plead for the use of systematic and detailed assessment in order to identify self-harming behavior as well as their situational and cognitive/affective triggers. Making use of standardized questionnaires for this purpose has several advantages. First, the presence of behaviors that the patient is ashamed of (self-harming is a typical example) can be explored in a less threatening way than during an interview. Second, most patients find it easier to check particular symptoms on a questionnaire than to verbally describe them in their own words (e.g., the description of dissociative experiences). Third, a broad and systematic assessment of these behaviors decreases the risk of overlooking particular actions or symptoms. Finally, the pre- and post-treatment assessment can be helpful in evaluating the results of the therapy.

Additionally, our newly developed way of analyzing a patient's situation-behavior profile and guiding cognitive and affective processes has specific advantages. First, the functional analysis of the self-harming behavior is completely based on personal data from the patients themselves. The procedure allows in/outpatients to describe their problems in their own words. Feedback can further be given to them with their own examples and in their own terms, which may be especially useful for intellectually less sophisticated patients. Otherwise, the fact that the procedure may be based on highly individualized data may make its results more acceptable and understandable for the patient. Second, the method generates some meaningful structure in the patient's cognitions and affects, such as their functional equivalence, their hierarchical relationships, and their link with particular situational and/or behavioral features. The graphical representation of the results makes them more understandable and useful for the patient. Finally, the assessment procedure offers "evidence-based" suggestions as to the choice of therapeutic interventions.

The greatest stumbling block with this type of therapy-related assessment procedure is that it is very time consuming. To some degree, this problem can be resolved by computerized assessment and scoring. Nevertheless, the best way for clinicians to learn about the usefulness of this approach is to test it in practice, which we hope the reader will do.

References

Arrindell, W. A., & Ettema, J. H. M. (1986). SCL-90: Handleiding bij een multidimensionelepsychopathologie-indicator. Lisse: Swets & Zeitlinger.

Claes, L., Vandereycken, W., & Vertommen, H. (2001). Self-injurious behaviors in eating-disordered patients. *Eating Behaviors, 2/3*, 263–272.

Claes, L., Van Mechelen, I., & Vertommen, H. (2001). A procedure for the assessment of situation-behavior profiles and their guiding cognitive and affective processes: Principles and illustration with a case study from the domain of aggressive behaviors. Manuscript submitted for publication.

De Boeck, P., & Rosenberg, S. (1988). Hierarchical classes: Model and data analysis. *Psychometrika, 53*, 361–381.

Fahy, T., & Eisler, I. (1993). Impulsivity and eating disorders. *British Journal of Psychiatry, 162*, 193–197.

Garner, D. M. (1991). Eating Disorder Inventory-2: Professional manual. Odessa, FL: Psychological Assessment Resources.

Lacey, J. H., & Evans, D. H. (1986). The impulsivist: A multi-impulsive personality disorder. *British Journal of Addiction, 81*, 641–649.

Linehan, M. M. (1993). Cognitive-behavioral treatment of borderline personality disorder. New York: Guilford Press.

Nijenhuis, E. R. S., van der Hart, O., & Vanderlinden, J. (1995). Vragenlijst belastende ervaringen [Traumatic Experiences Questionnaire]. University of Amsterdam, Department of Psychology.

Probst, M., Vandereycken, W., Van Coppenolle, H., & Vanderlinden, J. (1995). The Body Attitude Test for patients with an eating disorder: Psychometric characteristics of a new questionnaire. *Eating Disorders: The Journal of Treatment and Prevention, 3*, 133–144.

Schotte, C. K. W., De Doncker, D., Vankerckhoven, C., Vertommen, H., & Cosyns, P. (1998). Self-report assessment of the DSM-IV personality disorders: Measurement of trait and distress characteristics: the ADP-IV. *Psychological Medicine, 28*, 1179–1188.

Vandereycken, W. (1993). The Eating Disorders Evaluation Scale. *Eating Disorders: The Journal of Treatment and Prevention, 1*, 115–122.

Vanderlinden, J., & Vandereycken, W. (1997). Trauma, dissociation, and impulse dyscontrol in eating disorders. New York: Brunner/Mazel.

Vanderlinden, J., Van Dyck, R., Vandereycken, W., Vertommen, H., & Verkes, R.J. (1993). The Dissociation Questionnaire (DIS-Q): Development of a new self-report questionnaire. *Clinical Psychology and Psychotherapy, 1*, 21–27.

Walburg, J. A., & Limbeek, J., van (1985). München Alcohol Test. Lisse: Swets & Zeitlinger.

CHAPTER 11

Dialectical Behavior Therapy Strategies in the Management of Self-Harm Behavior in Patients with Eating Disorders

ELIZABETH BLOCHER MCCABE AND MARSHA D. MARCUS

Introduction

Self-injury is not uncommon among individuals with eating disorders, and significant numbers engage in self-injurious or suicidal behavior (Lacey, 1993). In this chapter, we will describe the complex relationship between eating disorders and self-injury as well as definitions and conceptualizations of self-injury as they relate to eating disorders. We will also discuss comorbidity and prevalence of such behaviors among patients with eating disorders and theories relating to the function of self-injury. Finally, we will describe the use of Dialectical Behavior Therapy (DBT) strategies to manage self-injurious behavior in individuals with eating disorders.

Defining Self-Injury

The issues associated with defining self-injury in the population with eating disorders are complex. Aside from semantic complexities, such as the use of multiple terms (e.g., self-injury, self-harm, self-mutilation, parasuicide) and definitions, there are issues that relate to the very nature and function of eating disorder behaviors. Specifically, behaviors such as severely restricting intake, binge eating and purging, and misuse of

147

substances that affect weight have, themselves, been conceptualized as forms of self-injurious and self-destructive behavior (Conterio & Lader, 1998; Favazza, 1987; Miller, 1994; van der Kolk, Perry, & Herman, 1991). Other conceptualizations have focused on the presence of more explicit forms of self-injury such as skin cutting and burning in conjunction with eating disorder behaviors (Favazza, DeRosear, & Conterio, 1989; Favaro & Santonastaso, 1998, 1999, 2000; Lacey 1993; Mitchell, Pyle, Eckert, Hatsukami, & Soll, 1990; Welch & Fairburn, 1996). Finally, some definitions distinguish between self-injury and suicidal behavior (Simeon, Stein, & Hollander, 1995).

Favazza and Rosenthal (1990) developed a useful classification system for what they term "pathological self-mutilation," which aids in our understanding of the types and functions of self-injury found in patients with eating disorders. They define three categories of self-mutilation: major, stereotypic, and moderate/superficial. Major self-mutilation refers to dramatic acts such as eye enucleation and castration, and is typically associated with psychotic disorders. Stereotypic self-mutilation refers to repetitive behaviors such as head banging and biting, and is most commonly associated with mental retardation. Moderate/superficial self-mutilation refers to behaviors such as skin cutting, scratching, burning, and picking, and nail biting. Favazza and Simeon (1995) subdivide this last category into two subcategories, compulsive and impulsive behaviors. Compulsive self-mutilation behaviors are those that are repetitive and habitual in nature, as well as ego dystonic (e.g., hair pulling and skin picking). Impulsive self-mutilation occurs episodically, perhaps in response to aversive affective states, and, unlike other forms of moderate/superficial self-injury, is ego syntonic. Examples include skin cutting and burning. Impulsive self-injury appears most often associated with eating disorders, and these behaviors are the focus of this chapter.

We concur with others (e.g., Anderson, Carter, Mcintosh, Joyce, & Bulik, 2002; Favaro & Santonastaso, 2002) who conceptualize the distinction between self-injury and suicidal behavior in dimensional rather than categorical terms. We believe that self-injury is best understood as existing along a continuum, ranging from behaviors that are intended to inflict mild injury to those behaviors that are intended to end life. Because the term "parasuicide" encompasses this perspective, it will be used in this chapter to describe the spectrum of behavior and motivations that include self-injurious and suicidal (non-fatal) behavior.

Finally, this chapter will limit its focus to explicit parasuicidal behaviors that occur in patients with eating disorders; we will not address the debate of whether eating disorder symptoms are themselves parasuicidal. We next turn to an examination of the relevant literature on the comorbid relationships and prevalence of parasuicidal behavior in patients with eating disorders.

Comorbidity and Prevalence

Parasuicidal behavior occurs in substantial numbers of individuals diagnosed with eating disorders; however, it is unclear if parasuicidal behavior has a specific link to eating disorders or whether parasuicidal behavior is associated with general or comorbid psychopathology. Research indicates that parasuicidal behavior and comorbid eating disorder pathology are often associated with drug dependence (Anderson et al., 2002; Casper & Lyubomirsky, 1997; Favaro & Santonastaso, 1997; Lacey, 1993; Welch & Fairburn, 1996), borderline personality disorder (Dulit, Fyer, Leon, Brodsky, & Frances, 1994; Schmidt & Telch, 1990), and dissociation (Brown, Russell, Thornton, & Dunn, 1999). Relationships have also been found between parasuicidal behavior in patients with eating disorders and histories of childhood victimization (Fullerton, Wonderlich, & Gosnell, 1995; van der Kolk, McFarlane, & Weisaeth, 1996); although childhood abuse appears to be a nonspecific risk factor for psychiatric illness in general rather than for disordered eating per se (Kendler et al., 2000; Wonderlich, Brewerton, Jocic, Dansky, & Abbot, 1997; Wonderlich, Wilsnack, Wilsnack, & Harris, 1996). The combination of parasuicidal behavior and eating disorders appears to be associated with increased severity of psychiatric illness (Herzog, Keller, Lavori, Kenny, & Sacks, 1992; Newton, Freeman, & Munroe, 1993) and treatment-resistant eating disorder symptoms (Nagata, Kawarada, Kiriike, & Iketani, 2000).

Studies attempting to clarify the relationship between eating disorder subtype and parasuicidal behavior have found strong associations between bulimic symptomatology and impulsive behaviors, including parasuicidal behavior (Paul, Schroeter, Dahme, & Nutzinger, 2002; Corcos et al., 2002). In contrast, some studies report a similarly high prevalence of parasuicidal behavior in women with restricting anorexia nervosa (Baral, Kora, Yuksel, & Sezgin, 1998), a disorder typically characterized by an inhibited and harm-avoidant personality style. These data suggest that there are mechanisms other than impulsivity involved in the pathogenesis of parasuicidal behavior in patients with eating disorders, and suggest a complex relationship between parasuicidal behavior and eating disorders.

Sansone and Levitt (2002) conducted a review of epidemiological studies examining the prevalence of self-harm behavior among individuals with eating disorders. Results are summarized in Table 11.1. Note that self-injury and suicide attempts were common in both patients with anorexia

TABLE 11.1 The Prevalence of Suicide Attempts and Self-Injury among Patients with Eating Disorders

Behavior	Prevalence
Suicide Attempts	
Outpatients with BN ($N = 1,211$)	23%
Inpatients with BN ($N = 26$)	39%
Patients with BN + alcohol abuse ($N = 76$)	54%
Outpatients with AN ($N = 261$)	16%
Self-Injury	
Outpatients with BN ($N = 574$)	25%
Inpatients with BN ($N = 260$)	25%
Outpatients with AN ($N = 52$)	23%

Note: AN = anorexia nervosa, BN = bulimia nervosa.
Source: Data adapted from Sansone & Levitt [2002]

and those with bulimia, but suicide attempts were most prevalent among inpatients with bulimia nervosa and patients with bulimia nervosa and comorbid alcohol abuse. The finding that suicide attempts are common in hospitalized patients is not surprising, as they are frequently the impetus for the inpatient hospitalization of patients with bulimia, who usually are managed on an outpatient basis.

To summarize, the evaluation of the relationship between eating disorder behaviors and parasuicidal behavior is complicated by the existence of comorbid diagnoses and conditions, and the inconsistent use of terminology. Some comorbid conditions such as substance abuse, Cluster B personality pathology, and a history of childhood abuse may increase one's vulnerability to, or exacerbate, parasuicidal behaviors. Conversely, other conditions, such as Cluster C personality pathology, may function as a protective factor against parasuicidal behavior among some individuals. Sansone and Sansone (2002) note that there are currently no available assessment tools to simultaneously diagnose eating disorders and assess parasuicidal behavior. Both the lack of precise assessment and the definitional difficulties previously described hamper our ability to explicate the relationship between parasuicidal behavior and eating disorders. Consequently, more precise assessment of the coexistence of parasuicidal behavior and eating disorders, and more consistent use of terminology describing self-injury and suicidal behavior, are needed in future research designed to examine the relationship between eating disorders and parasuicide.

Functions of Self-Injury

Why individuals engage in parasuicidal behavior has been a topic of clinical interest for many years. Numerous descriptive accounts can be found in the clinical literature illustrating parasuicidal behavior patterns and the responses of treating clinicians. Despite its widespread presence in clinical populations and the difficulty it presents for patients and clinicians, there has been limited empirical attention given to the question of why individuals engage in parasuicide.

It is clear that parasuicide is a complex behavior, which may be one factor contributing to the paucity of empirical studies. Biological, psychological, cultural, and social factors have been implicated and are thought to interact in such a way as to explain the etiology as well as maintenance of parasuicidal behavior (e.g., Favazza & Rosenthal, 1993). Although this chapter will focus on the intrapsychic and interpersonal functions of the behavior, it is important to note that there is emerging research on the physiological and biological mechanisms of parasuicidal behavior (e.g., Haines, Williams, Brain, & Wilson, 1995; Herpertz, Sass, & Favazza, 1997; Pies & Popli, 1995; Simeon et al., 1992). These studies suggest that problems in the modulation of serotonin are involved in the regulation of mood and behavior, and that such neurochemical perturbations consequently are involved in the pathogenesis of parasuicidal behavior.

The theoretical and empirical literature examining parasuicidal behavior suggests that the functions served by these behaviors are overdetermined and contextually bound. That is, parasuicidal behavior is likely to have multiple meanings and functions. Further, as previously noted, parasuicidal behavior has been linked to multiple factors including diagnoses, symptoms, and past experiences. Consequently, examining the function of parasuicidal behavior requires close analysis.

Little is known about the function of parasuicidal behavior in individuals with eating disorders. However, several of the conceptual models advanced to explain parasuicidal behavior in general clinical populations appear to be relevant to our understanding of its functions in patients with eating disorders. The putative functions of parasuicidal behavior in patients with eating disorders can be classified into two broad categories: (a) mood- and affect-regulating functions, and (b) interpersonal functions. Determining the function of parasuicidal behavior in particular individuals, however, requires (among other things) careful analysis of the environmental context, precipitating factors, and consequences.

In her review of the clinical literature, Suyemoto (1998) concludes that self-injury serves to express and externalize intolerable and overwhelming emotions, create a sense of control over the emotions, validate internal experience, and communicate the intensity of the internal experience to others. Gratz (2003) emphasizes the function of affect regulation in her review of parasuicidal behavior, noting that such behaviors serve to relieve anxiety, anger, stress, tension, guilt, loneliness, alienation, self-hatred, and depression, and to provide a sense of control, safety, protection, and security. She also describes, as functions of self-harm, attempts to escape, externalize, and concretize emotional pain. Brown, Comtois, and Linehan (2002) found that almost all participants in a study of 75 women reported that parasuicidal behavior was intended to relieve negative emotions.

Both Gratz (2003) and Suyemoto (1998) note that self-harm may play a role in ending dissociative states (e.g., Allen, 1995; Herpertz, 1995). Similarly, Brown and colleagues (2002) note that patients with borderline personality disorder frequently cite the need to feel something and/or to stop feeling numb or dead as reasons for nonsuicidal self-injury. The mechanism by which parasuicide ends dissociative states is unclear; however, some have hypothesized that it may be related to the shock of seeing blood (Miller & Bashkin, 1974) or to experiencing the physical sensation of pain. Conversely, some have noted that self-injury may induce dissociation, with its attendant numbing and escape from aversive affective states (Himber, 1994).

In line with these observations, we consider affect regulation to be a primary function of parasuicidal and eating disorder behaviors in patients. We have described eating disorder behaviors as being effective, albeit maladaptive, strategies for regulating mood and managing aversive affect (McCabe & Marcus, 2002; McCabe, LaVia & Marcus, in press). Further, given the substantial rates of comorbid mood and personality disorders among patients with eating disorders, it is not surprising that parasuicidal behavior would be included in their repertoire of strategies for relieving aversive affective states.

Linehan's (1993a) conceptualization of the role of parasuicidal behavior in regulating affect is compatible with our understanding of the function of eating disorder behaviors and parasuicidal behavior in eating disorder patients (McCabe, LaVia, & Marcus, in press). Parasuicidal behavior and eating disorder behaviors (e.g., severe calorie restriction, binge eating, purging) effectively numb, soothe, or enable patients to avoid negative affect. Moreover, the relief experienced following the use of these behaviors negatively reinforces parasuicidal and aberrant eating behaviors, thus increasing their likelihood of recurrence and establishing these behaviors as coping mechanisms. It may be that parasuicide and eating disorder behaviors work via a similar mechanism of action to relieve aversive affect.

It is also critical to understand the role of the environmental context in precipitating and maintaining parasuicidal behaviors. Our conceptualization of the role of environment is based on behavior and systems theory and posits that parasuicidal behavior is initiated or maintained by interactions between the individual and the environment. Linehan (1993a) also highlights the importance of environment in her biosocial theory of borderline personality disorder. Her work has elucidated the role of the environment in creating and maintaining complex, problematic behaviors. Biosocial theory postulates that complex behaviors, such as those associated with severe eating disorders and parasuicide, are created and maintained over time by the transaction between a biological vulnerability to emotion dysregulation and an invalidating environment (Linehan, 1993a). The invalidating environment is characterized by pervasive communications that the individual's responses and emotional reactions are incorrect, inappropriate, or faulty. Further, an invalidating environment fails to validate private experiences, oversimplifies the ease of problem solving, and punishes or intermittently reinforces emotional displays. The construct of the invalidating environment, although difficult to evaluate empirically, has clinical relevance to our understanding of eating disorder and parasuicidal behaviors.

We believe the environment may work to reinforce eating disorder and parasuicidal behaviors in a similar fashion. Eating disorder and parasuicidal behaviors each elicit strong reactions from others. For example, patients engaging in either or both types of behaviors are frequently characterized as manipulative; that is, others assume that individuals engage in these behaviors with the express purpose of eliciting attention or concern. Contrary to conventional clinical wisdom, research evidence has failed to document that the primary intent of parasuicidal behavior is to elicit a caring response from the environment (e.g., Gratz, 2003; Brown et al., 2002). Therefore, it is critically important not to assume that parasuicidal behavior is intended to elicit care, attention, or concern from others, and to therefore carefully analyze the patient's intrapsychic and interpersonal aspects in a given episode of parasuicide. Although some parasuicidal behavior may be intended to affect the behavior of others, to assume that this is the case generally constitutes a fundamental therapeutic error.

Linehan (1993a) has stressed the importance of distinguishing the intent from the function of parasuicidal behavior. This distinction serves two important functions. First, it challenges the notion that those who engage in parasuicidal behavior (and eating disorder behaviors) are invariably trying to manipulate the responses of others, thus destigmatizing these patients and perhaps increasing clinicians' willingness to work with them. Second, the distinction helps to emphasize how the environment reinforces dysfunctional behavior. The concept of secondary gain is relevant to our understanding of the functions of parasuicidal behavior and, more specifically, how the environment operates to reinforce dysfunctional behavior.

Secondary gain refers to the benefits obtained by the individual by engaging in symptomatic or aberrant behaviors independent of the causes of the behaviors. For example, an individual may cut her forearms to relieve intolerable stress and tension. Although the cutting works to moderate stress and tension, another benefit (i.e., a secondary gain) is the secondary response of her boyfriend. He responds by altering his plans in order to spend time with her and by being extra supportive. Although his response was not the intended function of the cutting behavior, the attention and support are nonetheless reinforcing. This individual may not have intended to elicit the boyfriend's attention and support, but his response nonetheless functions to strengthen the patient's dysfunctional behavior and increases the likelihood of it occurring again. The concept of secondary gain provides a plausible explanation for how these behaviors are reinforced by the environment, and also how parasuicidal behavior impacts interpersonal relationships.

Patients with eating disorder often have deficits in interpersonal skills that interfere with their ability to assertively communicate feelings and make requests (McCabe, LaVia, & Marcus, in press). Thus parasuicidal and eating disorder behaviors also may serve to communicate indirectly the suffering and confusion that patients are unable to directly express. Lack of interpersonal skills, rather than efforts to manipulate, may drive the use of parasuicidal and eating disorder behaviors in interpersonal situations. This observation is consistent with findings from Brown and colleagues (2002). These investigators report that 63% of their sample endorsed the expression of anger as a reason for nonsuicidal self-injury, an emotion that frequently poses difficulties for patients with eating disorders.

To summarize, we believe that affect regulation is the primary function of parasuicidal behavior in patients with eating disorders. Parasuicidal acts effectively work to help individuals avoid, reduce, or eliminate negative mood and aversive affective states. Parasuicidal and eating disorder behaviors also influence and are influenced by the environment. This is notable in the context of interpersonal relationships where the dysfunctional behavior often is inadvertently reinforced. Parasuicidal and eating disorder behavior may also function in the interpersonal context to communicate that which individuals are unable to express in a more assertive and effective fashion.

Treatment with DBT

We have found DBT to be a useful framework for conceptualizing and treating co-occurring parasuicidal and eating disorder behaviors. The DBT treatment structure, philosophy, and interventions are readily applicable to the management of complex problem behaviors. Moreover, the conceptual basis of DBT is readily understood by therapists, patients, and families.

Parasuicidal behavior is an explicit target of DBT and is specifically addressed in its treatment philosophy and interventions. The DBT treatment philosophy balances an unwavering insistence on change with an acknowledgment that parasuicidal behavior represents a legitimate effort to deal with life circumstances. The dialectic of balancing acceptance and change is fundamental to the practice of DBT and the effectiveness of the treatment.

In conjunction with its philosophical stance, DBT employs a treatment structure and specific interventions to manage parasuicidal behavior. We will highlight the structure and several of these interventions because we find them to have particular relevance and applicability to the management of parasuicidal and eating disorder behaviors. Use of the treatment structure, therapeutic relationship, treatment agreements, and cognitive-behavioral techniques will be discussed. A full explication of DBT is beyond the scope of this chapter and thus the present chapter does not represent a comprehensive description of DBT or an exhaustive exploration of its utility in managing parasuicide. The reader is directed to Marsha Linehan's text (Linehan, 1993a) and accompanying skills manual (Linehan, 1993b) for a complete description of DBT.

Treatment Modes

The DBT treatment structure defines four modes of treatment that work in a complementary fashion to decrease the occurrence of parasuicidal behavior. In the first mode of treatment, *individual therapy,* parasuicidal behavior is managed by using a variety of cognitive and behavioral techniques, validation strategies, reliance on agreements and previous commitments, and overt reliance on the strength of the therapeutic relationship. Second, the *DBT skills training group* addresses parasuicidal behavior by teaching a variety of behavioral skills designed to promote affective stability and mood regulation, and thus decrease the likelihood of parasuicidal behavior. The group provides didactic instruction and an opportunity for skills practice and feedback. The third mode of treatment, *telephone consultation,* is used to provide coaching on the use of skills in a parasuicidal crisis. Use of the telephone extends the therapy session into the context of real life circumstances occurring in real time. Finally, DBT recognizes that therapists treating parasuicidal patients need support. The *consultation team* provides nonjudgmental coaching and support to the individual therapist so the therapist will remain willing and able to continue treating the patient.

Use of the Therapeutic Relationship

DBT emphasizes the necessity of a strong, positive interpersonal relationship between patient and clinician as the basis for treatment and behavior change. The DBT therapist works to establish a strong relationship and then makes explicit use of the relationship to elicit behavior change. This is accomplished by openly acknowledging that the patient and therapist exert an influence on, and are influenced by, each other. The DBT therapist will make deliberate use of this interpersonal influence to achieve behavior that is consistent with treatment objectives. The importance and utility of the therapeutic relationship is highlighted during patient crises, when parasuicidal urges are strong and the therapist has exhausted other strategies. At these moments, the therapist must rely on the strength of the therapeutic relationship. For example, the patient in a parasuicidal crisis may ask the therapist "Why shouldn't I kill myself?" After other strategies have failed, a DBT therapist may respond, "You and I have an agreement to work together. I know that things are intolerable at this moment, but I also know that things will improve. I care about you and I'm asking you not to do this." This intervention conveys genuineness, and a sense of trust and faith in the relationship and the treatment. Moreover, it emphasizes a reliance on prior agreements and an expectation that agreements made at the start of treatment (i.e., to work together and to eliminate parasuicidal behavior) will be kept. Reliance on the strength of the relationship can provide a powerful and effective intervention that gets the patient and therapist safely through the parasuicidal crisis, and also strengthens the therapeutic relationship.

Treatment Agreements and Commitments

As the above example illustrates, agreements between therapist and patient are an essential element of DBT and are emphasized throughout the treatment. DBT requires that treatment targets and procedures be explicitly discussed and agreed upon prior to initiating treatment. Agreements are necessary to the treatment and are an important element in the building of a strong therapeutic relationship. Agreements to address specific symptoms or behaviors and commitment to building a life worth living are negotiated at the start of treatment and revisited throughout treatment whenever commitment wanes. Because DBT emphasizes the necessity of agreements, it also defines specific strategies for obtaining and maintaining commitment. These strategies address, clarify, and strengthen commitment, minimize ambivalence, and increase compliance with specific goals or behaviors. Reminding patients of prior agreements, expecting patients to honor their treatment commitments and highlighting the differing effects on the therapeutic relationship of keeping and breaking agreements are DBT strategies used to promote behavior change.

DBT specifies that at a minimum, patients agree to participate in weekly individual therapy and skills group training for a specified length of time (the initial commitment is usually 1 year), and to focus on particular symptom behaviors. Agreements may also be negotiated to address other problem behaviors, including eating disorder symptoms. For example, for patients with eating disorders, the therapist and patient make an agreement that specifies a minimally acceptable weight that the patient must maintain in order to remain in DBT. Other agreements may include the extent to which the family will be involved in treatment, the conditions under which medical intervention will be required consequent to self-injury or eating disorder behaviors, and the parameters of between-session or after-hours contact.

Since parasuicidal behavior is inherently incompatible with the DBT goals of balancing extreme thoughts and behaviors and building a life worth living, specific agreements and commitments are made to eliminate parasuicidal acts. As with other DBT agreements, those that focus on managing and eliminating parasuicidal behavior are secured prior to the occurrence of the behavior. The initial agreement to participate in DBT explicitly acknowledges that reduction and elimination of parasuicidal behavior will be a primary goal of treatment; however, specific agreements targeting parasuicide are also built into the treatment. For example, a standard agreement in DBT is that the patient will call for coaching before acting on parasuicidal urges. The therapist and patient thoroughly discuss the details and implications of this agreement, including among other things the expected behavior of the patient and therapist during the call and consequences for not adhering to the agreement. The therapist agrees to provide behavioral skills coaching via telephone during parasuicidal crises. The therapist makes it clear to the patient that he or she will not necessarily be immediately available, but does commit to returning the call as soon as possible. Thus the patient commits to telephone contact with the therapist prior to engaging in any parasuicide regardless of how long it takes for the therapist to respond to the call. The patient agrees to be open to and make use of the behavioral skills coaching offered by the therapist during the coaching call. That is, the patient agrees to try at least one of the behavioral skills suggested by the therapist to reduce parasuicidal urges. This agreement is an effective strategy for managing parasuicidal crises. The coaching call extends the therapy session to real time circumstances in which the behavioral skills can be applied. Keeping the agreement to call before engaging in parasuicidal behavior and responding as promised to the call is also an effective method for establishing and maintaining trust between patient and therapist and thus strengthening the therapeutic relationship.

24-Hour Rule

Despite these agreements, parasuicidal behavior will sometimes still occur. The DBT therapist plans for this possibility by explaining, in advance of parasuicidal behavior, the 24-hour rule. The 24-hour rule specifies that the patient is not to have contact with the therapist (outside of a regularly scheduled therapy appointment) for 24 hours following an act of parasuicide. Essentially, the 24-hour rule is a behavioral intervention designed to increase compliance with the previously described agreements and reduce the occurrence of parasuicidal behavior by withholding attention from the therapist following parasuicidal behavior. This rationale is explained so that the patient understands that it is only *prior* to an act of parasuicide that the therapist can provide coaching and assist the patient in their efforts to overcome urges to self-injure.

The effectiveness of the 24-hour rule rests on the fact that patients are made aware of the rule prior to the occurrence of parasuicidal behavior. That is, they are not learning about the rule in the midst of or following a parasuicidal crisis, but are aware and considering the effect of the 24-hour rule as they contemplate the consequences of parasuicidal behavior. The intent of the rule is to use the strength of the therapeutic relationship, and prior commitments, to influence the patient not to engage in parasuicidal behavior. Conversely, enacting this rule without the prior knowledge of the patient would be inconsistent with the philosophical stance of collaboration and respect for the patient, and would likely be experienced by the patient as punitive and rejecting.

Treatment Hierarchy

The DBT treatment hierarchy provides a framework for organizing treatment and prioritizing treatment targets. The complexity, dangerousness, and sheer multitude of problems associated with parasuicidal and eating disorder behaviors can overwhelm and discourage the most experienced and skilled therapist. Thus, DBT presents a hierarchy of treatment goals to provide the treating clinician and the patient with a framework designed to address the multiple problems presented by patients with parasuicide. The DBT treatment hierarchy dictates that parasuicidal behavior is given the highest priority during the individual session. That is, no other symptoms, behaviors, or issues are addressed if parasuicidal ideation or behavior is present or has occurred since the last session.

Behavior Chain Analysis

The first individual session following parasuicidal behavior is always used to conduct a behavior chain analysis (BCA) of the environmental and intrapersonal circumstances preceding, during, and following the parasuicidal act. The BCA is a cognitive-behavioral tool used to explore, in detail, the antecedents and precipitating factors, problem behavior (e.g., parasuicide), and consequences of the problem behavior. The BCA is also used to generate a solution analysis and a plan to repair any damage to relationships caused by the parasuicide.

A chain starts with a review of environmental and intrapersonal factors that may have increased the patient's vulnerability to emotion dysregulation and subsequent parasuicidal behavior. Factors such as an argument with a friend, a poor grade on a test, work stress, physical illness, fatigue, and hunger are examples of potential vulnerability factors. Next, the BCA is used to examine the immediate precipitant or event(s) that triggered the parasuicidal behavior. The parasuicidal behavior is next described and an exhaustive list of the positive and negative, short- and long-term consequences of the behavior is generated.

The review of consequences provides an opportunity to remind patients of prior agreements, and to highlight the damaging effects of breaking agreements. Importantly, it is also an opportunity for the therapist to acknowledge and validate that symptom behaviors serve a meaningful function and represent legitimate efforts to deal with life circumstances. However, although there is an explicit acknowledgment that symptoms are understandable, they are also associated with profoundly negative consequences, and thus DBT focuses on the need for behavior change.

The BCA concludes with a solution analysis generated by the patient and therapist to identify alternative, adaptive coping strategies for future use and, if necessary, a plan to repair any damage to the therapeutic or other relationships resulting from the parasuicidal behavior.

The content of the BCA provides important information linking environmental and individual factors, cognitions, feelings, and behaviors to the occurrence of symptom behaviors, thus increasing the patient's and the therapist's understanding of the behavior and identifying alternative solutions. The process of completing a BCA is an opportunity for the therapist to validate the function of the behavior while simultaneously applying behavior-change technology, thus highlighting one of the fundamental dialectics in DBT, the balance between acceptance and change. Although patients find the BCA helpful, ultimately the amount of time and effort to conduct a thorough analysis is experienced as aversive and thus serves to minimize parasuicide.

Conclusion

We have found the conceptual framework of DBT and its armamentarium of therapeutic interventions to be extremely useful in the management of parasuicidal behavior and other symptoms in patients with eating disorders. DBT provides a systematic application of behavior-change technology in a treatment context that persistently promotes change while concurrently validating and accepting the difficulties associated with recovery. The DBT stance of respect for the patient and the treating clinician encourages patients and therapists to persist together until therapeutic objectives are realized. This is particularly important in working with a patient population known for ambivalence about treatment and recovery, and for whom the consequences of symptom behavior can be life threatening. We have found that DBT offers effective strategies, hope, and promise in work with parasuicidal patients.

References

Allen, C. (1995). Helping with deliberate self-harm: Some practical guidelines. *Journal of Mental Health, 4*, 243–250.

Anderson, C. B., Carter, F. A., McIntosh, V. V., Joyce, P. R., & Bulik, C. M. (2002). Self-harm and suicide attempts in individuals with bulimia nervosa. *Eating Disorders: The Journal of Treatment and Prevention, 10*, 227–243.

Baral, I., Kora, K., Yuksel, S., & Sezgin, U. (1998). Self-mutilating behavior sexually abused female adults in Turkey. *Journal of Interpersonal Violence, 13*, 427–437.

Brown, M. Z., Comtois, K. A., & Linehan, M. M. (2002). Reasons for suicide attempts and nonsuicidal self-injury in women with borderline personality disorder. *Journal of Abnormal Psychology, 111*, 198–202.

Brown, L., Russell, J., Thornton, C., & Dunn, S. (1999). Dissociation, abuse and the eating disorders: Evidence from an Australian population. *Australian and New Zealand Journal of Psychiatry, 33*, 521–528.

Casper, R. C., & Lyubomirsky, S. (1997). Individual psychopathology relative to reports of unwanted sexual experiences as predictor of bulimic eating pattern. *International Journal of Eating Disorders, 21*, 229–236.

Conterio, K., & Lader, W. (1998). *Bodily harm: The breakthrough treatment program for self-injurers.* New York: Hyperion.

Corcos, M., Taieb, O., Benoit-Lamy, S., Paterniti, S., Jeammet, P., & Flament, M. F. (2002). Suicide attempts in women with bulimia nervosa: Frequency and characteristics. *Acta Psychiatrica Scandinavica, 106*, 381–386.

Dulit, R. A., Fyer, M. R., Leon, A. C., Brodsky, B. S., & Frances, A. J. (1994). Clinical correlates of self-mutilation in borderline personality disorder. *American Journal of Psychiatry, 151,* 1305–1311.

Favaro, A., & Santonastaso, P. (1997). Suicidality in eating disorders: Clinical and psychological correlates. *Acta Psychiatrica Scandinavica, 95,* 508–514.

Favaro, A., & Santonastaso, P. (1998). Impulsive and compulsive self-injurious behavior in bulimia nervosa: Prevalence and psychological correlates. *Journal of Nervous and Mental Disease, 186,* 157–165.

Favaro, A., & Santonastaso, P. (1999). Different types of self-injurious behavior in bulimia nervosa. *Comprehensive Psychiatry, 40,* 57–60.

Favaro, A., & Santonastaso, P. (2000). Self-injurious behavior in anorexia nervosa. *Journal of Nervous and Mental Disease, 188,* 537–542.

Favaro, A., & Santonastaso, P. (2002). The spectrum of self-injurious behavior in eating disorders. *Eating Disorders: The Journal of Treatment and Prevention, 10,* 215–225.

Favazza, A. R. (1987). *Bodies under siege: Self-mutilation in culture and psychiatry.* Baltimore: Johns Hopkins University Press.

Favazza, A. R., DeRosear, L., & Conterio, K. (1989). Self-mutilation and eating disorders. *Suicide and Life-Threatening Behavior, 19,* 352–361.

Favazza, A. R., & Rosenthal, R. J. (1990). Varieties of pathological self-mutilation. *Behavioral Neurology, 3,* 77–85.

Favazza, A. R., & Rosenthal, R. J. (1993). Diagnostic issues in self-mutilation. *Hospital and Community Psychiatry, 44,* 134–140.

Favazza, A. R., & Simeon, D. (1995). Self-mutilation. In E. Hollander & D. Stein (Eds.), *Impulsivity and aggression* (pp. 185–200). Sussex, England: John Wiley & Sons.

Fullerton, D. T., Wonderlich, S. A., & Gosnell, B. A. (1995). Clinical characteristics of eating disorder patients who report sexual or physical abuse. *International Journal of Eating Disorders, 17,* 243–249.

Gratz, K. L. (2003). Risk factors for and functions of deliberate self-harm: An empirical and conceptual review. *Clinical Psychology: Science and Practice, 10,* 192–205.

Haines, J., Williams, C. L., Brain, K. L., & Wilson, G. V. (1995). The psychophysiology of self-mutilation. *Journal of Abnormal Psychology, 104,* 471–489.

Herpertz, S. (1995). Self-injurious behavior: Psychopathological and nosological characteristics in subtypes of self-injurers. *Acta Psychiatrica Scandinavica, 91,* 57–68.

Herpertz, S., Sass, H., & Favazza, A. (1997). Impulsivity in self-mutilative behavior: Psychometric and biological findings. *Journal of Psychiatric Research, 31,* 451–465.

Herzog, D. B., Keller, M. B., Lavori, P. W., Kenny, G. M., & Sacks, N. R. (1992). The prevalence of personality disorders in 210 women with eating disorders. *Journal of Clinical Psychiatry, 53,* 147–152.

Himber, J. (1994). Blood rituals: Self-cutting in female psychiatric inpatients. *Psychotherapy, 31,* 620–631.

Kendler, K. S., Bulik, C. M., Silberg, J., Hettema, J. M., Myers, J., & Prescott, C. A. (2000). Childhood sexual abuse and adult psychiatric and substance use disorders in women: An epidemiological and cotwin control analysis. *Archives of General Psychiatry, 57,* 953–959.

Lacey, J. H. (1993). Self-damaging and addictive behaviour in bulimia nervosa. A catchment area study. *British Journal of Psychiatry, 163,* 190–194.

Linehan, M. M. (1993a). *Cognitive behavioral treatment of borderline personality disorder.* New York: Guilford Press.

Linehan, M. M. (1993b). *Skills training for treating borderline personality disorder.* New York: Guilford Press.

McCabe, E. B., & Marcus, M. D. (2002). Question: Is dialectical behavior therapy useful in the management of anorexia nervosa? *Eating Disorders: The Journal of Treatment and Prevention, 10,* 335–337.

McCabe, E. B., LaVia, M. C., & Marcus, M. D. (in press). Dialectical behavior therapy for eating disorders. In J. K. Thompson (Ed.), *Handbook of eating disorders and obesity.* New York: John Wiley & Sons.

Miller, D. (1994). *Women who hurt themselves.* New York: Basic.

Miller, F., & Bashkin, E. A. (1974). Depersonalization and self-mutilation. *Psychoanalytic Quarterly, 43,* 638–649.

Mitchell, J. E., Pyle, R. L., Eckert, E. D., Hatsukami, D., & Soll, E. (1990). Bulimia nervosa in overweight individuals. *Journal of Nervous and Mental Disease, 178,* 324–327.

Nagata, T., Kawarada, Y., Kiriike, N., & Iketani, T. (2000). Multi-impulsivity of Japanese patients with eating disorders: Primary and secondary impulsivity. *Psychiatry Research, 94,* 239–250.

Newton, J. R., Freeman, C. P., & Munroe, J. (1993). Impulsivity and dyscontrol in bulimia nervosa: Is impulsivity an independent phenomenon or a marker of severity? *Acta Psychiatrica Scandinavica, 87,* 389–394.

Paul, T., Schroeter, K., Dahme, B., & Nutzinger, D. O. (2002). Self-injurious behavior in women with eating disorders. *American Journal of Psychiatry, 159,* 408–411.

Pies, R. W., & Popli, A. P. (1995). Self-injurious behavior: Pathophysiology and implications for treatment. *Journal of Clinical Psychiatry, 56,* 580–588.

Sansone, R. A., & Levitt, J. L. (2002). Self-harm behaviors among those with eating disorders: An overview. *Eating Disorders: The Journal of Treatment and Prevention, 10,* 205–213.

Sansone, R. A., & Sansone, L. A. (2002). Assessment tools for self-harm behavior among those with eating disorders. *Eating Disorders: The Journal of Treatment and Prevention, 10,* 193–203.

Schmidt, N. B., & Telch, M. J. (1990). Prevalence of personality disorders among bulimics, non-bulimic binge eaters, and normal controls. *Journal of Psychopathology and Behavioral Assessment, 12,* 169–185.

Simeon, D., Stanley, B., Frances, A., Mann, J. J., Winchel, R., & Stanley, M. (1992). Self-mutilation in personality disorders: Psychological and biological correlates. *American Journal of Psychiatry, 149,* 221–226.

Simeon, D., Stein, D. J., & Hollander, E. (1995). Depersonalization disorder and self-injurious behavior. *Journal of Clinical Psychiatry, 56(Suppl. 4),* 36–39.

Suyemoto, K. L. (1998). The functions of self-mutilation. *Clinical Psychology Review, 18,* 531–554.

van der Kolk, B. A., Perry, J. C., & Herman, J. L. (1991). Childhood origins of self-destructive behavior. *American Journal of Psychiatry, 148,* 1665–1671.

van der Kolk, B. A., McFarlane, A. C., & Weisaeth, L. (Eds.). (1996). *Traumatic stress: The effects of overwhelming experience on mind, body, and society.* New York: Guilford.

Welch, S. L., & Fairburn, C. G. (1996). Impulsivity or comorbidity in bulimia nervosa. A controlled study of deliberate self-harm and alcohol and drug misuse in a community sample. *British Journal of Psychiatry, 169,* 451–458.

Wonderlich, S. A., Brewerton, T. D., Jocic, Z., Dansky, B. S., & Abbott, D. W. (1997). Relationship of childhood sexual abuse and eating disorders. *Journal of the American Academy of Child and Adolescent Psychiatry, 36,* 1107–1115.

Wonderlich, S. A., Wilsnack, R. W., Wilsnack, S. C., & Harris, T. R. (1996). Childhood sexual abuse and bulimic behavior in a nationally representative sample. *American Journal of Public Health, 86,* 1082–1086.

CHAPTER 12

An Integrative Cognitive Therapy Approach to the Treatment of Multi-Impulsive Bulimia Nervosa

TRICIA COOK MYERS, STEPHEN WONDERLICH,
MARGO NORTON, AND ROSS D. CROSBY*

Introduction

Approximately a quarter of individuals with bulimia nervosa will engage in some form of self-harm behavior (SHB) during their lifetime, a percentage far greater than in the general psychiatric population (Paul, Schroeter, Dahme & Nutzinger, 2002). In fact, various studies have found that over half of patients who engage in SHB also meet criteria for an eating disorder (Favazza & Rosenthal, 1993). Commonalities between these two psychopathologies frequently exist, including a history of sexual trauma and dissociation (Zlotnick et al., 1996), and, more generally, poor impulse control (Fichter, Quadflieg, & Rief, 1994). Yet little is known about the complexities of the interaction between bulimia nervosa, SHB, and the associated constructs of multi-impulsive bulimia (MIB) and borderline personality disorder (BPD).

In this chapter, we present preliminary findings from an ongoing study at our institution comparing bulimia nervosa and MIB, and we also briefly review the potential implications of childhood sexual abuse

*The material presented in this chapter was supported by a grant awarded to Dr. Wonderlich by the National Institute of Mental Health (R01 MH59674-01A1).

and neurotransmitter disturbances in the occurrence of SHB. Following this information, we discuss the potential applications of Integrative Cognitive Therapy (ICT), a personality-focused treatment protocol for patients with bulimia nervosa that can be adapted to address SHB.

The Empirical Relationship between Bulimia Nervosa, BPD, MIB, and SHB

We are presently concluding a federally funded National Institutes of Mental Health (NIMH) grant that explores the connection between BPD, SHB, and MIB in individuals with bulimia nervosa. In this study, information is gathered via several semi-structured interviews including the Structured Clinical Interview for *DSM-IV* (SCID-I/P; First, Spitzer, Gibbon, & Williams, 1994), Hamilton Depression Inventory (HDRS; Hamilton, 1960), Eating Disorders Examination (EDE; Fairburn & Cooper, 1993), and Diagnostic Interview for Borderlines-Revised (DIB-R; Zanarini, Gunderson, Frankenburg, & Chauncey, 1989). In addition, participants are asked to carry a Palm Pilot for a 2-week duration. During this time, they are asked to record eating episodes and other impulsive behaviors multiple times per day when randomly prompted as well as following any impulsive behaviors.

The DIB-R (Zanarini et al., 1989), a well-known, semi-structured diagnostic interview, was selected to assess BPD due to its widespread use in research settings. This measure is comprised of four different subsections that are considered to be diagnostic of BPD: Affect, Cognition, Impulse Action Patterns, and Interpersonal Relationships. For the purpose of this study, individuals who accrue scores > 7 on a 10-point scale are considered to have BPD.

Patients with MIB tend to display impulsive behaviors such as alcohol abuse, drug abuse, shoplifting, suicide attempts, SHB, and sexual promiscuity. Individual items from several of the above measures are used to assess the concept of MIB as defined by Fichter (Fichter, Quadflieg, & Reif, 1994). For example, the SCID I/P is used to assess *DSM-IV* diagnoses of alcohol and non-alcohol substance abuse and dependence; a question on the initial phone screen interview is used to determine the presence of shoplifting; and the DIB-R is used to assess suicide attempts, SHB, and sexual promiscuity. Lifetime diagnoses are assessed using 2-year time periods since age 18 (or 16 if currently 18), with only one incident of each impulsive behavior necessary to meet criteria (with the exceptions of sexual promiscuity, which requires ≥ 5 episodes of impulsive sexual relationships, and alcohol and drug abuse, which are based on *DSM-IV* diagnoses).

So far, statistical analyses have been conducted on data from 46 women with bulimia (Wonderlich, Myers, Norton, & Crosby, 2002). Initial results indicate that 33% of participants met full criteria for BPD on the DIB-R and that 39% of participants endorsed ≥ 3 of the 6 impulsive behaviors for MIB. Additionally, SHB such as cutting, burning, punching, and head banging were endorsed by 47% of participants who met criteria for BPD, while 27% reported suicidal gestures. Participants who met criteria for MIB were even more likely than those with BPD to endorse these same self-harm (61%) and suicidal behaviors (33%). Interestingly, while the occurrence of self-harm or suicidal gestures was a strong predictor of MIB or BPD, the presence of MIB or BPD was not as predictive of self-harm or suicidal behaviors. Fifty three percent of those participants who met criteria for MIB or BPD denied a lifetime history of these self-destructive behaviors. Therefore, endorsement of SHB or suicidal gestures is quite predictive of a BPD or MIB diagnosis, while the opposite is not true. It seems that a significant number of participants with MIB or BPD do not engage in self-harming or suicidal behaviors.

In summary, while the vast majority of participants with bulimia who report a history of self-destructive behaviors will meet diagnostic criteria for MIB or BPD, only half of the participants with BPD or MIB endorse engaging in any SHB. Fewer than 50% of the participants who scored in the borderline range on the DIB-R indicated that they had engaged in SHB, and only slightly more than 25% had ever made suicidal gestures or attempts. This is quite astonishing given the fact that self-harm is the most commonly identified symptom of BPD. This evidence suggests that the conceptualization of BPD should be more expansive and not focused explicitly on SHB. Of note, while the number of participants with BPD who engage in SHB might have been more substantial if a broader definition of self-harm had been used, the occurrence of self-harm and suicidal behaviors in our sample was less common than was expected. These findings, if supported, could have substantial implications in eating disorders treatment as researchers work to subcategorize bulimia (e.g., bulimia nervosa with or without SHB) and match each with the most effective intervention for that subtype.

Potential Causes of Self-Harm in Individuals with Bulimia

In general, many factors have been identified as potential causes of self-destructive behavior, with the majority of authorities agreeing that the cause is most likely multi-factorial and due to a very complex relationship between psychological, social, and biological factors (Paris, 1997; Zanarini

& Frankenburg, 1997). Although a number of variables are implicated as the cause of SHB, only two will be briefly reviewed in this chapter.

First, childhood maltreatment or trauma has been linked to the occurrence of SHB in individuals with eating disorders (Deep, Lilenfield, Plotniciv, Pollice, & Kaye 1999; Favaro & Santonastaso, 1998). Evidence from both adults and children who have been victims of trauma suggests that maltreatment during childhood may increase the risk for eating disturbances, impulsive behavior, and SHB (Wonderlich et al., 2000a; Wonderlich et al., 2001a). In one study of young girls who were sexually abused, impulsive and self-destructive behaviors seemed to mediate the relationship between childhood sexual abuse and eating disturbances (Wonderlich et al., 2001b). In addition, there is suggestion that the MIB syndrome identified above is correlated with a history of childhood maltreatment (Wonderlich et al., 2001a). However, it is not yet clear which of the various mechanisms mediate the relationship between abuse during childhood, and either SHB or disturbed eating.

Second, disturbances in biological and neurotransmitter systems, serotonergic and hypothalamic–pituitary-adrenal systems (HPA) in particular, may also be related to SHB. Steiger and colleagues (2001b) found that bulimic women with a history of SHB have a greater likelihood of significant serotonergic disturbances. Additionally, irregularities in HPA functioning (i.e., decreased plasma cortisol) and serotonin are more notable in those individuals with bulimia nervosa who were abused as children versus women with bulimia who were not abused (Steiger et al., 2001a). These results highlight a growing literature emphasizing the many ways in which SHB may be impacted by an array of psychobiological variables in individuals with bulimia. Therefore, it seems unlikely that the identification of a single variable will shed much light on what is responsible for self-destructive behaviors. It is also apparent that the interactive relationship between biological and psychological variables will need to be taken into consideration when conceptualizing self-destructive behaviors in those with bulimia nervosa.

ICT Treatment of SHB in Individuals with Bulimia

Although the relationship between bulimia nervosa and SHB is not yet fully understood, it appears that interventions that are more personality-centered may be a viable approach to treatment. One example of such a treatment is ICT (Wonderlich, Peterson, Mitchell, & Crow, 2000b); based largely on Benjamin's (1993) work on the treatment of personality disorders. ICT continues to be developed, and may offer promise as a treatment for individuals with bulimia nervosa, including those who engage in SHB.

ICT was developed because of the concern that traditional therapies such as cognitive therapy fail to give adequate attention to interpersonal issues, emotional responses, and the therapist-patient relationship, while at the same time placing too much importance on conscious controlled thoughts (Clark, 1995). At this time, CBT is considered to be the treatment of choice for bulimia nervosa, yet it is helpful in only about 50% of the cases at treatment endpoint (Craighead & Agras, 1991), with an even lower success rate during follow-up (Mitchell, Davis, & Goff, 1985). Cognitive Behavior Therapy (CBT) also fails to address commonly occurring self-destructive behaviors, which may limit treatment success as a result. While ICT includes fundamental cognitive-behavioral techniques for bulimia nervosa, it also addresses some of the above criticisms of standard treatments by integrating elements of motivational enhancement, interpersonal therapy, emotion-focused therapy, and feminist theory.

In general, ICT places more emphasis than traditional CBT on cultural factors, self-oriented cognition, interpersonal patterns and schemas, and emotional reactions. As seen in Figure 12.1, the underlying theory is that a person's temperament (e.g., harm avoidance) and negative life experiences (e.g., loss, rejection, criticism) interact to formulate cognitive schemas of the self and others, which then impact future thoughts and interactions. This discrepancy between perception of the actual self and standards for evaluating the actual self results in feelings of inadequacy, which are thought to increase the likelihood of appearance-related concerns and associated negative affect. In order to cope with this negative affect, the person develops unhealthy interpersonal (e.g., submission, attack) and/or self-regulatory styles (e.g., self-control, self-attack, self-neglect), which may include SHB.

Individuals with bulimia and with borderline traits are thought to adopt an interpersonal pattern of friendly submission to others, as long as they are readily available and are positively reinforcing. However, when other individuals are perceived as more withdrawn or rejecting, the typical borderline response is to initiate an interpersonal attack. Benjamin (1993) hypothesizes that one example of this type of attack is when an individual with BPD attempts to prevent the other person from disengagement by harming him/herself. In addition, the individual with BPD is thought to display a self-attacking regulatory style when he/she engages in self-harm in response to criticism, rejection, or withdrawal from important others. Developing an awareness of these unhealthy interpersonal and regulatory patterns, identifying their function, and establishing more appropriate means of interacting with others and the self are the focus of this treatment.

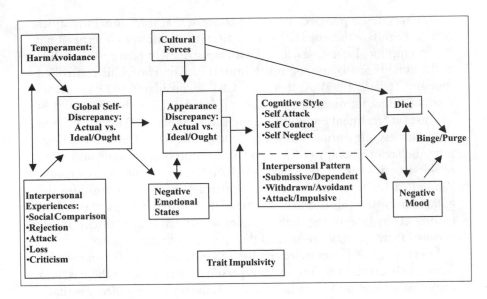

Fig. 12.1

ICT has been pilot tested with 9 patients with bulimia over the course of 20 sessions at the University of North Dakota and the University of Minnesota with significant success (Peterson, Wonderlich, Mitchell, & Crow, in press). At the conclusion of treatment, 8 of the 9 participants were abstinent from purging, with a decrease from 6.7 to 0.3 in the average number of purging episodes per week. Seven of the 9 were abstinent from binge eating, with a reduction from 4.3 to 0.6 in the average number of binge episodes per week. Although in the early stages of validation, this new treatment continues to be investigated as a viable alternative to CBT and includes a clinician manual and patient workbook. Ultimately, randomized clinical trials will be necessary to determine its efficacy, and plans for this are already underway. Although the above study did not monitor changes in self-harm, given its potential applications, future studies should examine ICT's effectiveness in addressing self-destructive behaviors. Below is a more specific discussion of the ICT approach to the treatment of SHB in the context of bulimia nervosa.

Stages of ICT

ICT is typically presented over the course of 20 individual sessions. Patients are seen biweekly for the first month, with weekly sessions thereafter. Although the focus of clinical attention may vary at times, it differs little from that in CBT. Over the course of treatment, the therapist takes an active, collaborative approach to providing education and identifying interpersonal patterns and self-regulatory styles. The therapist focuses on the here-and-now when identifying affective responses in session as well as outside of sessions. As with CBT, there is an emphasis on homework assignments in between sessions. ICT is not intended for patients who are medically unstable or significantly underweight, nor for those with cognitive impairments.

The treatment is composed of four phases: Phase One—Enhancing Motivation and Education; Phase Two—Normalization of Eating and Coping Skills; Phase Three—Interpersonal Patterns and Self-Regulatory Styles; and Phase Four—Relapse Prevention and Lifestyle Management. Phase One takes place over three sessions and utilizes motivational enhancement techniques. The focus is on labeling emotional responses and beginning to identify any self-discrepancies. This provides access to core beliefs and appraisals and helps to clarify the link to SHB. Typically, the therapist starts out focusing on general discrepancies and progresses to discrepancies related to appearance.

Phase Two (sessions 4–8) includes many of the behavioral strategies integral to CBT for bulimia nervosa, including the establishment of a regular pattern of eating, alternative behaviors, and exposure to feared foods. In contrast to CBT, however, ICT therapists recommend that the patient consume a specific number of exchanges each day based on a three-tier system. Patients are not informed of the exact calorie goal but rather are instructed to eat similarly to examples of daily meal plans at Level I (1,500 calories), Level II (2,000 calories), or Level III (2,500 calories). Level II is ideal for most patients. In the case of a patient with MIB, it would be helpful to alter the daily food recording log and include a column to monitor the occurrence of any SHB as well as a range of other impulsive actions. In addition, patients are encouraged to work on coping skills via a handheld computer, including the identification, expression, and tolerance of emotional states. We have created an interactive 10-module Palm Pilot application for this purpose that aims to serve as an extension of the therapy hour. It includes modules on binge cues, alternative behaviors, cognitive restructuring, problem solving, body image, and interpersonal patterns, among others.

During Phase Three (sessions 9–18), the focus is on identifying how interpersonal patterns and self-regulatory styles, such as SHB, represent efforts to cope with self-discrepancy. Development of more appropriate patterns and a self-affirming regulatory style are the core aspects of this phase and are rehearsed through roleplay. Finally, relapse prevention is addressed in the last phase.

ICT and SHB

Although the focus of Phase Three is quite broad, it can be tailored to specifically address SHB. Interpersonal patterns (i.e., affirm, control, attack, ignore, express, submit, withdraw, separate) and self-regulatory styles (i.e., self-affirm, self-control, self-attack, self-neglect) are identified through exploration of social interactions and identification of affect. Patients are encouraged to be more assertive (i.e., express) and self-affirming. Although Benjamin (1993) identifies self-attack as the pattern responsible for self-harm in individuals with BPD, this may not always be the case. A thorough pattern analysis will be helpful in identifying these difficult interpersonal and intrapersonal patterns.

In the treatment of SHB, the therapist should continue to begin each session by reviewing the patient's meal plan, albeit more briefly than during Phase Two. This is helpful in identifying any triggers or problematic circumstances that might lead to binging/purging as well as SHB. The therapist should use Pattern Analysis, based on the work of Benjamin (1993) and examined by others in a population with eating disorder (e.g., Wonderlich & Swift, 1990), to identify interpersonal patterns (affirm, control, attack, ignore, express, submit, withdraw, separate) and self-regulatory styles (self-affirm, self-control, self-attack, self-neglect). Not only should the self-harming patient with bulimia complete a pattern analysis in response to binge/purge episodes or negative affect, but he/she should also be asked to complete this process in regard to SHB. Worksheets in the patient manual are assigned to help the patient become more aware of these typical responses to self and others.

The core concept of self-discrepancy is introduced by comparing the "actual self" (i.e., the patient's perception) and the "desired self" (i.e., how the patient would like to be), initially focusing on appearance-related discrepancies. As the patient begins to focus more on discrepancies between how he/she perceives him/herself to be and how he/she wishes to be, the therapist should begin to help the patient identify discrepancies, or perceived "flaws," in terms of other aspects of self-concept. The goal is to enable the patient to alter unrealistic standards, and at the same time to begin to evaluate self in a more accurate manner.

The focus on affect is key during Phase Three. Patients will likely react with strong emotions as they begin to focus on perceived "flaws" and difficult interpersonal interactions they have experienced. Therapists should aid the patient in identifying and labeling these emotions and should also encourage expression of emotions during session. A main objective of Phase Three is to help the patient balance differentiation with dependence in their interpersonal relationships. Patients are encouraged to test hypotheses in a useful desensitization exercise. Rather than attacking or avoiding, patients are supported in their efforts to interact with others in an assertive manner. This balance between differentiation and dependence is further addressed in appropriate worksheets in the Patient Workbook, which suggest various methods of change.

Potential Limitations of ICT for Clinicians

The addition of Palm Pilot technology to ICT is a potential limitation to the widespread use of this intervention by clinicians. ICT clinicians may either request that patients purchase a handheld computer or have one available for their use over the course of treatment. Clinicians will also need to obtain the modules and upload them on each portable computer. Of note, due to the affordability of this technology, many people already own a handheld computer, and at this time there are no plans to charge for the ICT software. However, if one of these options is not reasonable, ICT can ultimately be conducted without using the Palm Pilot modules. Future recommendations may change on this topic as research determines if this technology is integral to the ICT approach.

In addition, many clinicians will not be familiar with implementation of specific ICT interventions. As with any treatment that a clinician is unfamiliar with, he or she should read the available literature, attend training workshops, and seek appropriate supervision. A clinician manual and patient workbook are currently under development and will be made available to the professional community after effectiveness trials are completed. Additional training opportunities would most likely become available as this approach is validated.

Additional Treatment Considerations

ICT therapists should also keep in mind other valuable information. Baker-Dennis and Sansone (1997) suggest that when initially treating patients with BPD and with eating disorder, individual therapy should be the primary source of treatment, and that additional treatments (e.g., dietary counseling, group treatment, support groups) should not be implemented until a stable therapeutic alliance has been established. They also recommend that until this occurs, the focus of treatment should be on more general matters, such as the management of SHB and self-regulation, rather than the goal of eliminating eating disorder symptomatology. This recommendation fits well within the confines of ICT, which can easily be adapted to focus on the containment of SHB. In fact, the therapist may wish to introduce Phase Three material earlier in the course of treatment.

SHB can be monitored on daily food recording logs and addressed throughout the various phases of treatment. As always, when working with individuals who self-harm, therapists should contract with the patient about plans for managing self-destructive behaviors in between sessions. When necessary, the therapist should be willing and able to set firm limits, but should usually wait until these problematic behaviors dictate a response. Self-destructive behaviors should always be confronted when they occur and precipitants, associated emotions, and consequences of their behavior be identified. It is also essential to identify any problematic interpersonal patterns that occur during sessions, which are assessed in a manner similar to the pattern analysis in Phase Three.

Conclusion

Although there is a high prevalence of patients with bulimia who engage in SHB, data-based evidence on the relationship between self-harm and eating disorders is limited. It remains unclear whether SHB should be conceptualized as an associated yet separate symptomatology of eating disorders or if they should be thought of in terms of a more comprehensive psychological disorder such at BPD or MIB. In treating this type of patient, no matter what the nature of the relationship is determined to be, it is important to have a comprehensive treatment approach. The field of personality disorders has been at the forefront of treating those patients who self-harm, and offers viable strategies to contain this destructive behavior. ICT incorporates the best of CBT with more general strategies based on personality theory, motivational enhancement, and interpersonal therapy. ICT shows promise, at least in an initial pilot study, as a treatment for bulimia nervosa. However, further research is needed to examine the effectiveness of this protocol for SHB in patients with bulimia.

References

Baker-Dennis, A., & Sansone, R. A. (1997). Treatment of patients with personality disorders. In D. M. Garner, & P. E. Garfinkel (Eds.), Handbook of treatment for eating disorders (2nd ed.) (pp. 437–449). New York: Guildford Press.

Benjamin, L. S. (1993). An interpersonal approach to the diagnosis and treatment of personality disorders. New York: Guilford Press.

Clark, D. A. (1995). Perceived limitation of standard cognitive therapy: A consideration of efforts to revise Beck's theory and therapy. Journal of Cognitive Psychotherapy: An International Quarterly, 9(3), 153–172.

Craighead, L. W., & Agras, W. S. (1991). Mechanisms of action in cognitive-behavioral and pharmacological interventions for obesity and bulimia nervosa. Journal of Consulting and Clinical Psychology, 59, 115–125.

Deep, A. L., Lilenfeld, L. R., Plotniciv, K. H., Pollice, C., & Kaye, W. H. (1999). Sexual abuse in eating disorder subtypes and control women: The role of comorbid substance dependence in bulimia nervosa. International Journal of Eating Disorders, 25, 1–10.

Fairburn, C. G., & Cooper, Z. (1993). The eating disorders examination. In C. G. Fairburn & G. T. Wilson (Eds.), *Binge eating: Nature, assessment, and treatment* (pp. 317–360). New York: Guilford Press.

Favaro, A., & Santonastaso, P. (1998). Purging behaviors, suicide attempts, and psychiatric symptoms in 398 eating disordered subjects. *International Journal of Eating Disorders, 20,* 99–103.

Favazza, A. R., & Rosenthal R. J. (1993). Diagnostic issues in self-mutilation. *Hospital and Community Psychiatry, 44,* 134–140.

Fichter, M. M., Quadflieg, N., & Rief, W. (1994). Course of multi-impulsive bulimia. *Psychological Medicine, 24,* 591–604.

First, M. B., Spitzer, R., Gibbon, M., & Williams, J. B. W. (1994). *Structured Clinical Interview for DSM-IV Axis I Disorders, Patient Edition (SCID-I/P).* New York: Biometrics Research Department, New York State Psychiatric Institute.

Hamilton, M. (1960). A rating scale for depression. *Journal of Neurological and Neurosurgical Psychiatry, 23,* 56–62.

Mitchell, J. E., Davis, L., & Goff, G. (1985). The process of relapse in patients with bulimia. *International Journal of Eating Disorders, 4,* 457–463.

Paris, J. (1997). Childhood trauma as an etiological factor in the personality disorders. *Journal of Personality Disorders, 11,* 34–49.

Paul, T., Schroeter, K., Dahme, B., & Nutzinger, D. O. (2002). Self-injurious behavior in women with eating disorders. *American Journal of Psychiatry, 159,* 408–411.

Peterson, C. B., Wonderlich, S. A., Mitchell, J. E., & Crow, S. J. (in press). Integrative Cognitive Therapy for bulimia nervosa. In J. K. Thompson (Ed.), *Handbook of eating disorders and obesity.* Hoboken, NJ: John Wiley & Sons.

Steiger, H., Gauvin, L., Israel, M., Koerner, N., Kin, N. M. K., Paris, J., & Young, S.N. (2001a). Association of serotonin and cortisol indices with childhood abuse in bulimia nervosa. *Archives of General Psychiatry, 58,* 837–843.

Steiger, H., Koerner, N., Engelberg, M. J., Israel, M., Kin, N. M. K., & Young, S. N. (2001b). Self-destructiveness and serotonin function in bulimia nervosa. *Psychiatry Research, 103,* 15–26.

Wonderlich, S. A., & Swift, W. J. (1990). Borderline versus other personality disorders in the eating disorders: Clinical description. *International Journal of Eating Disorders, 9,* 629–638.

Wonderlich, S. A., Crosby, R., Mitchell, J. E., Roberts, J., Haseltine, B., DeMuth, G., & Thompson, K. (2000a). The relationship of childhood sexual abuse and eating disturbance in children. *Journal of the American Academy of Child and Adolescent Psychiatry, 39,* 1277–1283.

Wonderlich, S. A., Peterson, C. B., Mitchell, J. E., & Crow, S. J. (2000b). Integrative cognitive therapy for bulimia nervosa. In K. J. Miller & J. S. Mizes (Eds.), *Comparative treatments for eating disorders, Springer Series on comparative treatments for psychological disorders* (pp. 258–282). New York: Springer Publishing Co.

Wonderlich, S., Crosby, R., Mitchell, J. E., Thompson, K. M., Redlin, J., DeMuth, G., Smyth, J., & Haseltine, B. (2001a). Eating disturbance and sexual trauma in childhood and adulthood. *International Journal of Eating Disorders, 30,* 401–412.

Wonderlich, S. A., Crosby, R., Mitchell, J. E., Thompson, K. M., Redlin, J., DeMuth, G., & Smyth, J. (2001b). Pathways mediating sexual abuse and eating disturbance in children. *International Journal of Eating Disorders, 29,* 270–279.

Wonderlich, S. A., Myers, T. C., Norton, M, & Crosby, R. (2002). Self-harm and bulimia nervosa: A complex connection. *Eating Disorders: The Journal of Treatment and Prevention, 10,* 257–267.

Zanarini, M., & Frankenburg, F. R. (1997). Pathways to the development of borderline personality disorder. *Journal of Personality Disorders, 11,* 93–104.

Zanarini, M. C., Gunderson, J. G., Frankenburg, F. R., & Chauncey, D. L. (1989). The Revised Diagnostic Interview for Borderlines: Discriminating borderline personality disorder from other Axis II disorders. *Journal of Personality Disorders, 3,* 10–18.

Zlotnick, C., Shea, M. T., Perlstein, T., Simpson, E., Costello, E., & Begin, A. (1996). The relationship between dissociative symptoms, alexithymia, impulsivity, sexual abuse, and self-mutiliation. *Comprehensive Psychiatry, 37,* 12–16.

CHAPTER 13

Eclectic Treatment of Eating Disorders and Self-Injury: A Case Illustration

MONIKA OSTROFF

Introduction

There are a variety of available techniques for the treatment of patients with eating disorders who self-injure. The following case presentation illustrates an effective and integrated approach in a young woman in which the goals were to decrease parasuicidal behaviors while increasing healthy coping skills and subjective feelings of self-worth. The treatment itself spanned a year and integrated several approaches and philosophies into a comprehensive treatment package.

Melissa is a 22-year-old woman who struggled with anorexia nervosa for 7 years and, when she presented for treatment, had recently begun cutting her arms and legs. Melissa's trauma history likely contributed to her intense difficulty in regulating emotions. Melissa often used cutting along with purging to cope with intense and painful emotions.

Formulation: Understanding Melissa through Theoretical Lenses

Melissa's childhood was laden with chaos. Her alcoholic father and depressed mother had frequent and violent arguments, which compromised her sense of safety and well-being. Ideally, fathers support and protect their daughters, helping them to form secure boundaries. Melissa's father did the opposite. At the onset of adolescence, he began to sexually abuse her, effectively annihilating any shreds of safety that she had developed. Due to depression and extramarital affairs, Melissa's mother was both unavailable and unable to provide the kind of protection and nurturing required for normal childhood development. The mutual failure of these central caretakers to emotionally provide for Melissa clearly contributed to her symptomatology. Zerbe (1995) posits that in families with a history of depression or alcoholism, there may be a predisposition to eating disorders. "An obsession with food and weight can be an effective way to 'disappear' from these unhappy family situations or, in contrast, to take the focus away from other problems at home" (Hall & Ostroff, 1999, p.26). Melissa openly reports that her anorexia served these functions for her, while cutting provided a way of externalizing the internal pain she felt from being abused.

Miller and Stiver (1997) see symptoms as reflections of the "central relational paradox," in which the patient uses symptoms as a way of staying out of relationships and hiding the coexisting deep yearning for connectedness. In Melissa's case, her fears of being hurt indirectly reflected her longing for being cared about by others. Yet, this same fear of being hurt caused her to distance herself from others. She restricted close relationships and used her eating disorder as a protective barrier to keep people out. Melissa admits that "no one knows the real Melissa." Melissa will also admit that this disconnection extends from her interpersonal relationships to her intrapersonal relationship, as "I don't even know me" (Miller & Stiver, 1997).

Many survivors of sexual assault feel unsafe in their bodies and consciously or unconsciously reason that a body resembling a preadolescent is no longer sexually desirable. Thus, losing weight becomes a viable means of protecting oneself and feeling safer. Indeed, the onset of Melissa's problems with food and weight directly coincided with the cessation of abuse from her father. The anorexia, then, may be partially understood as Melissa's way of protecting herself from potential future sexual assaults (Hall & Ostroff, 1999; Marx, 1992).

Another widely accepted theory proposes that people who were sexually abused had no emotional control over what happened to their bodies; thus, they develop eating disorders as a way of regaining that emotional control. Restricting food intake and/or purging become viable ways to alleviate immediate feelings of discomfort and powerlessness. "Disappearing" becomes a way of hiding the body, shame, and feelings of innate "badness" (Hall & Ostroff, 1999; Zerbe, 1995; Kearney-Cooke & Striegle-Moore, 1996). This clearly applies to Melissa, who described her "core of badness," which she held responsible for the abuse she had suffered. Similarly, Melissa's cutting may also be understood as another way of simultaneously relieving uncomfortable feelings. Melissa often spoke about the "sense of relief" cutting brought to her. "It's like I'm going to explode, and then I cut, and that horrible feeling just vanishes," she explained.

Eating disorder symptoms and self-injury may also serve as a means of communication. People struggling with these issues often use their behaviors to tell others things like their lives are unmanageable, they loathe who they are, they are in unbearable pain, and they are desperately in need of comfort (Hall & Ostroff, 1999). Unfortunately, others are often unable to understand the complicated, frightening language of eating disorders and self-injury. In order for Melissa to free herself from the grips of her self-injurious behavior, she needed to develop effective communication skills to convey the vast realm of feelings and thoughts her behaviors had been communicating for her.

In summary, anorexia, in tandem with cutting, functioned as extraordinary—albeit dangerous—coping mechanisms for Melissa. Losing weight distracted her by providing a "concrete goal that requires energy, planning, and effort; time spent tallying calories, exercising, and worrying about weight is time not spent thinking about pain" (Hall & Ostroff, 1999, p. 24). True feelings are superceded by thoughts about food and weight. Moreover, restricting food and purging both numbed and comforted her (Hall & Ostroff, 1999; Marx, 1992; Rorty & Yager, 1996; Thompson, 1996). For Melissa, cutting functioned much the same way as her anorexia. The unsightly cuts lining her arms and legs were powerful distractions within the treatment setting. Melissa reported:

> All of my previous doctors and therapists spent so much time focusing on how ugly my arms were that everyone forgot to ask why I was doing it. It got to the point that I think I was cutting and throwing up before my feelings ever reached conscious awareness. It was a reflex. I always felt like no one understood me, because no one took the time to get to know me beyond my "appalling behaviors"—that's a quote.

Clearly, not feeling her feelings became central to Melissa's survival.

Melissa's difficulty in feeling her feelings also stemmed from being frightened of them—something she outwardly admitted. The avoidance of feeling and thinking about painful trauma was central to Melissa's survival. Van der Kolk (1996) posits, "After having been chronically aroused, without being able to do much to change this level of arousal, persons with Post Traumatic Stress Disorder (PTSD) may (correctly) experience just having feelings as dangerous" (p. 219). Coupled with her invalidating home environment, where the expression of feelings was met with punishment and criticism, experiencing feelings became even more dangerous. van der Kolk (1996) goes on to say, "In PTSD, extreme feelings of anger and helplessness can be understood as the reliving of memories of the trauma; like other memories of the trauma, they become reminders that are to be avoided" (p. 219). It would be important for Melissa to understand that she is both entitled to and worthy of feeling her feelings. Increasing her distress tolerance would be necessary in order to prepare her for the emotionally demanding work of healing from trauma.

Leading clinicians on trauma and recovery assert that survivors must have the opportunity to process and reintegrate the traumatic experiences in order to heal. Without such an opportunity, the traumatic experiences will manifest themselves in a vast array of distressing symptoms such as depression, anxiety, eating disorders, parasuicidal behaviors, and the perpetuation of the victim role, to name a few (Herman, 1992; Linehan, 1993a van der Kolk, 1996). In Melissa's case this is evidenced by the maintenance of her anorexia nervosa, nausea at the thought of being intimate with a male, inability to have emotionally intimate relationships, and low distress tolerance and cutting. In order to reverse these destructive trends, an opportunity to process and integrate her painful past in a safe, respectful, and compassionate environment was needed (Herman, 1992). However, exploring feelings of powerlessness while analyzing and correcting maladaptive, self-sabotaging behaviors might be the first step in Melissa's empowerment (Herman, 1992; Linehan, 1993a). For Melissa, the actual integration of traumatic events would be a long-term process.

Goal Setting and Baseline Data Collection

Although Melissa's abuse was at the root of her symptoms, it would be contraindicated to delve into trauma work before she had the ability to cope with the accompanying intense emotions. With this in mind, Melissa and I sat down to discuss goals. In order to get a clear sense of these goals, I used the Solution-Focused Miracle Question, which asks:

> Suppose that tonight, while you are sleeping, a miracle happens. The miracle is that all the problems that brought you here (to therapy) are solved. But you don't know that this miracle happened. When you wake up, what will be some of the first things you notice that are different—that tell you that this miracle happened?

This initial query can be expanded to clarify who will be the first person to notice, what will they notice that is different, who else will notice, and so on. Melissa was able to describe a "miracle day" in great detail emphasizing, "I'm not purging or cutting as much." Through this exercise, Melissa was able to recognize that she often purged or hurt herself in response to distressing thoughts or feelings. She also stated that she sometimes had difficulty identifying and expressing her feelings. She added that she would like to be able to sit with and tolerate her feelings better. Not surprisingly, her last complaint was feeling "worthless." She thought it would be "nice to have a better view of myself as a person." In summary, Melissa's goals were to decrease purging and cutting while simultaneously increasing distress tolerance and feelings of self-worth. (This would prepare her to do the necessary future trauma work at a later date; Tohn & Oshlag, 1997.)

Before setting specific objectives, Melissa collected baseline data for 10 days. She filled out a daily purging log, which indicated that she purged an average of 10 times per week. She also filled out a "Feelings of Worth" scale. The scale ranges from a low score of 1, "I am a worthless piece of crap" to a high score of 5, "I have value as a human being." She routinely rated herself a 1. Her daily cutting log indicated that she cut herself an average of twice weekly.

Given this baseline data, we established the following objectives. Melissa would decrease her purging behavior incrementally to an average of seven times per week by the end of month one; five times per week by the end of month two; three times per week by the end of month four; once per week by the end of month five, and no purging at all by the end of month six. Melissa would cut only once per week by the end of month one, twice a month by the end of month two, once per month by the end of month three, and cease entirely by the end of month four. In addition, Melissa would tolerate one distressing feeling per day without cutting or purging and would use new coping skills to "survive" it by week two. By the end of month three, she would tolerate all distressing feelings before noon without purging or cutting, increasing this by half-hour increments each week. Lastly, Melissa would increase in feelings of self worth such that by the end of month five, the "Feelings of Worth" scores would average a neutral 3. By month ten, scores would average a positive 4.5. These changes would be gradual, but steady, and would help us to determine whether the treatment was on track.

Therapeutic Interventions and Their Integration

The Feminist Relational Model and Winnicott's Theory

Increasing Melissa's subjective feelings of self-worth came, in large part, from the actual therapy environment, in which I drew from both the Feminist Relational Model and Donald Winnicott's work. From a Feminist Relational Perspective, which emphasizes the therapist's respect, compassion, and willingness to work collaboratively with patients, I adopted the following stance: "Anorexia and cutting have served you in some very important ways. They have helped you to survive intolerable circumstances, and we need to honor them for that. But now, let's work together to find ways for you to not only survive but to thrive in life." This approach emphasized collaboration while indicating that the therapeutic relationship is the vehicle for change and healing. Most importantly, it encouraged Melissa to move forward without shaming her.

The Feminist Relational Model posits that women heal in part from the "zest" they glean from connected relationships. It allows the therapist to be an active participant with feelings of her/his own. In practical terms, it allowed me to be open to the ways that Melissa emotionally moved me. Reflecting this to her allowed me to mirror her self-worth directly to her (e.g., if someone cares, it logically follows that one must have value). This, then, was the fabric of a corrective emotional experience for Melissa. (For further discussion of the Feminist Relational Model, see Miller 1986, 1987; Miller & Stiver, 1997.)

Weaving Winnicott's theories into this fabric enriched the therapy. According to Winnicott, the consistency, continuity, and reliability of the therapy relationship are transformative for the individual whose troubles of self stem from environmental deprivation and trauma (Applegate, 1996). Through a supportive and "good-enough" therapeutic relationship that maintains an empathic holding environment and emphasizes her right to her "true self," Melissa felt safe enough to begin and sustain the process of change. It was paramount to maintain this environment throughout the concomitant psychoeducation and cognitive behavioral work.

Linehan (1993a) asserts that therapists must frequently and sympathetically acknowledge the client's emotional desperation while emphasizing the building of a positive, collaborative relationship. She suggests accomplishing this by "warm acceptance and empathy" to validate experience and emotion, "occasionally mixed with blunt, irreverent confrontational comments" to address behavior (Linehan, 1993a, p. 29). Linehan's "warm acceptance and empathy" melds nicely with Winnicott's theory.

Whether Melissa chose to discuss behaviors, thoughts, feelings, or events, I offered empathy, validation, and understanding. When Melissa described excessive if not outlandish purging or cutting behaviors, I maintained the empathic holding environment by focusing on the intense, underlying pain she experienced. It was invaluable to validate the intensity of discomfort Melissa was fleeing from when she purged or cut. Between an empathic facial expression, soft tone of voice, and words that acknowledged her pain, Melissa's experiences were lent credence and validated. Sometimes Melissa responded tearfully, voicing her belief that she was unworthy and undeserving, which often led to a productive conversation about the ways in which her history trampled her boundaries and sense of self. I often reaffirmed that part of her healing entailed reclaiming what was lost, broken, or stolen long ago. At other times, Melissa seemed to have great difficulty sitting with the affect my empathy stirred in her. Her eyes would fill with tears and she would seem to will those tears to recede. At those times, I refocused on the here-and-now, while calling attention to her specific reaction. Encouraging Melissa to embrace the emotion without changing it allowed her to occasionally bear her feelings within the context of a supportive environment (Herman, 1992; Linehan, 1993; van der Kolk et al., 1994).

As previously stated, part of Melissa's difficulty in feeling her feelings was derived from her not always being fully aware of them. Winnicott states that the basis for feeling real is the "true self," which incorporates "being adequately held, establishing ego relatedness with others, finding means for self-soothing, and integrating libidinal and aggressive drives" (Applegate, 1996, p.90). Because her mother was unavailable and her home life was both invalidating and unsafe, Melissa's true self was supplanted by a false self. Just as Winnicott suggested, Melissa became adept at tuning into her caregivers' needs at the expense of alienating her own inner self. Melissa was good at caring for everyone else. In fact, she plans on making a virtual career out of being hypersensitive to the needs of others; her major is psychology and she aspires to be a psychologist. Winnicott posits that therapists "must understand such client's spontaneous gestures, both loving and hating, as they are becoming comfortable in experimenting with their true selves in a safe, reliable, undemanding relationship" (Applegate, 1996, p. 91). Empathic questions to gain deeper understanding coupled with validating Melissa's feelings and experiences as legitimate and valuable were my ways of recognizing her right to her true self.

Dialectical Behavior Therapy (DBT)

The initial phase of treatment consisted of educating Melissa in identifying and expressing feelings. DBT worksheets on emotion regulation, which describe emotions as well as ways in which people express and experience them, were the tools of choice (Linehan, 1993b). It was simultaneously imperative that Melissa learn new skills to help her manage both urges and feelings. DBT's "Crisis Survival Strategies" were critical in this regard (Linehan, 1993b). DBT provides a Crisis Strategy Worksheet that served as a quick reference list for Melissa, which simultaneously allowed us to track the skills she used.

Melissa tracked the number of times per day she purged, and twice weekly she completed a DBT Behavioral Analysis (Linehan, 1993a). The behavior analysis, a form of cognitive restructuring, views a "slip" as an opportunity for learning, growth, and change as opposed to an excuse for self-denigration. The DBT analysis asks the patient to specifically describe the problem behavior, the precipitating event, vulnerability factors, chain of events, consequences of the behavior, alternative solutions, a prevention strategy, and ways to make restitution. These analyses were the foci of many therapy sessions. Reviewing the analysis enabled Melissa to dissect her behavior within the context of her feelings in a compassionate, reliable environment. It enhanced her insight and understanding of self, which in turn planted the seeds of change. Reviewing the analyses allowed us to devise "alternative strategies" to purging and cutting. Or simply, it was a coaching opportunity to encourage the transfer of new coping skills into her daily life (Linehan, 1993a).

At various points in the treatment, DBT techniques were incorporated into other techniques, as the reader will note in the material that follows.

Exposure/Response Prevention

A tailored form of exposure and response prevention was also intermittently used to help decrease the frequency of purging; this included coaching Melissa in "urge surfing." Classic exposure/response prevention allows a binge, but prevents purging. It has been touted as effective, although controversial (Garner, Vitousek & Pike, 1997; Polivy & Federoff, 1997). A modified version requires the patient to eat one "risk food," and sit with the fear and discomfort without engaging in compensatory behaviors. This is the format that we used in Melissa's treatment.

As an example, Melissa brought in one food that she was terrified of eating without purging. After she ate it, she was allowed to go through her usual processes of panicking or planning to skip a meal while experiencing her intense urges to purge. After five minutes of experiencing intense panic and urges, she was asked to challenge her beliefs and reassure herself. Melissa was then redirected to distract herself from any remaining anxiety by engaging in an activity or conversation, or using her survival kit in my presence.

In a variation of this exercise, before eating the risk food, we reviewed the concept of an urge as an ocean wave that will roll in, crest, and subside. Drawing a straight line across a sheet of paper, I explained that this line is "baseline" where she has no urges and feels okay. Drawing out the first half of a bell-shaped curve, we discussed the incline as the increase in the urge. At the top, or the point of highest intensity, we discussed her "usual reaction" which was to purge or cut. Drawing a vertical line down from the top of the curve to the baseline illustrated the effect of purging. We discussed urges naturally subsiding and drew the rest of the curve back down to baseline. Melissa was able to see that she eventually got to the same spot, whether she purged, cut, or used a healthy method. We noted that the "trick" was surfing the wave and riding out the time between the point of highest intensity and the wave subsiding on its own. Melissa correctly postulated that filling that time with coping skills would help her successfully ride the wave. Thus we used the time after eating to practice "urge surfing." Repetition of this exercise led to a decrease in food-related anxiety and seemed to be useful in decreasing and eliminating her purging. Generally, as people become more proficient in "urge surfing," the waves become incrementally smaller. Eventually patients become aware of their triggers and immediately begin applying coping skills, thus circumventing the urge entirely.

Approaches to Self-Esteem

For Melissa, like most people struggling with eating disorders and self-injury, recovery entails learning to care about oneself as much as one cares about others—and feeling okay about doing that. Thus, Melissa worked on the "10 Steps to Fostering Gentleness and Compassion in Yourself" (available at http://www.caringonline.com/eatdis/editorials/ostroff/ten-steps.htm). Recognizing that it is the patient's self-hate that drives the critical voices and behaviors of anorexia nervosa, this approach seeks to reverse self-hate by teaching patients to treat themselves with gentleness and compassion. In turn, the destructive behaviors will eventually be extinguished. The underlying logic is simple—it is impossible to hurt something you care about. The specific 10 steps are undertaken slowly throughout the course of therapy.

This particular cognitive behavioral approach requires a fair amount of time before change is effected. Melissa often struggled with not doing a step "perfectly." For example, she was upset that she could not make it through an entire day without judging herself. I frequently reassured her that there was no "one right way" to work through a step. It was helpful to refocus her on the process itself, viewing it as a learning experience that provided her with more information about herself as an individual.

"Saying It Anyway"

I recognized that we could not simply sit back and wait until Melissa felt like a worthy, valuable person before she could use her own authentic voice to communicate and meet her needs. I introduced the concept of "saying it anyway" (similar to the AA "Fake it 'til you make it" philosophy). The underlying idea was for Melissa to voice her feelings and needs regardless of feeling unentitled to do so. Through time and practice, Melissa worked through the attached guilt and eventually began to spontaneously voice her needs and feelings instead of acting them out. Sometimes Melissa would begin with, "I don't have any right to say this, but I feel really angry." Sometimes, we worked on having her feel entitled, while at other times, we focused directly on the anger, entirely ignoring the fact that she felt unentitled to it. Working on feeling entitled was a slow process, but she clearly made gains, as occasionally she would express herself without the disclaimer, "I have no right to say this...." It was always beneficial to talk about the anger itself, because 5 minutes into the discussion, she would forget all about feeling unentitled and would talk freely, able to experience the feeling while receiving validation and encouragement from me.

Enhancing Distress Tolerance

Melissa was terrified of becoming completely overwhelmed and dysfunctional by the emotions her behaviors held at bay. Thus it was important for us to problem solve regarding her distress tolerance. Given Melissa's low distress tolerance, mindfulness skills, consciously experiencing and observing oneself and surrounding events, were essential (Linehan, 1993a). This skill greatly enhances distress tolerance. It is not uncommon for people of Western cultures to be unwilling to sit with distressing feelings until they naturally shift. Instead, many people engage in mood-altering behaviors (e.g., substance abuse, eating disorder, parasuicidal behaviors) which short circuit the healing process in addition to the feelings. In Melissa's case, purging and cutting were the short-circuiting agents. I actively encouraged her to adopt a willing attitude to endure and walk through her feelings, as that is the first step to their healthy resolution and permanent behavior change. Because the idea of experiencing feelings was so foreign to Melissa, it was necessary to briefly revisit and practice mindfulness at each session.

Identifying Feelings

Because Melissa had historically spent little time in her feelings, she often had difficulty identifying them. In order to help her do this, she was given fourteen DBT worksheets on emotion regulation, which describe emotions as well as the ways people express and experience them (Linehan, 1993b, pp.139–152). Part of the first week's homework was to practice being mindful in relation to the feelings described in detail on these worksheets. Reviewing the worksheets together in session helped Melissa become more fluent in the language of feeling. For example, we explored a recent time when Melissa felt guilty and sad. We discussed in detail how it both resembled and differed from the descriptions found on the worksheets. Sometimes when Melissa was unable to name an emotion, we perused the worksheets for clues. With one exception, this exercise led her to identify and talk about the emotion she was experiencing at the time. Melissa reported that the combination of worksheets, discussions, and practice helped her become more aware of her feelings in general (Linehan, 1993b).

Developing Alternative Coping Skills

Because decreasing Melissa's purging and cutting behaviors effectively removed her most reliable and effective coping mechanisms, it was important, early on, to teach her healthier coping skills. She clearly needed them in order to experience the realm of feelings that her purging and cutting protected her from. Melissa was given worksheets and in-session guidance on self-soothing and relaxation (see, for example, Bourne, 1995, pp. 67–91, 103–137; Copeland, 1991, pp. 239–261; Linehan, 1993b, pp. 167–168). Melissa often reported that self-soothing skills worked best for her when she remembered to use them. In order to remind herself to use her skills, Melissa made a list of all her coping skills, which continued to grow as treatment progressed, and hung copies of it in her bathroom and bedroom so that she could see them when she was about to purge or cut.

Additionally, we used some session time to brainstorm and supplement these options with others that were more unique to Melissa. Creating a "crisis survival kit" proved to be most beneficial. Melissa decorated a plastic shoebox with affirmations and inspirational pictures. She then filled it with items that she could use to circumvent acting on an urge. Using DBT's concept of soothing through the five senses, Melissa chose one item for each of her five senses—a stress ball for touch, breath drops for taste, an aromatherapy candle for smell, a tape of her favorite music for hearing, and a bottle of bubbles for sight.

In addition, she made five positive affirmation cards as well as five challenge cards to include in her kit. To make a challenge card, Melissa took one of her negative beliefs and wrote it on one side of an index card. For example, on one card she wrote, "I deserve nothing because I am worth nothing." On the back of the card, she wrote three objective arguments refuting or disproving the statement. For example, for that card, one of her arguments was, "because I do not like myself very much I am not an accurate, objective judge of my worth."

Over time, Melissa reported turning to her crisis survival kit not only to cope with urges but also to soothe herself through her authentic emotions once they began to surface. "This was one thing that was fun to make and really helpful to use when trying to stop purging and cutting; it's also something I bet I'll use for a long time to come while I work through the rest of my issues," Melissa said. Later on, Melissa challenged herself to make a crisis survival kit small enough to keep on her at all times.

I occasionally asked Melissa to describe a distressing event and analyze her use of healthy coping skills. This provided her with an opportunity to receive both validation and coaching from me. As part of coaching, I always posed the question, "what other skills might have been useful?" Melissa would scan her list and could often name two or three other skills that would have been helpful to her. I also encouraged her to transfer these skills to other areas, as they could assist her in coping with intrusive thoughts or nightmares of her abuse when they occurred. At the end of the eighth month, Melissa began turning to these skills for support in these situations. With time, practice, and consistent coaching, Melissa became increasingly proficient in the use of healthy coping skills. It was my hope that these adaptive skills coupled with self-expression in therapy would "replace" her purging and cutting behaviors altogether, and by the end of the year that appeared to be the case.

Solution-Focused Interviewing and Motivational Techniques

To increase motivation for Melissa, I relied heavily on Solution-Focused interviewing techniques. For example, when Melissa purged 10 times during a week that she opted to use no skills, I directly asked, "How did purging make your life better this week?" Without thinking, she quickly replied, "It didn't." I encouraged her to take some time to think about it more carefully. She was then able to identify that purging had made her week more predictable, calmed her down, and distracted her from distressing events and feelings. We then explored alternative ways that she could meet these needs (e.g., building structure into her days, using relaxation techniques, engaging in healthy distractions such as calling friends or watching a funny movie). Then I asked, "On a scale of 1 to 10, where 10 is that all the problems that brought you here are solved and 1 is that they are the worst ever, where would you rank yourself right now?" Melissa, at that point, ranked herself a 2. My next question was, "On a scale of 1 to 10 where 10 is the most willing you could ever be to change your behavior and 1 is not remotely willing to change, where are you right now?" Melissa ranked herself a 6. Because Melissa was somewhat motivated to change, I phrased my next question in the active voice: "Between now and the next time we meet, what is one thing that you can do to move one half point up the scale to problem resolution?" She stated that consistently using the skills we had identified together in session would accomplish this (Tohn & Oshlang, 1997).

There were times when Melissa was not so motivated or willing. On those occasions, I was careful to phrase my questions differently. For example, at one point I asked Melissa to scale her motivation. Using a scale of 1 to 10 where 10 was the most motivated she could be, she ranked herself a 2. Before proceeding, I stopped to phrase my next question more passively: "Between today and two days from now, *what needs to happen for you to move one half point up the motivation scale?*" Using the passive voice afforded Melissa enough space to see the bigger picture. Had I asked Melissa *what she could do* to move herself up the scale, she likely would have become frustrated with me. Using the active voice inherently presupposes that motivation exists, and she had just clearly told me that she was not motivated. Before moving on to the benefits of her behavior and changing it, it was important to scale her willingness in precisely the same manner in which we scaled her motivation. Motivation and willingness work in tandem to effect change. If she is motivated but unwilling, change is unlikely to occur (Tohn & Oshlang, 1997).

In order to maintain motivation and address fears related to recovery, I frequently asked, "How will your life change if you stop purging and cutting?" or "How will your life be different if you are no longer cutting and purging?" While these questions are essentially one and the same, Melissa seemed to hear them differently. To her, "change" implied some momentous event that might catch her off guard, whereas "different" allowed her to explore some of the subtleties that recovery brings. These questions were most fruitful in leading us to explore Melissa's deep-seated fears about recovery. One of her primary fears was of disappearing and feeling as though no one would care about her. This was an excellent opportunity to explore the concept of Melissa developing and using her authentic voice to express herself and meet her needs.

It was important for Melissa to learn to use her voice to convey all of the things her purging and cutting communicated for her. We reviewed and practiced the basic assertive statement, "When you _____, I feel _____, I prefer that _____." Additionally, I taught Melissa the DBT skills DEAR MAN, GIVE, and FAST. She practiced them in sessions as well as at home. Becoming well versed in effectively using her voice made Melissa feel more secure within herself, which in turn made the process and prospect of recovery less frightening. She learned that she could ask for acknowledgment when she felt invisible and she could ask for reassurance when she felt that no one cared.

"What Is Being Communicated?"

I was careful to consistently ask Melissa to think about the message her behavior might be communicating to other people. In order for Melissa to change this behavior and use her voice, it was imperative that she understood her behavior's concomitant message. Thus, insight coupled with using healthy coping skills ultimately led to behavior change. Through my persistent questioning, Melissa was able to dissect her behavior within the context of her feelings. She articulated on several occasions that her purging was clearly an attempt to "numb out," while cutting herself was an attempt to let others know that she was hurting and needed comfort. Identifying any behavior's purpose is the first step in developing the ability to verbalize it in the future.

Relaxation Techniques

We also devoted session time to practicing relaxation techniques. Melissa responded fairly well to progressive relaxation in which she flexed and relaxed major muscle groups beginning with her feet and working up to the muscles in her face. She also was able to quickly learn diaphragmatic breathing while repeating the word "relax" as she exhaled. "That was a quick, easy way to bring my anxiety down," she noted. Melissa reported, "Relaxation, as stupid as I thought it was in the beginning, really did help with the anxiety" that often led to purging or cutting. She did not use relaxation techniques consistently, however, and I noticed that purging, in particular, tended to occur when her anxiety was quite high. As a result, I encouraged her to set aside at least 10 to 15 minutes three times per day to practice some form of relaxation. I had hoped that a less anxious state would help her center and remember that her most important work was learning to experience and express her feelings without purging or cutting. When she was able to be more consistent with this practice, her purging and cutting did decrease.

Other Aspects of the Treatment

Our sessions provided a multitude of opportunities for working through feelings, reframing perceptions, and simultaneously affirming Melissa's right to her true self. For example, every now and then, Melissa would occasionally misperceive a look of mine or become flustered if I did not immediately understand something. By compassionately and patiently working through her frustration and disappointment, she learned that my not immediately understanding did not necessarily preclude my caring about her or her situation. During these times, I was careful to give her positive feedback about her ability to verbally express her emotions and acknowledge their validity, which in turn served to validate her right to her true self. Through time and practice, Melissa improved her communication skills and distress tolerance while correcting some of her cognitive distortions. Consistently encouraging her to rely on her own inner strength and skills, while voicing my admiration and praise when she did so, helped circumvent her from becoming overly dependent on the therapeutic relationship.

Occasionally, Melissa tried to talk about the details of her abuse. While I never interrupted or "forbade" this, I was careful to avoid depth in conversations about it because she did not yet have the requisite skills to survive the full emotional fallout. For Melissa, these types of discussions had previously been set-ups for setbacks (her behaviors spiraled out of control and she was consequently hospitalized). I invariably validated her horror and pain and immediately asked what she was doing to take care of herself in relation to it. This immediately led to a discussion about available skills/ tools she could use to help her tolerate her distress—one of her treatment goals (Linehan, 1993a).

We continued to work in the manner described, exploring the here and now, with me empathetically supporting her, encouraging her to experience and express her feelings while simultaneously coaching her in the use of healthy coping skills. We collaboratively worked on alternative solutions to purging, such as using her voice, engaging in relaxation exercises, using positive self-talk, challenging her negative beliefs, self-soothing through the five senses, etc.

Data Collection and Analysis

The primary indicator of intervention success was the reduction of Melissa's purging and cutting behaviors. These reductions were measured primarily by reviewing her daily log, which tracked the number of purges and cutting per day. At the end of each week, these data were transferred onto a graph, which highlighted the target number of purges and cutting for that week. This provided a quick visual reference for us to track the frequency of her purging and cutting. It allowed us to visually see a steady decline in her behaviors.

The "Feelings of Worth" scale tracked Melissa's subjective feelings of self-worth. The scale was filled out weekly and again the data was transferred to a graph. This allowed us to view whether her feelings of self-worth were increasing, decreasing, or unchanged. The last method of tracking was Melissa's use of amended DBT Survival Strategies worksheets (see Linehan, 1993b). This worksheet is devised in a way that allows the therapist to track which strategies a patient is using as well as the level of distress tolerance on a scale of 0–100, both before and after employing the specific skill. We deleted certain DBT skills from the worksheets and added other coping skills that Melissa would use. The data for distress tolerance can also be graphed weekly. By comparing Melissa's Survival Strategies sheets to the purging and cutting frequency graphs, we were able to see whether there was a correlation between the use of coping skills and purging and cutting. Graphing and color coding the number of skills used directly on the cutting and purging graphs had tremendous impact on Melissa, as she could then most clearly see the correlation between coping skills usage and her purging and cutting.

Melissa brought these logs into session twice a month and we graphed the data together. I remained cognizant of evidence of change and provided her with positive feedback and encouragement regarding her efforts to change. (None of these instruments are standardized and there is no available information on reliability and validity.) However, given the fact that the goal was to change Melissa's subjective experiences from Time 1 to Time 2, these subjective self-reports would suffice for the purpose of confirming a change.

The Treatment Outcome

Melissa was initially concerned with meeting the objectives perfectly and on time, a response that is not surprising. I reassured her that all that was required was effortful participation in the therapy process. I further explained that there is no one or "right" way to do therapy; rather, it is through the unfolding process that we learn more about who she is and what she needs. Objectives are not "set in stone" and could be reset at different intervals. Furthermore, I explained that it was important for us to remember that what works for one person does not necessarily work for another, and that we needed to be flexible. Thus we were able to anticipate that certain interventions would not be right for her. Melissa thought that perhaps when she was more in touch with her inner self, she might naturally gravitate toward other exercises that would be more beneficial to her, which did in fact occur.

Purging and Cutting Behaviors

We often referred to the graphs throughout the interventions, as they clearly illustrated the progression toward her treatment goals. For example, one of Melissa's long-term goals was to cease all purging behaviors by the end of month six. Recall the baseline data indicating that Melissa purged an average of 10 times per week. At week four, she showed the first decrease in purging. With the exception of week five, we saw a slow but persistent decrease in purging behaviors until they ceased entirely near the end of month eight. Melissa also had the goal of ceasing all cutting by the end of the fourth month. While this behavior fluctuated some, she was able to extinguish the behavior in the beginning of the sixth month of treatment. Note that we often needed to reevaluate and readjust the objectives. Some of the objectives were met early, some late, and some right on schedule.

Distress Tolerance

Melissa's second goal was to increase her overall distress tolerance. Her first objective was, by the end of week two, to be able to use one new skill to tolerate one distressing feeling without purging or cutting. Melissa met this objective during week two of the intervention phase, but regressed during the third week. By the end of the first month, Melissa was able to use coping skills more regularly.

During the fourth and fifth weeks, Melissa used coping skills 5 out of 7 days per week. When I inquired as to why she was not using them on the other 2 days per week, she reported "not feeling like it," believing that it was unnecessary on the days she attended therapy. Explaining the importance of using and practicing coping skills every day of the week was critical. I offered that it sometimes takes a little while before skills feel helpful. I used the analogy of buying a pair of sneakers. One must often try them on and wear them around for a while before they feel comfortable. Thus, the more practiced one becomes in using coping skills, the more comfortable they are and the better the skills function for that person. Furthermore, it was important for her to know that therapy sometimes uncovers difficult material, evoking painful feelings. If and when this happened, it would be important that she know how to take care of herself without turning to purging or cutting for comfort. Shortly after this conversation, Melissa began to use her skills more consistently. The "coping skills usage" graph coupled with the "days of skills usage" graph illustrated that the number of different skills in her repertoire increased as she learned and practiced—evidence that she was becoming more proficient in using healthy coping skills.

Feelings of Self-Worth

Melissa's third treatment goal was to increase subjective feelings of self worth by the end of six months. During the baseline phase, Melissa routinely ranked herself at a low 1 on the "Feelings of Worth" scale. Her first objective was to rank herself a neutral 3 by the end of month three. Near the end of month two, she was regularly ranking herself at a more positive 2. By the end of month six, she ranked herself at a neutral 3 and by the end of month ten, she was fluctuating between a 4 and 4.5.

Behavioral Inter-Relationships

For Melissa, the number of days she used skills and the actual number of skills she used on those days appeared to be directly correlated with her purging and cutting behaviors. For example, during the first week of the intervention stage, Melissa used no active coping skills, purged an average of 10 times weekly, cut twice, and rated herself as feeling completely worthless. During the second week of intervention, Melissa was able to use two different DBT skills and progressive muscle relaxation 5 out of 7 days that week, and although we saw no change in her feelings of self-worth, her purging behavior decreased to an average of eight times per week with no cutting at all. Almost predictably, during the third week of intervention, when Melissa used no active coping skills, her purging behavior increased back to baseline. In fact, she cut three times that week, as well. When we reviewed the graphs together, Melissa was able to see the decrease in purging and cutting in tandem with an increase in skills usage. This gave Melissa added incentive to regularly work on and practice her skills.

Conclusion

I have used this eclectic approach with good results with many patients who struggle with self-injury and eating disorders. I have noted that one approach alone has not produced successful results. Thus, I am led to hypothesize that Melissa's success was one more testimony to the utility of an eclectic approach. The most important clinically significant aspect is that Melissa was able to reach the goals and objectives outlined in her treatment plan. The evaluative process indicated that this intervention was successful. However, the integration of these various techniques resides in the ever-changing terrain of the therapeutic relationship, which is the challenge, as well as the satisfaction, of an integrative approach.

References

Applegate, J. (1996). The good enough social worker. In J. Edward & J. Sanville (Eds.), *Fostering healing and growth* (pp. 77–97). Northvale, NJ: Jason Aronson, Inc.

Bourne, E. (1995). *The anxiety and phobia workbook.* Oakland, CA: New Harbinger.

Copeland, M. (1991). *The depression workbook: A guide for living with depression and manic depression.* Oakland, CA: New Harbinger.

Garner, D., Vitousek, K., & Pike, K. (1997). Cognitive behavioral therapy for anorexia nervosa. In D. Garner & P. Garfinkel (Eds.), *Handbook of treatment for eating disorders* (pp. 94–145). New York: Guilford.

Hall, L., & Ostroff, M. (1999). *Anorexia nervosa: A guide to recovery.* Carlsbad, CA: Gürze Books.

Herman, J. L. (1992). *Trauma and recovery.* New York: Basic Books.

Kearney-Cooke, A., & Striegel-Moore, R. (1996). Treatment of childhood sexual abuse in anorexia nervosa and bulimia nervosa: A feminist psychodynamic approach. In M. Schwartz & L. Cohn (Eds.), *Sexual abuse and eating disorders* (pp. 155–179). New York: Bruner Mazel.

Linehan, M. (1993a). *Cognitive behavioral treatment of borderline personality disorder.* New York: Guilford.

Linehan, M. (1993b). *Skills training manual for treating borderline personality disorder.* New York: Guilford.

Marx, R. (1992) *It's not your fault: Overcoming anorexia and bulimia through biopsychiatry.* New York: Plume.

Miller, J. B. (1986). Domination and subordination. In P. Rothenberg (Ed.), *Race, class, and gender in the United States* (4th ed.) (pp. 73–79). New York: St. Martin's Press.

Miller, J. B. (1987). Connection, disconnection and violations. *Works in Progress, 33.* Wellesley, MA: Wellesley College Stone Center for Developmental Services and Studies.

Miller, J. B., & Stiver, I. (1997) *The healing connection: How women form relations in therapy and life.* Boston: Beacon Press.

Polivy, J., & Federoff, I. (1997). Group psychotherapy. In D. Garner & P. Garfinkel (Eds.), *Handbook of treatment for eating disorders* (pp. 462–476). New York: Guilford.

Rorty, M., & Yager, J. (1996). Speculations on the role of childhood abuse in the development of eating disorders among women. In M. Schwartz & L. Cohn (Eds.), *Sexual abuse and eating disorders* (pp. 23–36). New York: Bruner Mazel.

Thompson, B. (1996). *A hunger so wide and so deep: A multiracial view of eating disorders.* Minneapolis: University of Minnesota Press.

Tohn, S., & Oshlag, J. (1997). *Crossing the bridge: Integrating solution focused therapy into clinical practice.* Sudbury: Solutions Press.

van der Kolk, B., Dreyfuss, D., Michaels, M., Shera, D., Berkowitz, R, Fisler, R., et al. (1994). Trauma and the development of borderline personality disorder. *Journal of Clinical Psychiatry, 55,* 715–731.

van der Kolk, B. (1996). The body keeps score: Approaches to the psychobiology of Posttraumatic Stress Disorder. In B. van der Kolk, A. McFarlane, & L. Weisaeth (Eds.), *Traumatic stress: The effects of overwhelming experience on mind, body, and society* (pp. 214–242). New York: Guilford Press.

Zerbe, K. (1995). *The body betrayed: A deeper understanding of women, eating disorders and treatment.* Carlsbad, CA: Gürze Books.

CHAPTER 14

Interventions and Strategies for Families and Friends of the Self-Harming Patient with an Eating Disorder

CAROLYN COSTIN

Introduction

Healthy support and connection are critical to the long-term recovery of individuals with eating disorders and with self-harm behavior (SHB). The intention of this chapter is to discuss working with significant others including family, spouses, lovers, and friends. I find it useful to work with available significant others whenever I can, and this chapter will provide examples of considerations, strategies, and interventions.

Family and friends find it difficult to understand the cause and function of eating disorder behavior. Add SHB to this and you usually have significant others either in an uproar or in despair. How one could willingly starve, purge, or purposely hurt oneself is often a matter of household inquisition and arguments. Typical reactions include anger, disgust, and fear, combined with threats of varying consequences in hope and desperation to make the behavior(s) stop.

Intervention with the family, no matter what the age of the patient, is critical even if in-person sessions are contraindicated. The family is the backdrop and the context for the patient's life. Whether currently living with the family or on their own, the patient's symptoms developed in a context. For various reasons, if someone has eating disorder and self-harm symptoms, he or she did not form sufficiently healthy attachments in order to build trust and self-reliance and did not achieve an appropriate balance between dependency and separation needs. In response to anything from benign neglect to abuse, the patient uses his or her behaviors to replace the support that was unavailable or inappropriate from others. This does not mean that the family or a certain family member causes the symptoms. It is more complicated than that. Two children growing up in the same home may turn out quite differently. One may develop an eating disorder and SHB while the other develops neither. Heredity, the presence of other comorbid conditions, and social/environmental conditions are all potential contributory factors.

In order to heal, patients must learn how to get their needs met from healthy relationships or from their own inner healthy self. To do this requires establishing healthy relationships in the present. The clinician must decide if healthy, or at least healthier, relationships can be developed in the family (with a strong emphasis to attempt this unless otherwise contraindicated). Other than the family, clinicians must rely on themselves and significant others for providing the patient with a context and healthy attachments to facilitate the patient's development of his or her own internal sense of trust, safety, and self-esteem. People heal by being able to understand what they are experiencing inside, being able to communicate this, and having this validated. I always say to my patients that "The more congruent you are with what is going on inside of you, what you say, and finally how it is received and reflected back to you, the healthier you are." This kind of congruence is developed in healthy attachments.

Family members can be involved at various levels. How directly one works with family members will need to be determined on a case-by-case basis. With an adolescent living at home, the need for family sessions is critical, but they might also be critical for a 38-year-old who has not lived at home for 20 years. My philosophy is that unless there is a compelling reason not to do so (due to the limitations of this chapter, clinicians will have to determine this individually), get the family members in for sessions. How many sessions will depend on the patient's history and what happens once the therapy is initiated.

An overriding theme of family intervention is to demystify the patient's behaviors while helping significant others develop healthy responses. In working with the family, the therapist can explain how the behaviors have developed as coping mechanisms. Family dynamics will be exposed in the session and be available for comment, therapeutic intervention, and hopefully change. A critical father who thinks that he can punish his daughter into not cutting herself will soon learn that this is not the case. His daughter is more likely to hide her behavior better or even increase it as a result.

A mother who tries taking her daughter's car away until she gains weight might discover that her daughter has gained the weight but now scratches herself with safety pins and nail files in places that cannot be seen. All of these and similar topics are the material for family therapy, where all involved have to learn new ways of communicating, understanding, and dealing with each other.

Observe the family and you may see the dynamics that created, or perpetuate, the reason for the patient's dysfunctional behaviors. Even in cases of abuse, it is not just the abuse that caused the developmental derailment, but all of the other concomitant issues in a family where such abuse can even occur such as inconsistency, lack of validation, or absence of safety. What you see might be subtler. For example, a very kind and seemingly "perfect" family might present themselves in your office; mother and father both listen to the daughter's concerns, stating how much they love her and that they would do anything to help. There is no arguing and the parents state they have never had any problems with their daughter until now. In this family, it could be that being good and doing one's best were the only qualities the daughter saw being valued. When she did not feel like she did her best, she had no way to resolve those feelings of shame, frustration, or fear. Somewhere during development, starving and cutting helped her to deal with feelings by numbing them, or distracting her from them, or at least transforming the psychological pain into more tolerable and controllable physical pain.

In some cases, family therapy might be difficult and troubling. Consider a case in which there was physical or sexual abuse by a family member. There are many resources out there for the reader that detail family therapy for abuse victims, but one important task is for the therapist to help both the patient and the family see how certain behaviors like binging, purging, and cutting may be a reenactment of the trauma. In this case, the patient has often learned to connect both love and pain together.

Meredith was a patient who suffered from bulimia nervosa and would also masturbate to the point of rubbing herself raw and bloody. Her stepfather had sexually abused her from the time she was 6 years old until age 15. This man also cared for her more than anyone ever had. He bought her things, took her places, paid attention to her, and told her he loved her. In therapy, this patient discovered to her own dismay that both her binge/purge episodes and masturbation were serving an unconscious purpose. In some way, she was reenacting the abuse by her stepfather. She symbolically binged and purged him out of her, but she also masturbated to pain because this brought him (or at least the memory of him) close to her. When he died, she suffered from his loss even though she had anger and terrible feelings associated with him as well. For her, and for many self-harming patients with eating disorders, love and pain are connected and their seemingly disordered symptoms are a way of reenacting this duality unconsciously. Helping Meredith see how her behaviors were related to her past abuse was healing for her. It gave her an understanding of her self-inflicted pain and was the beginning of her ability to control it. In this case, there was no need to discuss this with her mother, who was too emotionally troubled to deal with it appropriately. Her father and stepfather were deceased. In this case, "family work" took place without the family members present. Discussing her stepfather's abuse and her mother's negligence of Meredith in general helped Meredith come to an understanding of why she turned to these behaviors. Furthermore, explaining all of this to her husband was very useful. He had understood the eating disorder as a lack of willpower on her part to maintain her weight in a healthy way and her masturbation as a rejection of him. Meredith had often masturbated to the point of being unavailable for healthy sexual relations. After understanding her behaviors as reenactments of her family trauma, Meredith's husband had more empathy and patience during her recovery.

I always approach family therapy with the concept that I want to teach family and/or friends to do for the patient what I am doing for him or her such as to empathize, understand, guide without controlling, step in when necessary, foster self-esteem, and facilitate independence. If the therapist can help the family and significant others to provide for the patient what a healing therapeutic relationship provides, therapy becomes less important and eventually unnecessary.

In a sense, my job as a therapist is to put myself out of business with every patient. One way is by helping patients learn how to constructively handle their problems on their own. The other way is by helping them to meet their needs in healthy relationships with others. In addition, clinicians must teach and facilitate significant others to understand their role, if any, in the etiology and/or perpetuation of the eating disorder or SHB, and their role in helping the patient to access other methods of coping.

Family therapists should keep in mind the following important tasks: establish rapport, educate the family, explore the impact of the illness on the family, uncover parental expectations and aspirations, set goals, discover the role of the patient in the family, and improve family communication patterns. *The Eating Disorder Sourcebook* (Costin, 1996) is an excellent source for further explanation of these different tasks. Other useful resources include *Surviving an Eating Disorder* (Brisman, Siegel, & Weinshel, 1997), *Cutting* (Levenkron, 1999), *Women Who Hurt Themselves* (Miller, 1994), and *Self Injury* (Aronson, 2000).

Assessments

In addition to assessing the patients, I assess all parents through a mailed intake form. I have found that some of the most valuable material in therapy comes from these assessments. I want to compare the parent reports with the information my patient tells me about his/her life, growing up in his/her family, significant events or problems, family meal times, mother's and father's home life, and communication styles. Some of this information is evident in how the paperwork is even filled out by the family members. Are there substance abuse disorders, eating disorders, and other mental health problems in my patient's parents and grandparents? What concerns do mother and father both have about the patient and at what age did they begin to have them? Do their perceptions match or differ radically? What is each parent's relationship to the other parent and to my patient? Have there been any traumatic or at least very upsetting events in the lives of the parents? Therapists may find that they have to be the ones to connect these kinds of traumas or stressful events with the development of symptoms in the patient. The family may not have made this connection at all. Overall, I am usually able to piece together the development of certain feelings and perceptions about the world, and even symptoms, based in large part on some evidence found in these assessments. I believe clinicians can benefit by spending time creating their own family assessment forms and being tenacious in getting them filled out. A separate one for spouses can also be valuable.

Revealing the SHB

By the time a family therapy session is scheduled, the members may know about the eating disorder but often do not know about any SHB. Revealing this to the family is important but has to be done in a safe setting where trust has already been established with the patient, unless the behavior is seriously dangerous or life-threatening to the individual. Many eager or overly cautious therapists feel that they must reveal this information to family members as soon as they discover it, particularly if the patient is an adolescent. These are the issues to consider before disclosure. For example, has the therapist established trust with the patient and does the patient feel safe/comfortable with the therapist, particularly in regards to disclosing SHB? Has the therapist explained a general understanding of the functions of SHB and how these are related to eating disorder behaviors? Do the patient and the therapist have an understanding of the meaning of his or her SHB? What might the likely responses of the various family members be, and have the patient and the therapist discussed these? Is the SHB currently escalating, decreasing, or staying the same? Is the therapeutic work helping to decrease the behaviors? What are the patient's expectations regarding disclosure?

Patients who are pushed to disclose too soon may feel exposed, frightened, ashamed, or angry. It is always important to keep in mind that there will be loyalty to parents and other caregivers even if there are serious family problems, such as current abuse. The patient will often want to protect family members from blame and the disappointment and/or anger he or she is sure they will experience when they find out about the SHB. The need for disclosure on the patient's behalf has to be kept in balance with his or her need for safety and control. Obviously, age and whether the patient is living at home are relevant issues to be considered.

Once the patient feels enough trust and safety with the therapist to begin to discuss the truth in family sessions, the therapist has to make sure that there is sufficient time spent educating and working with the family to ensure that they can hear information, understand what it means, and what they can and cannot do about it. There has to be sufficient time spent talking about an appropriate plan of action if any is warranted.

Plans of Action: What Significant Others Cannot Do

In helping patients to begin to talk about their SHB, it is important for the therapist to let the family and significant others know that the patient will continue to use the behaviors as long as he/she feels the need to. This is not to condone the behavior, but rather to let others know that simply revealing them will not stop them, nor will punishment or bribery. This is also true with eating disorder behaviors, but treatment professionals and significant others usually feel more pressured and compelled to stop SHB.

Therapists will continually need to point out the similar function of affect regulation achieved by both eating disorder behaviors and SHB. They may both be present at the same time, or one set of symptoms may emerge as another fades. It may be helpful for significant others to understand how both types of symptoms result in an attack on, or control of, the body to work out psychological conflicts, obtain relief from overwhelming feelings, or manage experiences such as flashbacks or hyperarousal. In this way, the patient turns psychological problems into physical problems and thus experiences them as more concrete and therefore more "controllable."

While the goal of the therapy is to stop all destructive eating disorder symptoms and SHB, yelling, grounding, threatening, or other punishments will not control these behaviors, and therapists should help significant others to desist such activity. Remaining neutral is the best way to react to seeing a new cut or hearing someone purge. Family and friends need to know that in order for the destructive behaviors to stop, the patient

must be able to talk about the behaviors and the feelings connected to them, and figure out new ways to deal with those feelings.

It can be helpful to figure out the etiology of the behaviors, but getting stuck in the "why" can lead to lack of progress. It is a common family reaction to want to know "Why?" "Why does my daughter starve herself?" "Why would my wife get any relief by cutting?" "I just don't understand it, we never had to worry about Karen and now just when we thought she was dealing with the binging and purging, she is burning herself; we don't understand why." Uncovering and directly dealing with events, relationships, behaviors, and beliefs that developed during childhood and throughout the patient's life helps to explain how certain current attitudes and coping behaviors have come about and, in some cases, are even necessary to healing. However, it is easy to get trapped into thinking that unless we know exactly why a patient started to binge, compulsively exercise, starve, and/or burn him/herself, we cannot help him or her. This is not so. Instead, we can help patients figure out how the function currently serves them and begin to help them find new ways to meet those same needs in the present. In this way, family and friends can be of significant help.

Plans of Action: What Significant Others Can Do

Acute Responses

As discussed earlier, remaining neutral to the behaviors is recommended. For example, I advise significant others to treat a self-harm injury like they would an accidental injury (i.e., help the person dress the wound, express empathy, offer to talk about it). A gentle questioning of how the incident happened may also be helpful. I also try to establish in the therapy sessions that significant others can and should bring up these incidents in the next session. There are certain situations in which the family member or friend might need to call me or take the patient to the hospital. A discussion of these parameters is important, and guidelines should be set up in advance.

Being There

Most importantly, the significant other's main responsibility is to be present and supportive. "I see that you are having a hard time and I am here for you if you want to talk about it," is the general attitude that works best.

Jenna is a patient who did extremely well in residential treatment and in her follow-up transitional living program. Upon returning home and re-enrolling in college, she began to relapse. She did not tell her therapist that she had started restricting and alternately binging. As the behaviors progressed, she also began to use small scissors to carve patterns on her stomach as she had done prior to treatment. Next, she stopped going to therapy. Jenna's relapse resulted in her having to drop out of school and return to residential treatment. In her first week back, Jenna was asked to share in multi-family group what had happened to her success in recovery.

> Carolyn: Jenna, I think it would be helpful to share with the family members and significant others what happened to your recovery after you left the transitional living program.

> Jenna: Well, I did really well here and at the transition. I mean, it was hard, but I was doing really well. Everyone here understood my feelings. If I wanted to binge or purge, I could always talk to someone. Talking it out helped and I did not need to actually do it. When I got home, I did not want to disappoint you guys (looking at her parents). It was clear, at least it seemed to me, that you wanted me to be over this and I understand that because you had spent so much money and everything. When I got stressed out and had the urges again, I felt afraid to tell you or anyone. The further I got into it, the harder it was to tell. I kept thinking that I just had to turn it around myself.

> Carolyn: Why were you so afraid to tell? We often talked here about reaching out.

> Jenna: It's weird. I was afraid of disappointing everyone, even myself. I think maybe I thought I could do it. Like I was a failure if I still wanted to binge and purge. I kept thinking of all the money spent and I also kept thinking I could fix things.

Jenna and her parents are in a common predicament. Earlier in this same family group session, another parent had expressed how angry he would be if he found out his daughter had binged and purged once she returned home after treatment. When I discussed the typical course of illness in bulimia nervosa and the long-term nature of recovery, he asked if we were not just setting up his daughter for failure by predicting continued behaviors and "giving her an excuse to continue after treatment." In outpatient therapy, significant others often expect the eating disorder and/or SHB to stop immediately, or at least soon, because the patient is "in therapy." Educating significant others regarding the long-term nature of probable continuance of behaviors for some time is a tricky issue. Treatment professionals have to present a healthy balance between the realities of what we know about the nature of recovery and each patient's personal responsibility for getting better and not making excuses for his or her behavior.

As Jenna's case illustrates, the important point is to educate significant others that they need to be there to listen, validate, empathize, and comfort without being judgmental. This is true throughout treatment, and is particularly important after discharge from a facility when the patient needs to replace the previously readily available staff and peers. It is important for significant others to understand that just being there may be enough. No brilliant words need to be said, no interventions initiated, just being there can provide an alternative to the person who might otherwise turn to his or her disordered behaviors to cope.

Initiating Connections

In addition to preparing family and friends on how to be supportive, therapists need to teach and orchestrate their patients' reaching out to and connecting with significant others. There are many ways to do this. For example, I have patients bring in friends whom they have identified as someone they would be willing to call before they engage in a self-harm or eating disorder behavior. I make sure that the support person understands that all they need to do is be there and listen in a non-judgmental way (i.e., be empathic). I even role-play with them. I also suggest that the patient not wait until he or she "needs" to call, but rather to use the support person at random times, such as late at night, just to talk, even if he/she is not feeling the urge to act on anything. I assign this kind of calling as homework in order to provide practice and to normalize it. Often the patient complains that calling when there is no problem would be silly or, at best, not useful. I tell them that practice is an important part of learning any new skill or behavior and that it is easier to practice when the stakes are not high. Without practice, no one would learn how to drive and no team would ever win a real game. When patients are in a treatment program, I encourage and facilitate them in determining their support people as soon as possible so that when they are having a hard time, they can start reaching out to these people and not just staff.

Empathizing

A primary goal of family therapy is to teach everyone about empathic connecting. As oxygen is to the physical self, empathy is to the psychological self. When all goes well, parents provide a developing child with confirming, calming, and sustaining functions through empathy. Empathy becomes a psychological "holding" environment that silently facilitates development. Empathy enables a person to tolerate not getting certain needs met. In every parent–child relationship, just as in every patient–therapist relationship, failure to meet some needs will occur. If there is not an ongoing climate of empathy, then the "failures" will result in feelings of emptiness, loss, disappointment, and lowered self-esteem, and will become split off and/or repressed. Without empathy, the self begins to wither and to be replaced by defensive structures and behaviors to sustain them.

Through ongoing empathic psychotherapy, patients with eating disorders and SHB can usually "remember" a disturbance in empathic connecting or a "trauma," but this is not always in the sense that trauma is usually thought of. The trauma may just be the inability to integrate the intense affect around an experience. For some, the trauma is often that nothing happened when something should have happened. Thus, they experience emptiness or nothingness. Patients often say, "If I give up my eating disorder and SHB, I won't have anything; I feel empty inside; there is a big black hole in me," and, "I need to fill up the emptiness."

Without empathy, the patient has no context in which to experience his/her feelings of emptiness and is deprived of internalizing. The self loses its feeling of aliveness, cannot modulate the affective state, feels misunderstood, and is unable to borrow the parent's or the therapist's strength. This is, in part, why the therapist needs to be active and engaging in treatment in order to avoid "re-traumatizing" the patient. Patients may feel that "nothing is happening" and will avoid this repeat of the past. A familiar sentiment is that " Previous therapy was not helpful because the therapist just sat and listened, didn't say much, and there were long silent pauses."

The family therapist is continually exploring what kind of disturbance has happened and is still happening in the empathic connection between the patient and significant others. Understanding these empathic failures and how they specifically related to derailing the patient's development helps determine what needs to be done in the present and to provide what was not provided in the past. Therapists have to help significant others feel their way into the patient's reality and understand the world from her or his personal biased perspective, thus providing the necessary empathy that was not provided early on.

Therapeutic Strategies

Role Playing

I often have my patient and a family member or significant other switch roles for at least part of the session. I ask them to "be" the other person, answering from the perspective of the other person. This is a wonderful way to get people to empathize with each other. For example, if I ask a mother, who is role-playing her daughter, to tell me how the week was, she has to try to get inside her daughter's head to know how she would respond. And imagine a daughter, who is role-playing her mother, trying to figure out how to respond to the question, "How was it, knowing that your daughter was purging in the bathroom?" There are endless combinations of role plays with various significant others. The role plays can extend for any length of time. In fact, a large portion of the session can take place "in roles," with the remaining time spent processing the experience.

Letters

I use various kinds of letter writing or e-mailing when working with significant others. Letters are a way to bring people who are not there into the room. Letters also can make it easier for some people to express ideas or feelings that they have been afraid to say. With a letter, there is no way of being interrupted by the other person or stopping because of the other person's body language. A letter gives the writer full reign to say whatever he or she wishes. There is also time between sending the communication and getting a response, a built-in pause, allowing each party time to think before responding.

From Significant Others. I ask patients to tell me who are they closest to, or who is their best friend (i.e., a person they feel like they can trust). I then ask them if I can call that person and ask him or her to write me a letter describing what it is like to have a relationship with my patient. From the friend's perspective, I want to know my patient's strengths and weaknesses and how his/her behaviors get in the way of a relationship. What would the friend want my patient to know? What does the friend hope will happen in therapy? What is it like being friends with someone who has an eating disorder or harms him/herself? If the friend could wave a magic wand, what would they want to change about my patient? The friend is asked to comment about very personal and specific things relating to my patient. I explain that the letter will not be given to my patient but that it will really help me in understanding him or her.

After I get the letter, I ask the friend if I can show the letter to my patient or at least summarize the contents. Friends are sometimes wary of this, but I can usually reassure them that the information will be very important to my patient's understanding of how his/her illness affects others and ultimately helpful in healing. Some patients report that getting these letters stands out as a profoundly helpful aspect of their recovery. Sometimes, significant others write letters directly to the patient, but I find they are more honest when first asked to write just to me. I often ask family members to do this assignment as well.

To the Therapist. In some cases, I control family fighting and change family interaction patterns by having parents write to me, instead of confronting my patient, with some issue that comes up during the week. They send it to me ahead of time, bring it to the family session, or put it in a sealed envelope and give it to the patient to bring to the next session. I do this so that these parents have a way to get out their feelings and know that they will be heard and responded to while avoiding unnecessary arguing and power struggles. I have used this most with mothers who have a difficult time with empathy, are overly enmeshed, or are far too intrusive in their son's or daughter's life.

To Significant Others. I also have patients write letters to their significant others. These letters vary but include some explanation of the problem and a request for some specific kind of help. The letter might be the first time the patient has ever really told the truth and/or asked for help. Letters are an initial way to start communicating. After writing letters, patients often report finding it easier to tell the truth and ask for help in person.

Journal Assignments

There are certain journal assignments that I have patients do that are particularly useful in family sessions or in multi-family group.

How Is My Relationship with Food Like My Relationship with People? I have not tried this assignment using SHB, but comparing what people do with food and weight, and what they do with people, is an amazing and extraordinary assignment. When patients are first asked to do this, many of them stare with a blank expression on their face, but once you give them a few examples, they catch on and generate significant information and realizations. Encourage as many examples as they can provide. I give the following examples to help them get started:

> A girl with anorexia nervosa says that she always has to inspect and scrutinize every food she eats before letting it into her body and she has to do the same to any person, too, before letting them in.
>
> A woman with binge eating disorder says that she binges on food and on people. She feels that if she likes something or someone, she can never get enough of them and even panics about not getting enough.
>
> A young man with bulimia nervosa says that he does not trust food and he does not trust people. He wants certain food but then feels afraid of what it will do to him so he has to get rid of it. He does the same with his relationships.

Through this assignment, patients begin to see how their eating disorder behaviors are symbolic representations of themselves in relationships. Having patients read this assignment in family session or family group also gives significant others further insight into the behavior and indicators for change. Interventions made in the patient's relationship to food will help lead to changes in how they relate to people, and conversely, when the patient works on and improves his/her relationships with people, then the relationship with food also improves. It is useful to do this same assignment a few times during the course of therapy to see how things are changing.

One of My Worst Days. Very early in treatment, I will ask a patient to write out in detail one of the worst days he/she can remember in terms of eating and SHB. I find that patients often forget how bad it was once they start to get better. As soon as a little abstinence is achieved, many patients take a flight into health and recovery, and minimize how bad their problem is. This can be intensified for patients in treatment programs who are not exposed to the outside stressors and who have meals made for them in controlled portions at structured times throughout the day. It is also particularly true for patients with bulimia nervosa, who often feel, after a period of abstinence, that they will never return to the behavior again and feel ready to conquer the world. I use the "worst day" assignment at the beginning of treatment to get them to be graphic and specific about all of their obsessive, compulsive, and destructive thoughts and behaviors. I want them to personalize their behaviors in detail rather than have the more distant experience of just stating, for example, that they "binged and purged several times a day" or "cut somewhere." I have them re-read this assignment when they are feeling overly confident. I also find it useful to have patients read this to their significant others. Too often, significant others, even close family members, do not have any idea about the extent of the thoughts and behaviors that make up and rule the patient's life. This is a good way to let them in. The therapist needs to make sure he or she has the trust of the patient and can deal with the reactions of significant others.

Agreement to Self. A necessary part of treatment and healing is the patient making internal agreements with him/herself rather than stopping the behavior because of some external structure or control. It is the patient's internal agreements and true commitments to self that will be lasting and successful. Therefore, it is important for clinicians to look for ways to reinforce the patient in coming to terms with the internal agreements that he/she wants to and can make. This process can and should be done in many ways during the course of therapy. One example is to have the patient write up an agreement with him/herself that is like a vow for the future. This idea was taken from a book called *Nourishing Wisdom* (David, 1994), and is an adaptation from what was called an "Eater's Agreement." The agreement can be written whenever the patient feels ready. I have found it particularly powerful when done upon discharge from treatment, whether in an outpatient or inpatient setting. The agreement is read out loud to the therapist, staff, peers, and/or significant others just as marriage vows are read and recited at a wedding. Note the following example of one patient's agreement to herself.

Cutter's Agreement

To give up the knife, my attachment to it, and to lay it to rest, I must first acknowledge it for what it has provided in my life. The purpose it served, this seemingly trusty companion and savior of mine. I must honor the purpose it has served.

In the deepest and darkest moments and expressions of my disease and my battle with being in life, the knife has been my release, my relief, my comfort. It has always been there ready to give me a graphic expression of the pain, the real pain, I could not name. It has been the disciplinarian who could rein me in, absolve me, and keep me sane. It has been there for me in the darkest and most frightening hours of the night, the one thing I trusted, could depend on. It became my friend, my sentry, my guide. It wore the mask of comfort, release, absolution, and soothing—protecting me from the real hurt. It kept me cut off from my inner pain and my fear of the world around me. Indeed my knife became a way to prove to myself that I was worthy and strong and able to tolerate all levels of punishment and pain.

But now, with the encouragement and support of those around me whom I trust and who love and respect me, my soul, I recognize and acknowledge that the purpose my knife served is now bankrupt. Its usefulness in my life is expired—extinguished. While once it provided something, it can no longer. Because now I have new tools, a way to name the pain, places to go to sort it out. Now I will take my courage and express it not with a knife in hand, but heart in hand.

If I look from my soul, I see that the knife severed my connection to myself, to life, and to love. It robs me of being with what I'm feeling, and I know now that I deserve to experience the full range of my emotions. The knife turns my anger inwards, when perhaps that anger needs to be communicated and let go. It distracts me, keeps me in the dark, doesn't allow me to get to the heart of the matter to what I'm really needing in those fearful and painful moments. It keeps me deprived, refuses to honor me, who I am. It was a slow death. In not cutting myself anymore I step into letting love, or the warmth of someone's arms, bring me comfort. In the absence of the knife, I will learn to give myself permission to need, to want, to desire, to ask, to receive. In forsaking my knife, I admit once and for all that I am lovable and worthy.

Starting today, I take compassion upon myself and promise to listen to my soul's cries. I promise to try and determine what I'm really needing and seek that out in the appropriate place—be that solitude, with another, or in the expression of my emotions. That means I can be angry, sad, lonely, and honest all without the threat of punishment, penance, or guilt.

Cutting myself will not remove fear, anxiety, anger, sadness, depression, loneliness, desperation, confusion, or self-loathing. It will only deepen these things. Cutting is a slow death, and I choose life and forsake the knife. I choose all expression and experience of life. I am not alone. All of these things are an expression of me, and I can respond to them in a way that supports and nurtures me, comforts me. I deserve that. Pain and torture no longer need to absolve me or be my confirmation. I no longer need to prove my tolerance for pain, embrace pain, or seek it out. Now my life, the care of my soul, is entrusted to care for the part of me that is in pain, rather than turn to more pain for distraction.

I promise to recognize urges to cut as a sign that I am already hurting, in pain, and in need of something or someone. I know I can summon the courage in these moments to identify the need and act on that. I can find my voice, listen, and in doing so, let the hands that once punished me, comfort me. And this is where my healing begins.

Conclusion

When working with families and significant others, the multidimensional tasks of the therapist are extensive. The therapist must correct any dysfunctions occurring in the various relationships, for this may be where the underlying causal issues have partly developed or at least are sustained. Family and significant others need to be educated about eating disorder and self-harm symptoms, and particularly the patient's unique embodiment of them. Significant others need help in learning how to respond appropriately to the various situations they will encounter and what they might do that either sabotages the patient's progress or supports it. Serious conflicts between family members must be addressed. Parents may need to learn how to solve conflicts between themselves and how to nurture each other, which will then enable them to better nurture their child. Other problems may include faulty organizational structure in the family, miscommunication about expectations, and psychiatric difficulties among family members, all of which must be pointed out and corrected. The task of dealing with family members and significant others is so complex and at times overwhelming that therapists often shy away from it, preferring to work solely with individual patients. This is a great loss. I believe that working with the significant people in our patient's lives, as well as helping them to establish other new healthy connections, is imperative and that most therapists and treatment programs, because of time constraints, financial reasons, lack of training, or just lack of comfort with the idea, do not do enough of it.

References

Aronson, J. (2000). *Self injury.* Northvale, New Jersey: Jason Aronson, Inc.

Brisman, J., Siegel, M., & Weinshel, M. (1997). *Surviving an eating disorder.* New York: Harper Collins.

Costin, C. (1996). *The eating disorder sourcebook.* Los Angeles: Lowell House.

David, M. (1994). *Nourishing wisdom: A mind/body approach to nutrition and well being.* New York: Crown Publishing Group.

Levenkron, S. (1999). *Cutting.* New York: W. W. Norton & Company.

Miller, D. (1994). *Women who hurt themselves.* New York: Basic Books.

CHAPTER 15

A Self-Regulatory Approach to the Treatment of Eating Disorders and Self-Injury

JOHN L. LEVITT

Introduction

The eating disorders (ED), Anorexia and Bulimia Nervosa, Binge Eating Disorder, and Eating Disorder Not Otherwise Specified (NOS), represent complex, multidetermined symptom constellations (Brownell & Fairburn, 1995; Garner & Garfinkel, 1997; Hsu, 1990). These disorders are often accompanied by a number of psychological problems (e.g., Edelstein & Yager, 1992; Strober & Katz, 1988), medial complications (Mehler & Andersen, 1999; Mitchell, Pomeroy, & Adson, 1997; Powers, 1997), impulse and substance abuse problems (Johnson & Connors, 1987; Mitchell, Pyle, Specker, & Hanson, 1992), personality disorders (Swift & Wonderlich, 1982; Wonderlich & Mitchell, 1992), and sexual abuse (Schwartz & Cohn, 1996; Vanderlinden & Vandereycken, 1997). In addition, while ED symptoms are most often found in adolescent and adult women, recent research indicates an increased prevalence of such symptoms in children and adolescents (Lask & Brayant-Waugh, 2000) as well as in males (Andersen, Cohn, & Holbrook, 2000).

While there is little available information about the interrelationship between ED and self-injury in either the ED or the self-injury literature (Levitt & Sansone, 2002), the frequency of concomitant self-injury in patients with ED is receiving increased attention (Levitt & Sansone, 2002;

Levenkron, 1998). Indeed, clinicians often note that self-harm behavior (SHB) and ED symptoms co-occur in some individuals who present for treatment (Wonderlich, Myers, Norton, & Crosby, 2002), and current studies indicate that the general prevalence of self-injury among outpatients with anorexia or bulimia, and among inpatients with bulimia, is approximately 25% (Levitt & Sansone, 2002; Sansone & Levitt, 2002). Some authors suggest that the percentage of self-injurers who "cut" may be similar to those who have anorexia nervosa (Levenkron, 1998, pp. 19–20). In addition, the self-injury literature indicates that the SHB rate may be as high as 35% in anorexia nervosa, 25% in bulimic nervosa, and 40% in individuals with bulimia who use laxatives (Favazza, 1987, p. 204). Favazza suggests that up to 50% of patients who self-mutilate present with a history of anorexia or bulimia nervosa (p. 206), Conterio and Lader (1998) report that 61% of surveyed subjects who self-injure confirmed either current ED symptomotology or a past history of an ED (p. 60), and other authors (e.g., Conterio & Lader, 1998; Walsh & Rosen, 1988) report a relatively high rate of comorbidity between ED and SHB.

Clinical experience appears to mirror the empirical data. For example, Levitt and Sansone (2002) randomly surveyed a group of patients with ED who were attending a partial hospital program and determined that the sample endorsed a significant number of items on the Self-Harm Inventory (SHI; Sansone, Wiederman, & Sansone, 1998); the majority of these patients (8 out of 13) presented with concomitant self-harm symptoms.

Part of the difficulty in identifying the prevalence of SHB in patients with ED is the lack of assessment tools that are suitable for examining *both* ED and SHB (Sansone & Sansone, 2002). Indeed, there are no individual assessment tools that concurrently assess for both ED and SHB pathology (Sansone & Sansone, 2002, p. 1930).

While there are numerous approaches to ED treatment (Garner & Needleman, 1997), there are few that simultaneously address SHB. For example, the literature on the treatment of individuals with ED indicates the efficacy of several treatment approaches including cognitive-behavioral therapy (Fairburn, 1997; Garner, Vitousek, & Pike, 1997; Johnson & Connors, 1987), psycho-educational and nutritional approaches (Beaumont & Touyz, 1995; Garner, 1997; Weiss, Katzman, & Wolchik, 1985), family therapy (Minuchin, Rosman, & Baker, 1978; Honig, 2000), and interpersonal psychotherapy (Fairburn, 1997). While most authors emphasize that treatment approaches should be tailored and sequentially implemented on an individual basis (Andersen, 1985; Garner & Needleman, 1997), the ED literature is relatively unclear as to how one might undertake this among individuals with ED and with SHB (Levitt

& Sansone, 2002; Wonderlich et al., 2002). Even the popular handbooks for ED treatment do not adequately address this dilemma (e.g., Garner & Garfinkel, 1997), and, when addressed, most intervention approaches for these individuals are extrapolated from the literature on borderline personality disorder (Linehan, 1993; Wonderlich et al., 2002).

As a rare exception in the ED literature, Vanderlinden and Vandereycken (1997) describe SHB as sequelae of traumatic life events in the histories of patients with ED. These authors present an excellent overview of trauma and impulse dyscontrol, which subsequently lead to self-injury. In addition, they make specific suggestions regarding the management of self-injurious behaviors (pp. 87–89). However, their approach is focused on the *sequelae* of traumatic life histories in patients with ED—rather than presenting a general integrated approach to treating ED and SHB.

The Concept of Self-Regulation

What is self-regulation? Carver and Scheier (1998) view self-regulation as a way of understanding how behavior happens, or the processes that underlie behavior. Behavior is a "consequence of an internal guidance system [which is] inherent in the way that living beings are organized. The guidance system regulates a quality of experience that's important to it … we refer to the guidance process as … *self-regulation*" (p. 2). Baumeister, Heatherton, and Tice (1994) refer to self-regulation as "…any effort by a human being to alter its own responses" (p. 7).

Different perspectives of self-regulation have been discussed in the literature, including self-regulated learning, self-control, and self-management (Boekaerts, Pintrich, & Zeider, 2000; Carver & Scheier, 1998). While some look at self-regulation from the perspective of self-control (Baumeister et al., 1994), others view self-regulation in the context of emotion or affect. Siegel (1999), for example, views emotion as playing a central role in self-regulation, and Yates (1991) focuses on self-regulation of affect as central to ED.

While the self-regulation literature discusses eating (Baumeister et al., 1994) and addictive behaviors (Endler & Kocovski, 2000), the ED literature rarely discusses the role of self-regulation except as it pertains to affect (e.g., Kinoy, 1994; Yates, 1991). Similarly, self-regulation is rarely discussed in the self-harm or self-injury literature except perhaps as it pertains to affect (Simeon & Hollander, 2001). Self-regulation as a treatment approach is not evident in either the ED or self-harm literature.

In this chapter, an approach to the treatment of the self-injuring patient with ED is presented that is fundamentally based upon the concept of self-regulation—the Self-Regulatory Approach (SRA). The SRA is intended to offer a model, or framework, for delivering treatment to this comorbid population. It is not, however, intended to limit the choice of interventions but to function as an *additional* approach for clinicians who may utilize a variety of clinical and theoretical perspectives.

The SRA to the Treatment of ED and Self-Injury

Because patients with comorbid ED/SHB may be quite common, the SRA was designed to provide a treatment framework for these complex individuals and has been presented previously (Levitt, 2000a, 2000b). The following represents an overview of the general or "key" elements of the approach.

Self-Regulation

Initially, we broadly describe for the patient the concept of self-regulation and self-regulatory functions. We emphasize that individuals are constantly regulating their "self." From the SRA perspective, self-regulation essentially refers to one's ability to maintain a steady or constant behavioral, affective, or perceptual (i.e., psychological) state despite ongoing environmental demands. From the SRA perspective, ED and self-injury behaviors tend to create for the patient the subjective experience of psychological steadiness (e.g., safety, efficacy, well-being) or constancy. These behaviors, "elected" by the patient, may be characterized by the degree to which they are repeated and relied upon (i.e., the extent to which they are utilized over time). Indeed, in severe cases, both ED and SHB exhibit a general "resistance to extinction" (Conterio & Lader, 1998; Hsu, 1990).

Role or Function of the Symptoms

From the SRA perspective, ED and self-harm symptoms serve to protect the individual. They may help to manage strong affects, enable being alone, calm or soothe oneself, and/or prevent being overcome by guilt and shame. Keep in mind that self-regulatory functions serve as a backdrop for other self processes, including the development of standards for self-approval (i.e., being able to know when something is accomplished and derive satisfaction from it), patterns of attributions (i.e., connections between events, behaviors, and outcomes), approaches for experiencing "control," and intrinsic internal reward systems. Intact self-regulation enables one to organize a flow of information and give it meaning and self-relevance, and to develop (a) a belief system about oneself in relation to others, (b) the awareness and skill in predicting the effects one's behavior has on the environment, (c) the skill to manage psychological space (i.e., boundaries) and interpersonal safety, (d) a relationship to one's physical body, and (e) the skill to maintain activities of daily living.

The SRA views ED and SHB as functional equivalents whose purpose may include indirectly expressing feelings (e.g., anger) or needs, distraction, relief of tension, self-soothing, stimulation, analgesia, control, "purging," and so forth (Brownell & Foreyt, 1986; Conterio & Lader, 1998; Johnson & Connors, 1987). From this perspective, the symptoms tend to provide a sense of reliable "control" or constancy over time and situations, and through constant application, serve to regulate the patient. While ED and SHB symptoms may serve relatively similar functions, the role a particular symptom plays in an individual patient is unique and must be determined.

Patients with ED temporally utilize their comorbid ED and/or SHB in various ways. Many self-harm concomitantly with their ED symptoms. Others may begin to utilize SHB when ED symptoms start to remit. Patients may also alternate the use of symptoms. Again, from the perspective of the SRA, patients utilize either or both symptoms for similar reasons.

The Therapeutic Relationship

As in any intervention, the therapeutic relationship is a critical element of treatment. *How* one relates to the patient in the SRA is considered as important as what intervention one employs in the treatment. The primary focus of the relationship in the SRA is to consistently guide the patient so that he/she experiences a sense of empowerment. It is considered crucial that the patient experiences a sense of mastery, competency, hopefulness, control, and empowerment through the interaction with him/herself, situations, and the therapist. In order to consistently accomplish the goal of patient empowerment, the concept of *position* is incorporated into the treatment and practiced by both the patient and the therapist.

Position

Position is a central and vital concept in the SRA. Position refers to whether the patient is interacting as a "victim" (i.e., things happen *to* the patient, the patient is unable to address the particular challenge) or a "survivor" (i.e., the patient is responsible for his/her actions, the patient is able to face the challenge). Position focuses on the process of who is in charge of patient's choices and responses. This concept guides how the therapist interacts with the patient and provides information as to how the patient is interacting with a given situation or individual. For example, in general interactions, the therapist observes and regularly provides feedback to the patient regarding what position is being taken. In addition, the therapist regularly attends to the position that he/she is taking with the patient in any particular interaction.

Position is considered critical to promote a sense of self-regulation. From the perspective of the SRA, if the therapist takes a one-down position (i.e., passive, non-directive), the effect is to encourage and empower the patient to manage his/her own interactions and choices—to self-regulate (a "survivor position"). That is, when the therapist defers to the patient on a consistent basis, it communicates (i.e., empowers) to the patient a need to act and be involved, and it repeatedly supports the view that the patient is and can be capable and able to manage him/herself. If the therapist takes a one-up position (i.e., overly directive, controlling), this suggests that the therapist is regulating the patient and consequently encouraging dependency and reinforcing a sense of powerlessness (e.g., a "victim position").

The concept of position is taught to the patient and is used to evaluate the nature of interactions with others, noting opportunities for changing position and potentially creating a different type of interactional outcome. Position is flexible and under the patient's general control. The following example illustrates how the therapist explores with the patient what position he/she is taking in any particular interaction in order for the patient to learn how to make different future choices. A 14-year-old patient with bulimia reports to her therapist that whenever her mother begins to nag her about her eating, she gets so angry that she wants to cut herself. Using the SRA, the therapist's initial response in this situation would be to ask the patient, "What position are you taking with your mother around your eating?" The therapist would then explore options for altering the position in this interaction (i.e., shifting from a one-down type position where she is feeling dominated or intruded upon by the mother to a one-up type position where she can recognize the pattern, see alternatives, and be successful without cutting). While this response is certainly not atypical for many therapists, in the SRA, the therapist's priorities are to consistently empower the patient to *make* an active decision for himself/herself rather than to simply react. *Choice* of "position" is almost always the patient's to make in this and any other situation—including the way one interfaces with oneself.

Responsibilities

There are a number of responsibilities in the SRA. Some belong to the therapist and some to the patient. These are clearly defined and spelled out at the beginning of treatment. Clarification is very important and, in the SRA, is considered essential for a successful outcome. That is, the therapist clearly articulates and discusses responsibilities with the patient so that the patient can make a decision if this approach to treatment is appropriate for him/her.

One of the initial responsibilities of the therapist is to assist the patient in clarifying why he/she is in treatment and what the goals actually are. In the SRA, abstinence of the ED or SHB symptoms may, or may not, be the goal. The therapist asks the patient if he/she is willing to recover (e.g., become abstinent) or wanting to learn to live with the behaviors more effectively. While many therapists believe that recovery must be the goal, many patients are ambivalent about giving up symptoms. Indeed, if they have had the behaviors for an extensive period of time or are mandated by others to come to treatment, recovery may prove to be an elusive goal. In the SRA, it is essential that the therapist be completely honest about the need for direction with the patient's symptoms. That is, the patient must either decide to lead life as a symptomatically chronic individual or one who is able to make a choice about whether or not to rely on the ED/SHB. If the patient chooses to remain chronic (for the time being), other goals must be agreed upon. The patient has to be aware that the ED/SHB cannot interfere from pursuing these goals and the therapist has to agree that he/she is willing to assist the patient with these goals. If the patient chooses to be able to make a choice about his/her symptoms, then the ED/SHB are consistently going to be a focus for clinical discussion. The emphasis, here, is that the patient and the therapist clarify the therapeutic goal at the outset and establish a contract.

The second broad responsibility of the therapist is to teach to the patient the Structural-Process Model (SPM) of Self-Regulation. The SPM consists of three elements that are used by *both* the patient and therapist for organizing the treatment and monitoring the patient's self-regulation. These skills and processes are designed to be practiced in the office as well as at home. For the therapist, the SPM provides a guide for introducing therapeutic content, and focusing, timing, and pacing interventions. For the patient, the SPM provides a general approach for learning about oneself, identifying areas of difficulty, and focusing attention during recovery (i.e., being a "student of oneself" rather than a "sick" individual). In this way, the patient views therapy as a learning process. In the SRA, it is important for the patient to approach treatment from an empowered student position rather than as a defective person. Figure 15.1 and Table 15.1 provide a model and summary of the skills areas of the SPM.

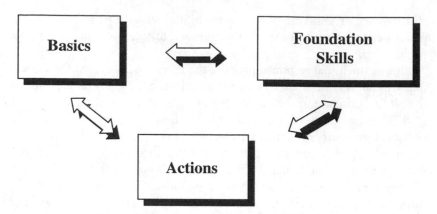

Fig. 15.1 The Structural-Process Model for Eating Disorders and Self-Harm Behavior

TABLE 15.1 Summary of Skill Areas of the Structural-Process Model

Basics

Safety: an internal and cognitive awareness of the elements of protecting oneself from psychological or behavioral self-injury, risk, or loss

Security: the skill to identify high-risk, potentially harmful external relationships or situations

Physical Well-Being: the ability to recognize and care for one's daily physiological and basic living needs

Framework for Recovery: an understanding and ability to articulate what recovery would look like for that individual as well as the elements of "how" one might recover

Foundation Skills

Communication: the ability to self-observe and be aware of "personal" cognitive, emotional, and behavioral information

Cooperation: being able to use personal information consistently within the context of one's framework for recovery

Connectedness: the observable ability to remain connected to the therapist and the therapeutic goals

Collaboration: the ability to utilize all of the above Foundation Skills with the therapist and significant others for effective recovery

Honesty: remaining open, and able and willing, to disclosing both overt and covert information that is relevant and essential for recovery

Actions

Focus: the ability to stay on-task with an identified therapeutic objective

Determination: the ability to stay focused over time

Direction: the ability to stay on task over time to achieve targeted goals

Commitment: the ability to maintain a psychological and emotional desire and obligation to the above Action elements

The "Basics" of SPM

For the patient, the Basics are *safety, security,* and *physical well-being.* When a patient is learning or applying the Basics, he/she must be able to develop and implement relatively safe thoughts and behaviors toward him/herself, engage in relatively secure interactions with other people and situations, and be able to demonstrate appropriate homeostasis with regard to well-being (e.g., nutrition, sleep, hygiene, exercise, socialization, rest and relaxation, adherence to medical regimens, avoidance of destructive drugs). The Basics refers to those elements and situations necessary for efficacious treatment and are monitored by both the patient and the therapist.

For the therapist, the Basics include introducing the patient to the therapy process. For example, it is essential for both therapist and patient to understand and agree upon how one improves or changes as a result of treatment and what that would look like if it were successful. In this case, it is equally important that the patient understands, and agrees, what the framework is for treatment.

Foundation Skills in SPM

Foundation skills generally refer to one's ability to monitor and utilize personal information for oneself. Thoughts, feelings, and relationship interactions are the predominant foci. Elements include communication with oneself and others, utilizing information effectively for oneself, remaining involved in treatment, working with others toward being successful, and being honest. Foundation Skills translate the Basics into therapeutic action.

Actions

Actions are those skills and processes that assist the patient in learning about attentional elements. These include the ability to stay on-task, over time, with purpose and conviction, and are the general elements necessary for goal accomplishment. They are a means to monitor motivation and represent areas that tell clinicians if motivation is on course or perhaps slipping. The ability to stay on-task is essential for any type of effective goal attainment and the ebbs and flows of recovery are hallmarks for both ED and self-harm symptoms (e.g., Miller 1994; Vanderlinden & Vandereycken, 1997).

Integrating Other Treatments

After the patient is more physiologically stable and oriented toward treatment through this structure, the more conventional therapeutic approaches may be integrated (e.g., cognitive-behavioral techniques). The therapist teaches a variety of skills (e.g., problem solving) that the patient practices in an effort to manage without the ED/SHB. The patient may practice these skills with the therapist as well as do homework assignments. Most importantly, the therapist is regularly giving the patient feedback as to the position he/she is taking in situations as well as between them. The patient is regularly encouraged to evaluate the data.

Case Examples

As SPM is utilized, the therapist and patient develop a common language, agreeing on targeting problems and focusing on the patient's concerns that are practical and accessible. Both the patient and the therapist monitor the areas of the SPM (i.e., the areas of the SPM are continually in the background as therapy progresses). At the beginning of therapy, the Basics are emphasized and the Actions and Foundation Skills are monitored. If the Actions (e.g., focus) are affected while focusing on the Basics, the therapy is redirected to examining motivational areas and skills (i.e., the ability to stay on-task). As therapy shifts to understanding thoughts and feelings and developing a repertoire of necessary behaviors, the Basics and the Actions are monitored. If the Basics and Actions are then affected, attention is then redirected to those areas. For example, after the patient's Basics are somewhat stabilized and consistent, the therapist and patient may begin working on an issue about the patient's relationship with his/her mother. As the therapy progresses, the therapist notes that the patient is beginning to demonstrate an increase in SHB, is not sleeping as well, and is having trouble focusing when at home. By noting a change in the Basics and Actions, the therapist might suggest that the patient is pushing too hard in those areas and may need to focus on the Basics for a short time and then get back to reexamining his/her relationship with mother. After this is improved, the therapist might suggest to the patient, as they delve into the relationship with mother, that they might want to go a bit slower. In addition, the therapist might encourage the patient to monitor for changes and recognize for him/herself, using the above data, when issues are moving too quickly. In this way, the therapy might be able to hold on course, a relapse might be minimized, and the patient might improve his/her self-monitoring skills.

It is important to note that any element of any self-regulatory area (i.e., Basics, Foundations Skills, Actions) needs to be evaluated and taught if the patient cannot access it. Indeed, some patients may not even have a concept of safety either cognitively or sensorily, so that talking about it may be a foreign concept. (We have experienced this frequently in patients who were abused as young children.) The patient may need to explore the concept and learn about, and even develop a sensory awareness of, safeness through successive approximation of the experience. It is also important to focus on teaching the patient to recognize and utilize this information.

The following case examples illustrate some practical application of the SPA and the SPM. These examples are only brief portions of patient sessions; the application of the approach is, of course, quite a bit more complex than can be demonstrated here.

Case Example 1

Betty is a 42-year-old, divorced woman who initially presented for treatment with anorexia nervosa and cutting. She reported a history of sexual abuse from a brother during childhood and from her ex-husband. Betty was taught the SPM, and after relatively intensive treatment was able to reach a healthy weight. However, she continued to cut herself at various times. In this interaction, she had begun dating again and was having a difficult time understanding the man's behaviors and her reactions.

B: I don't understand it. I just feel fat and I really want to cut myself.

T: Do you have any idea what's going on?

B: I was seeing this guy and we were fooling around and I really liked it and when I got home, I felt like hurting myself. Do you think I am fat?

T: You notice that your desire to lose weight and to cut increased after the interactions with that guy. Do you see any connections?

B: Well, it must be because I fooled around. I broke my rules not to fool around for at least 6 months, so I have to punish myself.

T: You might be correct that it is related to fooling around, but was there anything else you can think of? How about how the fooling around went?

B: What do you mean? I had a lot of fun.

T: Well, you say you had a lot of fun but now you need to be punished because you broke the rules. It's interesting that not only do you want to cut, but that you feel fat. Did you notice anything else?

B: I noticed that when I told him I didn't want to do something, he said I really did and went ahead anyway. But I really liked it.

T: What kind of position were you taking at that moment?

B: Position?

T: Being a student of yourself, what kind of position in that interaction were you taking?

B: I guess I was letting him make the decision for me. And, you know what—he didn't listen to me, did he?

T: What's your perspective? Look at how feeling fat and wanting to cut yourself have increased. Notice any connection?

B: I guess so. You mean that when I let someone make my decisions for me, I feel fat and want to hurt myself?

T: That's one explanation, but there may be others. Why don't you look at your data and let me know what you think might have happened. Maybe you'll be able to develop a different way of looking at things in the future.

Case Example 2

Samantha (Sam) is a 16-year-old high school student who has been bulimic for 3 years. She was brought to treatment by her mother, who noticed blood on the bathroom floor and found out that Sam had been cutting herself and scalding herself with hot water for over a year. Her mother was primarily concerned about the SHB and less about the bulimia because Sam's laboratory tests were normal. Sam appeared healthy and was a successful cheerleader. This brief vignette represents a period right after the introduction of treatment.

T: How are you doing, Sam?

S: Pretty good.

T: How's your eating?

S: My mom says that's not my problem. She just wants me to stop hurting myself.

T: That's pretty hard to just go do—what do you think?

S: I'll never get over this—it's just too hard and no one cares anyway!

T: Well, I don't read the future but I wonder ... have you ever learned something new? You know, something difficult that you never thought you would get?

S: Yeah, but this isn't the same.

T: Wait a minute, try to answer my questions first and then if you choose that you don't want to talk about this stuff, you can stop if you want. O.K.?

S: I'll see....

T: Have you ever learned something new?

S: Yeah.

T: Was it hard?

S: Yeah.

T: Did you ever get it at all?

S: I learned to be a cheerleader.

T: I hear you're pretty good.

S: I made the team.

T: I think that's pretty cool. But, if you can learn to do that, don't you imagine that you could learn to manage life without puking and hurting yourself?

S: I don't see how.

T: Is it possible?

S: I guess.

T: You know you're the expert on yourself, not me. If you are able to learn something new, I would imagine that you could also learn a new way to handle things. If you are open to it, I could teach you some skills that other patients have told me that they have found really effective for being able to take care of themselves differently. We would begin with learning the Basics, so that you would have a choice of what to do when you feel really bad and want to throw up or self-injure. But you need to tell me if you want to learn these things. You know, your mom may pay for your treatment but, in here, you're in charge and you get to choose.

S: But my mom will be mad if I don't do this.

T: Yep, maybe. But the choice is still yours. It is not your mother's choice whether you vomit or cut, it's yours. I would think that you would like to make that choice yourself.

S: I would.

Case Example 3

Amanda is a 19-year-old sophomore who is anorexic and cuts herself. When she came to treatment, she was unable to focus on school, feeling overwhelmed with her social life and spending inordinate amounts of time with her eating disorder and SHB. She has been in a treatment program and learned the SPM. Her weight, while low, has improved and she has been able to go without cutting for a month. She has just returned to school.

A: School sucks!

T: What's up?

A: I've only been back for two weeks and I already cut myself once and am having trouble eating.

T: Did you expect to be perfect? I think that maybe you're doing O.K. to start. I do think you need to focus on the Basics at this point.

A: What do you mean? Before I left the treatment program, everyone said I needed to get out more and look what that has done! Maybe I'm not cut out for school!

T: If you don't want to go to school right now, I guess that's an O.K. decision, but I'm wondering what happened that got you off focus. You certainly don't have to be perfect, but I am concerned that you seem to have stopped looking at how you manage yourself.

A: Maybe you're right.

T: What's that mean?

A: When I got back to school, everyone was looking at me and a bunch of people told me how good I looked.

T: And....

A: I heard fat. I heard they were telling me that I got fat and I got so angry with myself. How could I have let that happen? I'm such a loser. I got so mad that I was going to explode if I didn't do something. So I cut myself.

T: What do you think happened?

A: I just told you. I got fat and I hurt myself, but not as bad as before.

T: You know what I mean. Be a student of yourself. What really happened? We've talked about this before—many times. Look at your data.

A: I guess when I got back to school and got all that attention, the eating disorder stuff kicked in—I was triggered. I stopped doing the Basics. It's just that right then, I hated myself so much! I had to do something, I had to hurt myself.

T: I understand that was how you felt then. And, in general, I still think you're doing pretty good. Recovery is hard and I would expect some challenges. You were still restricting when you left the treatment program. I think you were still at the beginning of treatment, not the end. Let's look at this some more, shall we?

A: O.K.

T: What position were you taking?

A: I was acting like a victim.

T: Of?

A: Of the situation and my eating disorder.

T: And when you notice that you may be taking a one down, or victim position, what are some things you have found useful to focus on?

A: The Basics?

T: That's right! You have learned. Even when we know something, it doesn't mean we will use it perfectly—does it?

A: I suppose not.

T: So, since we're still learning, what have you learned today?

A: That I have to pay attention to my position and practice the Basics.

T: You see, you really *can* be a student of yourself.

Conclusion

In this chapter, the SRA for treating ED and self-harm symptoms has been reviewed. In the SRA, these symptoms are functionally similar and often appear together in some fashion. Patient presentations are, of course, quite varied, and each person and their symptoms must be evaluated individually. The SRA is useful for organizing treatment for these individuals. It emphasizes teaching and learning, moving away from pathology to learning, focusing on interactions, and empowering the patient as the expert of himself/herself. It does not limit the choice of therapeutic technique. It does require a consistent focus on the elements of self-regulation. We have found that for most patients, power struggles in treatment are kept to a minimum, patients tend to feel better about themselves (i.e., improved self-concept), and overall functioning is enhanced. The SRA is probably more suited to therapists who are action-oriented in treatment, are able to be more directive, and who are able to tolerate a sizeable amount of intensity in the patient's symptom presentation. The SRA therapist asks "directive questions;" that is, questions that guide. The SRA requires the therapist to participate, guide, and support the patient's exploration, learning, and decision-making processes. This is not always easy and the patient may make therapeutically unpopular decisions, including continuing to self-harm for extensive periods of time or terminating treatment when he/she is not doing well. It is essential for the therapist to remain in treatment with the patient even if they are not getting better. In this case, the therapist guides the patient to see if she may need alternative or even no treatment. The decision belongs to the patient.

References

Andersen, A. E. (1985). *Practical comprehensive treatment of anorexia nervosa and bulimia.* Baltimore: Johns Hopkins University Press.

Andersen, A. E., Cohn, L., & Holbrook, T. (2000). *Making weight: Men's conflicts with food, weight, shape, & appearance.* Carlsbad, CA: Gurze Books.

Baumeister, R. F., Heatherton, T. F., & Tice, D. M. (1994). *Losing control: How and why people fail at self-regulation.* New York: Academic Press.

Beaumont, P. J. V., & Touyz, S. W. (1995). The nutritional management of anorexia and bulimia nervosa. In K. D. Brownell & C. G. Fairburn (Eds.), *Eating disorders and obesity: A comprehensive handbook* (pp. 306–312). New York: Guilford Press.

Boekaerts, M., Pintrich, P. R., & Zeidner, M. (Eds.) (2000). *Handbook of self-regulation.* New York: Academic Press.

Boekaerts, M., Pintrich, P. R., & Zeider, M. (2000). Self-regulation: An introductory overview. In M. Boekaerts, P. R. Pintrich, & M. Zeidner (Eds.), *Handbook of self-regulation* (pp. 1–9). New York: Academic Press.

Brownell, K. D., & Fairburn, C. G. (Eds.) (1995). *Eating disorders and obesity: A comprehensive handbook.* New York: Guilford Press.

Brownell, K. D., & Foreyt, J. P. (Eds.) (1986). *Handbook of eating disorders: Physiology, psychology, and treatment of obesity, anorexia, and bulimia.* New York: Basic Books.

Carver, C. S., & Scheier, M. F. (1998). *On the self-regulation of behavior.* New York: Cambridge University Press.

Conterio, K., & Lader, W. (1998). *Bodily harm.* New York: Hyperion.

Edelstein, C. K., & Yager, J. (1992). Eating disorders and affective disorders. In J. Yager, H. E. Swordsman, & C. K. Edelstein (Eds.), *Special problems in managing eating disorders* (pp. 15–50). Washington, DC: American Psychiatric Press.

Endler, N. S., & Kocovski, N. L. (2000). Self-regulation distress in clinical psychology. In M. Boekaerts, P. R. Pintrich, & M. Zeidner (Eds.), *Handbook of self-regulation* (pp. 1–9). New York: Academic Press.

Fairburn, C. G. (1997). Interpersonal psychotherapy for bulimia nervosa. In D. M. Garner & P. E. Garfinkel (Eds.), *Handbook of treatment for eating disorders* (2nd ed.) (pp. 278–294). New York: Guilford Press.

Favazza, A. R. (1987). *Bodies under siege: Self-mutilation in culture and psychiatry.* Baltimore: Johns Hopkins University Press.

Garner, D. M. (1997). Psychoeducational principles in treatment. In D. M. Garner & P. E. Garfinkel (Eds.), *Handbook of treatment for eating disorders* (2nd ed.) (pp. 145–177). New York: Guilford Press.

Garner, D. M. & Garfinkel, P. E. (Eds.) (1997). *Handbook of treatment for eating disorders* (2nd ed.). New York: Guilford Press.

Garner, D. M., & Needleman, L. D. (1997). Sequencing and integration of treatments. In D. M. Garner & P. E. Garfinkel (Eds.), *Handbook of treatment for eating disorders* (2nd ed.) (pp. 50–63). New York: Guilford Press.

Garner, D. M., Vitousek, K. M., & Pike, K. M. (1997). Cognitive behavioral therapy for anorexia nervosa. In D. M. Garner & P. E. Garfinkel (Eds.), *Handbook of treatment for eating disorders* (2nd ed.) (pp. 94–144). New York: Guilford Press.

Honig, P. (2000). Family work. In B. Lask & R. Bryant-Waugh (Eds.), *Anorexia nervosa and related eating disorders in childhood and adolescence* (2nd ed.) (pp. 187–204). East Sussex, UK: Psychology Press.

Hsu, L. K. G. (1990). *Eating disorders.* New York: Guilford Press.

Johnson, C., & Connors, M. E. (1987). *The etiology and treatment of bulimia nervosa: A biopsychosocial perspective.* New York: Basic Books.

Kinoy, B. (Ed.) (1994). *Eating disorders: New directions in treatment and recovery.* New York: Columbia University Press.

Lask, B., & Bryant-Waugh, R. (Eds.) (2000). *Anorexia nervosa and related disorders in childhood and adolescence* (2nd ed.). East Sussex, UK: Psychology Press.

Levenkron, S. (1998). *Cutting: Understanding and overcoming self-mutilation.* New York: W. W. Norton.

Levitt, J. L. (1998). The disorganized client: New management strategies. *Paradigm, 2,* 20.

Levitt, J. L. (2000a). Nature and treatment of the symptomatically complex eating disordered clients: Trauma, self-injury, and dual diagnosis. Invited workshop given at Pinecrest Christian Hospital, Professional Lecture Series, Grand Rapids, MI, March.

Levitt, J. L. (2000b). Surviving the storm: Treating the complex eating disordered client. Institute presented at the International Association of Eating Disorder Professional, Annual Conference, Orlando, FL, August.

Levitt, J. L., & Sansone, R. A. (2002). Searching for the answers: Eating disorders and self-harm. *Eating Disorders: The journal of treatment and prevention, 10* (3) 189–191.

Linehan, M. M. (1993). *Cognitive-behavioral treatment of borderline personality disorder*. New York: Guilford Press.

Mehler, P. S., & Andersen, A. E. (Eds.) (1999). *Eating disorders: A guide to medical care and complications*. Baltimore: Johns Hopkins University Press.

Miller, D. (1994). *Women who hurt themselves*. New York: Basic Books.

Minuchin, S., Rosman, B. L., & Baker, L. (1978). *Psychosomatic families: Anorexia nervosa in context*. Massachusetts: Harvard University Press.

Mitchell, J. E., Pomeroy, C., & Adson, D. E. (1997). Managing medical complications. In D. M. Garner & P. E. Garfinkel (Eds.), *Handbook of treatment for eating disorders* (2nd ed.) (pp. 383–393). New York: Guilford Press.

Mitchell, J. E., Pyle, R. L., Specker, S., & Hanson, K. (1992). Eating disorders and chemical dependency. In J. Yager, H. E. Gwirtsman, & C. K. Edelstein (Eds.), *Special problems in managing eating disorders* (pp. 1–14). Washington, DC: American Psychiatric Press.

Powers, P. S. (1997). Management of patients with comorbid conditions. In D. M. Garner & P. E. Garfinkel (Eds.), *Handbook of treatment for eating disorders* (2nd ed.) (pp. 424–436). New York: Guilford Press.

Sansone, R. A., & Levitt, J. L. (2002). Self-harm behaviors among those with eating disorders: An overview. *Eating Disorders: The journal of treatment and prevention, 10* (3) 205–213.

Sansone, R. A., & Sansone, L. A. (2002). Assessment tools for self-harm behavior among those with eating disorders. *Eating Disorders: The journal of treatment and prevention, 10* (3)193–203.

Sansone, R. A., Wiederman, M. W., & Sansone, L. A. (1998). The Self-Harm Inventory (SHI): Development of a scale for identifying self-destructive behaviors and borderline personality disorder. *Journal of Clinical Psychology, 54*, 973–983.

Schwartz, M. F., & Cohn, L. (Eds.) (1996). *Sexual abuse and eating disorders*. New York: Brunner/Mazel.

Siegel, D. J. (1999). *The developing mind*. New York: Guildord Press.

Simeon, D., & Hollander, E. (2001). *Self-injurious behaviors: Assessment and treatment*. Washington, DC: American Psychiatric Press.

Strober, M., & Katz, J. L. (1988). Depression in the eating disorders: A review and analysis of descriptive, family, and biological findings. In D. M. Garner & P. E. Garfinkel (Eds.), *Diagnostic issues in anorexia nervosa and bulimia nervosa* (pp. 80–111). New York: Brunner/Mazel.

Swift, W. J., & Wonderlich, S. A. (1982). Personality factors and diagnosis in eating disorders: Traits, disorders, and structures. In D. M. Garner & P. E. Garfinkel (Eds.), *Diagnostic issues in anorexia nervosa and bulimia nervosa* (pp. 112–165). New York: Brunner/Mazel.

Vanderlinden, J., & Vandereycken, W. (1997). *Trauma, dissociation, and impulse dyscontrol in eating disorders*. Bristol, PA: Brunner/Mazel.

Walsh, B. W., & Rosen, P. M. (1988). *Self-mutilation: Theory, research, and treatment*. New York: Guilford Press.

Weiss, L., Katzman, M., & Wolchik, S. (1985). *Treating bulimia: A psychoeducational approach*. New York: Pergamon Press.

Wonderlich, S. A., & Mitchell, J. E. (1992). Eating disorders and personality disorders. In J. Yager, H. E. Gwirtsman, & C. K. Edelstein (Eds.), *Special problems in managing eating disorders* (pp. 51–87). Washington, DC: American Psychiatric Press.

Wonderlich, S., Myers, T., Norton, M., & Crosby, R. (2002). Self-harm and bulimia nervosa: A complex connection. *Eating Disorders: The journal of treatment and prevention, 10* (3) 257–267.

Yates, A. (1991). *Compulsive exercise and the eating disorders: Toward an integrated theory of activity*. New York: Brunner/Mazel.

CHAPTER 16

Group Therapy Approaches to the Treatment of Eating Disorders and Self-Injury

JOHN L. LEVITT AND RANDY A. SANSONE

I'm in tears, having a really bad time. I try to ignore this gross body, but there are times, like right now, when I can't. My stomach grows over my beltline every time I sit; my chest is out to there; nothing fits me anymore. I go through a mountain of clothes, trying to figure out what to wear that won't show the flagrant flaws of my body.

I can't get away from this body and how it makes me feel—fat, gross, and unacceptable. Shower time has become a bad trigger. While showering, I have strong thoughts of cutting my stomach and chest up. I even touch the razor blade to my stomach and think how easy it would be, envision the relief that would follow—the blood flowing from my body, the feeling of satisfaction in being able to strike back at the enemy, my body, and see the wounds that I inflict upon it.

Anonymous patient

Introduction

Eating disorders (ED) are complex, multidimensional problems that affect a wide range of patient functioning. In recent years, increasing numbers of such patients have begun to present with a variety of other comorbid conditions, especially self-injury (Levitt & Sansone, 2002). The literature is clear that for effective treatment outcomes, polysymptomatic patients generally require a multimodal approach to recovery, consisting of a mix of individual, family, group, and pharmacological therapies.

Group-based therapies have been documented for the treatment of patients presenting with ED as well as self-injury (SI) (Andersen, Bowers, & Evans, 1997; Crisp, 1997; Garner & Needleman, 1997; Polivy & Federoff, 1997; Walsh & Rosen, 1988). Specifically, group approaches have been utilized for treating anorexia nervosa (Andersen et al., 1997; Crisp, 1997), bulimia nervosa (Fairburn, 1995; Ries & Dockray-Miller, 2002), obesity (Cormillot, 1995), and SI (Conterio & Lader, 1998; Walsh & Rosen, 1988). Group approaches for patients with ED and patients with SI have been described in inpatient settings (Andersen et al., 1997) as well as partial hospitalization programs (Levitt & Sansone, 2003). Group treatment has also been effectively utilized for patients with ED and with issues related to SI, such as personality disorders (Dennis & Sansone, 1997), trauma and impulse control problems (Vanderlinden & Vandereycken, 1997), and a variety of related issues (Mehler & Andersen, 1999). In fact, some research has indicated that group therapy might be as efficacious as individual therapy, at least for those with bulimia nervosa (Richards et al., 2000).

In the ED literature, compared with individual and family approaches, there is considerably less available information about group treatment for SI. Likewise, the SI literature describes group therapy approaches, but these are discussed much less than other approaches. The ED and SI literatures, however, are relatively silent about the role of group treatment for patients who present with both ED and SI.

Basic Types of Groups

In this chapter, we describe various approaches to group therapy for patients with ED/SI. The underpinnings of several of the approaches that we describe are highly influenced by the Self-Regulation Approach (SRA) developed by Levitt (2000a, 2000b). The SRA provides a broad organizational "map" for delivering treatment. It provides guidance for selecting the general areas of focus, but does not restrict the choice of particular interventions employed (see Chapter 15 for further discussion of the SRA). In addition, these approaches are not limited to an SRA context.

With regard to group treatment, the SRA for treating patients with ED/SI focuses on three broad categories of group-based intervention: (a) skills development, (b) special issues, and (c) dynamic-relational intervention. Rather than being discrete from one another, the relationships between these areas of focused treatment are characterized by mutual overlap and intersection. That is, each area is likely to utilize elements and processes from other areas. The selection of a specific area is based upon treatment setting and patient needs. For example, symptomatically unstable patients may be more benefited by skills development. As stability increases, more emphasis may be placed on other areas, which may include special issues or dynamic-relational areas. These latter areas may be approached within an ongoing group, or may be undertaken in specifically designated groups. For example, an initial group therapy emphasis for a cohort of patients who are simultaneously entering a partial hospitalization program for ED/SI symptoms might be skills development. The explicit treatment foci would be nutritional rehabilitation, weight stabilization, and the interruption of SI patterns. Psychoeducational groups with less intra-group relational processing would be emphasized. As this cohort symptomatically improved, more emphasis would be placed upon intra-group relationships (e.g., interaction and feedback among members). The following is a brief description of these group-intervention areas, including specific examples of groups.

Skills-Based Groups

Many patients, particularly those in partial hospitalization or inpatient programs, benefit from skills-based groups. These groups are designed to accomplish two general goals. First, they emphasize symptom stabilization (i.e., containment). That is, they focus upon teaching and assisting the patient to implement those skills necessary for nutritional rehabilitation, weight stabilization, the reduction and elimination of related ED behaviors such as purging, and the reduction of SI behaviors. The group focus is learning how to develop alternatives to employing either ED or SI behaviors. Second, these groups focus on teaching and helping the patient to learn and practice those life skills that will help him/her to function effectively without ED/SI behaviors (i.e., adaptation). Examples of specific groups are described below.

Nutritional Groups. Generally psychoeducational in nature, nutritional groups are designed to help the patient to learn the basic aspects of healthy nutrition, normalized eating behaviors, appropriate and inappropriate psychological and emotional reactions to eating behaviors, healthy food selections, weight stabilization, and the elimination of associated eating disorder symptoms.

Body Image and Body Sensation Groups. These groups, generally a combination of psychoeducational and experiential elements, focus on the patient learning to discriminate and reconnect appropriate and accurate body sensations. The goal is for participants to experience their bodies as a positive component of self, rather than as an alien object or intruder. In addition, these groups assist the patient in reducing visual, internal, and kinesthetic distortions, and developing a more accurate sense of body self. With a more accurate body image and an ability to interpret body sensations and cues more accurately, the patient is able to rely less on ED/SI behaviors.

Expressive Therapy Groups. Expressive therapy groups, such as leisure, movement, and art therapies, are designed to promote skills that augment patients' abilities to express themselves—skills that can then be used as alternatives to ED/SI behaviors. While these groups are generally part of inpatient and intensive day treatment programs, some patients also participate in these types of groups during outpatient therapy.

Self-Management Groups. Self-management groups, often psychoeducational and interactional in nature, help the patient learn the skills that allow him/her to regulate self across a variety of areas given the supports, limitations, and demands of the environment. The general goals of these groups are to understand the difference between management and control, approach a situation/setting initially with some objectivity and neutrality (while titrating creativity, intuition, and feelings), and assess the requirements of the situation/setting as they actually are. In addition, participants learn to recognize personal resources (i.e., skills/assets) and identify their availability and accessibility, and practice implementing these personal resources in the situation/setting. These self-management skills are more fully described under the Structural-Process Model of the SRA (Levitt 2000a, 2000b, see Chapter 15). In partial hospitalization programs, these groups are often connected to daily goals groups, which focus on the patient's personal goals for the day and/or week.

Affect Management Groups. Affect management groups are designed to help the patient learn how to manage affect in a variety of situations. Some of these skills are similar to those described in Dialectal Behavior Therapy (DBT; Linehan, 1993). The initial goals for these groups are for patients to learn how to regulate or modulate affect, calm self, and express affect effectively (i.e., interpersonal expression skills) so that others will understand the intended message. Education, in-group practice, and feedback from group members are initially focused on.

Problem-Solving Groups. Problem solving is a cognitive approach that focuses on examining and utilizing new and/or alternative solutions. Many patients do not clearly understand what problem solving is and/or they ineffectively or inconsistently implement it. Some of the goals of problem-solving groups are the development of an approach that is readily accessible, the use of a problem-solving approach as a regular framework for developing new solutions, recognition of the need for pursuing new solutions versus focusing on problems (i.e., minimizing problems, which is often synonymous with simply reducing the negative affects related to the problem), and application of management skills (see above) in order to problem solve.

Pattern Recognition Groups. Pattern recognition groups focus on the skills necessary to be able to recognize and identify repeated sequences of cognitions (thoughts), affects (feelings), and behaviors that are contextually interdependent. From the perspective of SRA, recognition "makes the unseen accessible." These groups are especially useful for patients with SI and with bulimia, who need to learn how to identify the elements in their pattern of SI and to develop a variety of intervention options. Some of the goals of pattern recognition groups are for the patient to be able to recognize, identify, and accept the presence of patterns; to develop an awareness of patterns as regular processes of daily living; and to be able to anticipate patterns.

Relationship Management Groups. Relationships are often difficult for patients to manage. Indeed, many patients view their difficulties as primarily related to disturbances in relationships. Relationship management broadly refers to the development of the ability to manage oneself in, and appropriately respond to, the variety of relationships one has, given the requirements and circumstances of the relationship, situation, or setting. Goals for patients may include understanding the characteristics of relationships, identifying and anticipating relationship ambiguities, recognizing differences between one's needs and wants versus current relationship resources and demands, and being able to separate past from present relationship experiences. These groups combine psychoeducation, interactional experiences, and feedback within the group.

Cognitive Processing Groups. Cognitive processing groups entail cognitive-behavioral therapy (Fairburn, 1995; Garner & Garfinkel, 1997). The focus is on thought processes and cognitions, and the ways that these interact with feelings and behaviors. Goals include the identification and ongoing recognition of unhealthy cognitive schemas and distortions, how these distorted thoughts contribute to feelings and behaviors, problem solving around cognitive processes (e.g., hypothesis testing), and challenging and changing cognitive sequences.

Educational Resourcing Groups. Educational resourcing groups emphasize those skills related to the application of learning as a vital natural resource that must be cultivated and pursued for effective therapeutic outcomes. The emphasis is on learning and changing, rather than on pathology that is beyond one's control to change. Specific techniques include having the patient take on the role of being a "student of oneself," employing the concept of "learning" versus "judging" or "labeling," and developing a personal educational framework and orientation to organize information and practice new behaviors.

Special Issues Groups

Special issues therapy groups are those that focus on a very specific therapeutic issue, theme, or problem that affects some, but perhaps not all, patients. Among patients with ED/SI, this type of adjunctive treatment is often necessary as many have a number of other problems that may not initially be *a priori*ty for treatment, but will need to be subsequently addressed (Favazza, 1987; Garner & Garfinkel, 1997). Examples include sexual abuse or other trauma, and the use of alcohol or other chemical substances. At treatment entry, some of these problem areas may be addressed concurrently with presenting symptoms during skills development, but some will need to be addressed after stabilization. The themes of special issues groups are limitless, so only a few examples of these groups will be briefly described below.

Chemical Dependency Groups. A number of patients use alcohol and/or other illegal substances, or misuse prescription drugs, in a manner that requires intervention. Chemical dependency groups address the use of these substances and offer guidance in developing a lifestyle without them. Perhaps the best known organized approach to this is Alcoholics Anonymous.

Sexual Abuse or Trauma Groups. A number of patients present for treatment with a history of abuse or trauma. While the percentage of patients with such a history is unclear, the ED/SI literatures suggest a substantial number. Sexual abuse or trauma groups are designed to help patients understand their experiences and the sequelae of these experiences on their lives. Such groups help patients to address these effects in a healthier fashion and to not allow them to impede the development of healthy relationships with themselves or others.

Co-Dependency Groups. Co-dependency groups are designed to help patients learn about the complex ways in which they are involved in other people's problems and how others are involved in theirs. These groups are particularly useful for patients who need to learn how to separate themselves from the difficulties of others and focus attention on their own recovery.

Multiple-Family Groups. In multiple-family group treatment, the family is the patient and the group consists of a number of families. Here, families learn how they may be negatively reinforcing or interacting with the patient with ED/SI, as well as other individuals within the family. Family members obtain feedback about these unhealthy interactions and learn to develop alternatives to their "normal" mode of operation.

Assertiveness and Social Skills Groups. The goal of these groups is to help patients master new forms of social skills so that they are better able to speak out and manage themselves in social situations. Often, these groups are didactic as well as interactive (i.e., they incorporate practice) in nature.

Anger Management Groups. Like assertiveness training and social skills groups, anger management groups help patients to recognize, contain, and appropriately express anger. In many cases, patients with ED/SI express symptoms when they experience something that approximates anger. These groups provide a less self-destructive and more effective alternative strategy.

Women's Issues Groups. Research suggests that ED/SI symptoms may be associated with cultural aspects related to how women and their roles are viewed by society. These groups help patients to identify and understand these cultural effects, and to develop healthy counter-maneuvers (Garner & Garfinkel, 1997).

Support Groups. While support groups do not represent "special issue groups" per se, they are a unique type of group that is designed to provide a focused and limited function—support. Although some groups are closed, they are typically open to the public and provide general education and support for those struggling with ED/SI symptoms. Attendees may or may not be in treatment. Recovering patients or local professionals tend to facilitate these groups. Again, the general goal does not focus on change, but rather on providing support to those who are in any stage of their disorder.

Dynamic-Relational Groups

Dynamic-relational groups are designed to facilitate a "corrective emotional-relational experience." The primary emphasis in these groups is on what happens within the group itself. Feedback, confrontation, and interaction, often intense, are the hallmarks of these groups. The emphasis is upon facilitating those emotional experiences that occur via member interactions in an effort to help correct, or resolve, underlying deficits in emotional regulation, autonomy, identity, and self-esteem (Polivy & Federoff, 1997). These groups may also explore and connect dysfunctional family-of-origin patterns with current dysfunctional patterns in relationships. Members in these groups are able to explore problems related to interpersonal difficulties and develop more effective and successful ways of relating (Polivy & Federoff, 1997; Yalom, 1995).

In summary, groups can be utilized in highly flexible fashions. In addition, patients are continually working on interpersonal and dynamic themes as well as recovery in any type of group format. The particular group designation provides specific boundaries and guidelines as to how one might address these themes and elements. We regularly employ psychoeducational principles, and facilitate interpersonal feedback between the therapist and group members, in all of these groups. Thus, the amount of focus on different aspects of skills and interpersonal relationships is really a matter of degree. In the following section, we present the basic elements that serve as the foundation for setting up groups for patients with ED/SI.

The Construction of Groups for Patients with ED/SI

Regardless of the type of ED/SI group, thoughtful construction must be done before the group begins. Given that a group of patients with ED/SI is likely to be different from those who present with either "typical" ED or SI symptoms, we suggest an approach to group composition and construction that is appropriate for this population. Table 16.1 lists some of the basic elements that we have found essential for ED/SI groups.

To successfully focus on these elements, it is vital to create a successful ED/SI-group working environment. The following discussion describes those areas that we have found useful for group treatment with patients with ED/SI.

TABLE 16.1 The Basic Elements for Eating Disorder/Self-Injury Groups

Education
Containment, stabilization, and resolution of ED/SI symptoms
Identification of the interaction between eating disorder and self-injury behaviors
Development of a personal framework for recovery (Levitt, 2000a, 2000b)
Emotional support and reduced social isolation
Enhanced interpersonal functioning and social skills
Provision of a forum for education and learning
Provision of a setting for practicing new skills
Adaptation to functioning without the eating disorder or self-injury symptoms
Provision of an environment that creates hope for recovery

Special Considerations

At the outset, it is important to recognize that this group of patients is multi-symptomatic and often challenging. Within the group, the *relationship* between the ED and SI behaviors must be assessed, examined, monitored, and addressed. Furthermore, as symptom complexity, and perhaps chronicity, increases, the likelihood of having patients with comorbid personality disorders also increases. Group therapists need to be alert to and skilled in managing groups with these types of patients (Dennis & Sansone, 1997). For example, the risk of symptom contagion may be greater among characterological patients.

Group Membership and Composition

In general we have found that groups function most effectively with 5 to 8 members. Less than 5 members may result in somewhat limited and stilted interactions. In addition, the group needs a sufficient number of participants to maintain a "rotating ego" and, thus, an ongoing reality base. More than 8 members affect the therapist's ability to manage the interactions and give members ample time to participate.

Therapists need to be careful when evaluating patients for group participation. While therapists in inpatient and intensive day treatment programs generally have little choice in selection, outpatient therapists need to scrutinize group candidates. In our experience, patients who are adamant in their refusal to give up their reliance on either ED or SI behaviors are generally not good candidates for advanced groups, such as special issue or dynamic-relational groups. The more out of control a patient is with ED/SI symptoms, the more likely skill-based groups need to be emphasized.

Patients who acknowledge that they do not want to be in groups or have limited ability to tolerate a group situation should be, at least initially, directed to individual therapy or groups that are more psychoeducational and less interactive in nature. Some of these individuals may suffer from adjunctive difficulties such as social phobia, severe obsessive-compulsive disorder, intermittent psychotic symptoms, or exceptionally poor social skills. Some may even have been the victims of peer shunning and avoid such contact as an adaptation.

Another consideration for the therapist is whether to have a blended or a more heterogeneous ED group (i.e., anorexia/SI vs. bulimia/SI vs. binge eating disorder/SI). We generally favor blended groups. Advantages include broader opportunities for sharing, the development of realistic perspectives about other people and their ED, and the efficiency of service delivery. However, there are potential drawbacks, such as the individual with bulimia who wants to be more anorexic and "learn" faulty cognitive schemas from others, or the individual with binge eating disorder whose weight distracts other members.

The Role of the Patient

As part of group construction and member selection, the therapist needs to be clear about the group role of the patient. Ideally, each individual patient has three general responsibilities as a group member. First, each patient must be willing to be a "student of oneself" (Levitt, 2000a, 2000b), or a psychological detective in search of answers about oneself. That is, the patient must be willing to be open to learning new information, skills, and patterns of interaction that will allow them to function without ED/SI symptoms.

Second, each patient needs to come to group prepared. That is, the patient needs to focus on a specific objective or concern that is related in some way to ED/SI behaviors, and be willing to examine situations or skills that will support them in functioning without such symptoms. It is useful for the patient to contribute some specific examples of these concerns.

Third, patients need to come to group with a proactive attitude. That is, they need to participate, pay attention, and avoid rejecting provided support or information. Patients must make a commitment to what they are willing to do to address their ED/SI symptoms, both inside and outside of group. It is also essential that patients not become too dependent on others to address their concerns. Collectively, these preceding responsibilities, and their acceptability to the patient, provide the therapist with a sense of the patient's overall motivation, which is essential for progress.

The Role of the Therapist

The group therapist working with patients with ED/SI needs to have a variety of skills that will assist him/her to be most effective. In general, we see the therapist as a professional "guide" whose role is to provide feedback and assist with the ongoing direction and momentum of the group. The therapist also coaches and teaches certain skills, and guides patients in their learning and application of these skills. In this sense, the therapist responds to the material presented within the group and provides professional information that is in the best interest of the group, given the particular focus/type of group. Thus, therapists working with this population need to be active and direct in their interactions.

Therapists in ED/SI groups also need to be able to manage the relationships between the group members to keep them working together. The therapist, therefore, must be knowledgeable about group process in general (see Yalom, 1995).

Finally, the therapist must be vigilant of his/her own responses and reactions to group members and group process. Both ED and SI behaviors can be graphic and disturbing. It is important to recognize the potential for such emotionally distressing behaviors and dynamics to immobilize the group and the therapist. Due to the probability of characterological participants, there are also risks related to splitting, projective identification, and acting out by participants as well as the therapist. Again, experience in working with complex, characterological patients is essential.

Group Guidelines and Expectations

Each group must establish goals and guidelines. The goals of the group should reflect the expressed reasons for the group's creation and identify what members might hope to get from participation in the group. It is vital that the goals of each group be clearly explained to each patient, and that the group refocuses periodically on these to keep on task.

Group expectations and responsibilities are also important to clarify. They explain to patients what is expected of them in the group and how they should interact while in the group. We believe that it is useful to have members sign a contract. The contract explicitly establishes what the basic expectations are for members. Figure 16.1 provides an example of a group contract. It is important that the contract clarify exactly what is expected of the patient in order to continue to effectively participate in the group.

Group Process

It is essential that the group focus on the interplay between ED and SI symptoms, whether it is a skills development, special issues, or dynamic-relational group. That is, therapeutic interventions need to be directed to ED and SI *symptoms*, and the *relationships* between these as they relate to the various contexts of the patients' lives. The following vignette illustrates an interaction between the group therapist (T) and various group members (GM) in a general skills-development group.

FIGURE 16.1 Example of an ED/SI Group Contract

I understand that the ED/SI group is designed to promote my recovery by helping me to learn how to live without relying on, or using, my eating disorder or self-injury behaviors. I am joining this group because I am committed to my recovery and am aware that participation in the ED/SI groups will be beneficial for my recovery. I agree to the following guidelines for participation in the ED/SI group.

1. I will pay a fee of $_____ per group(s) for my participation (if applicable).
2. I will attend all group sessions that meet at_____(time) and will last 2 hours.
3. I agree to arrive on time and be ready for the group to begin on time.
4. I will leave a message at least 24 hours ahead if I am going to be absent.
5. I agree to no storytelling or sharing of ED/SI details other than in the context of how I am positively addressing them for my recovery.
6. I agree to have only one person talk at a time.
7. I agree to not use offensive language.
8. I agree to stay for the entire group session and not leave until it is over.
9. I agree to have no side conversations while others are talking.
10. I agree to be honest.
11. I agree to have a safety plan in case I have a crisis outside of group.
12. I agree to not come to group under the influence of drugs or alcohol.
13. I agree to turn off my cell phone or pager during group.
14. I agree to do my homework outside of group.
15. I agree to no outside relationships with group members outside of group.
16. I agree to not using my ED/SI behaviors during or immediately before or after the group.
17. I agree to consistently work on my recovery.
18. I agree to handle any problems with any other group member or with the group therapist(s) during group time and not outside of the group.
19. I agree to discuss any problems or concerns with the group and group therapist(s) before I decide to stop attending the group.
20. I agree that if I do not follow these guidelines, my ability to continue to participate in this group may be reevaluated.

_____   _____

Patient's signature   Date

_____   _____

Therapist's signature   Date

Note: ED = eating disorder, SI = self-injury

T: We have been discussing some of the elements of managing ourselves when we are in a difficult situation. GM3, you were talking about some of the problems you were having at home with your mom.

GM3: Yeah! My mom is always on my case. She just wants to make me eat and doesn't really care about me.

T: How are you handling that? When you think your mom is on your case?

GM3: I just want to puke! She's a bitch.

GM4: So what do you do?

GM3: She keeps following me around, so I can't get to the bathroom.

GM4: So what happens?

GM3: I just get pissed off. I get so angry that I just want to punch a wall.

T: This sounds like a very familiar pattern that we have been talking about lately in our skills groups. Do you remember when we were talking about the difference between control and management?

GM3: I get so pissed off that the only way I can calm down is to either throw up or cut myself. So, my mom is following me all the time and follows me to the bathroom. But, later when I'm alone in my bathroom, I take my scissors and....

T: Let's stay away from the specifics of what we do to harm ourselves and focus on how you can manage the situation. Okay?

GM5: Did it help? The cutting?

GM3: I was less angry.

T: What skills have we been talking about? Anyone?

GM2: We talked about looking at patterns.

T: Yep. Anything else?

GM1: Did you try to practice your breathing to calm down first and then talk to your mother?

GM3: She's a bitch.

GM1: Did you try anything to work the problem out? My mom makes me mad a lot, but I learned that when I talk to her when I am calmer and try to understand what she is saying, we get along better. The breathing exercise helps me—you know, the one where we grab our chest and breathe deep.

T: You mean diaphragmatic breathing, don't you?

GM1: Yeah.

GM3: No, she wouldn't listen anyway.

T: It's really important to use grounding skills, like the breathing technique that GM1 was talking about. It is also important to focus on when to use them most effectively. When practicing the pattern recognition skills, it's easier to predict which situations are likely to be most stressful and to approach them calmer and more focused. I think that GM1 makes a good point that when she can do this, and listen to others, she is better able to handle the situation. Before we are done, I think we should go over pattern recognition and grounding skills. Anybody else have any reactions?

GM6: It looks like GM3 is taking on a victim role. She is just reacting to her mother rather than dealing with the problem. I can tell when that is happening because then I don't want to eat or get rid of it, and later, I always feel like burning myself.

T: I think that many of you are bringing up some really good points. I suggest that we review some skills and then see if GM3 can come up with a different approach to her mother. A lot of you can figure out what situations you might use these in, as well. Okay?

This example illustrates, in a skills-focused group, the therapist's effort to integrate skills that had been learned in past groups into the present, and to challenge the group around their willingness to review and practice them. Skills groups allow the therapist, or group members, to redirect the group's energies to learning or practicing new or previously taught skills. In this example, there was also a strong emphasis upon interaction among the group members. It is important that the energy and emphasis within the group come primarily from the members rather than the therapist. It is easy to see how the elements of the three types of groups might be easily applicable to all of them.

Conclusion

Group therapy strategies for patients with ED/SI are obviously very similar to group therapies for other problems. What is critical for ED/SI groups is for the therapy to center on the immediate issues—to recognize, emphasize, and focus on those situations and dynamics that support ED and SI symptoms, and to actively explore the ways that these symptoms interact and reinforce one another. When accomplished, group therapy is a very efficient and effective modality for the treatment of patients with ED/SI.

References

Andersen, A. E., Bowers, W., & Evans, K. (1997). Inpatient treatment of anorexia nervosa. In D. M. Garner, & P.E. Garfinkel (Eds.), *Handbook of treatment for eating disorders* (2nd ed.) (pp. 327–353). New York: Guilford Press.

Conterio, K., & Lader, W. (1998). *Bodily harm.* New York: Hyperion.

Cormillot, A. (1995). Commercial and self-help approaches to weight management. In K. D. Brownell & C. G. Fairburn (Eds.), *Eating disorders and obesity: A comprehensive handbook* (pp. 498–503). New York: Guilford Press.

Crisp, A. (1997). Anorexia nervosa as flight from growth: Assessment and treatment based on the model. In D. M. Garner & P. E. Garfinkel (Eds.), *Handbook of treatment for eating disorders* (2nd ed.) (pp. 248–277). New York: Guilford Press.

Dennis, A. B., & Sansone, R. A. (1997). Treatment of patients with personality disorders. In D. M. Garner & P. E. Garfinkel (Eds.), *Handbook of treatment for eating disorders* (2nd ed.) (pp. 437–449). New York: Guilford Press.

Fairburn, C. G. (1995). Short-term psychological treatments for bulimia nervosa. In K. D. Brownell & C. G. Fairburn (Eds.), *Eating disorders and obesity: A comprehensive handbook* (pp. 344–353). New York: Guilford Press.

Favazza, A. R. (1987). *Bodies under siege: Self-mutilation in culture and psychiatry.* Baltimore: Johns Hopkins University Press.

Garner, D. M., & Garfinkel, P. E. (Eds.) (1997). *Handbook of treatment for eating disorders* (2nd ed.). New York: Guilford Press.

Garner, D. M., & Needleman, L. D. (1997). Sequencing and integration of treatments. In D. M. Garner & P. E. Garfinkel (Eds.), *Handbook of treatment for eating disorders* (2nd ed.) (pp. 50–63). New York: Guilford Press.

Levitt, J. L. (2000a). Nature and treatment of symptomatically complex eating disordered clients: Trauma, self-injury, and dual diagnosis. Invited workshop given at Pinecrest Christian Hospital, Professional Lecture Series, Grand Rapids, MI, March.

Levitt, J. L. (2000b). Surviving the storm: Treating the complex eating disordered client. Institute presented at the International Association of Eating Disorder Professionals, Annual Conference, Orlando, FL, August.

Levitt, J. L., & Sansone, R. A. (2002). Searching for the answers: Eating disorders and self-harm. *Eating Disorders: The Journal of Treatment and Prevention, 10,* 189–191.

Levitt, J. L., & Sansone, R. A. (2003). The treatment of eating disorder clients in a community-based partial hospitalization program. *Journal of Mental Health Counseling, 25,* 140–151.

Linehan, M. M. (1993). *Cognitive-behavioral treatment of borderline personality disorder.* New York: Guilford Press.

Mehler, P. S., & Andersen, A. E. (Eds.) (1999). *Eating disorders: A guide to medical care and complications*. Baltimore: Johns Hopkins University Press.

Polivy, J., & Federoff, I. (1997). Group psychotherapy. In D. M. Garner & P. E. Garfinkel (Eds.), *Handbook of treatment for eating disorders* (2nd ed.) (pp. 462–475). New York: Guilford Press.

Richards, P. S., Baldwin, B. M., Frost, H. A., Clark-Sly, J. B., Berrett, M. E., & Hardman, R. K. (2000). What works for treating eating disorders? Conclusions of 28 outcome reviews. *Eating Disorders: The Journal of Treatment and Prevention, 8,* 189–206.

Ries, H., & Dockray-Miller, M. (2002). *Integrative group treatment for bulimia nervosa*. New York: Columbia University Press.

Vanderlinden, J., & Vandereycken, W. (1997). *Trauma, dissociation, and impulse dyscontrol in eating disorders*. Bristol, PA: Brunner/Mazel.

Walsh, B. W., & Rosen, P. M. (1988). *Self-mutilation: Theory, research & treatment*. New York: Guilford Press.

Yalom, I. (1995). *The theory and practice of group psychotherapy* (4th ed.). New York: Basic Books.

CHAPTER 17

Psychotropic Medications, Self-Harm Behavior, and Eating Disorders

RANDY A. SANSONE, JOHN L. LEVITT, AND LORI A. SANSONE

Introduction

In this chapter, we discuss the various classes of psychotropic medication and their use in the management of self-harm behavior (SHB) among individuals with eating disorders (ED). Most authorities perceive medication as an adjunct to psychotherapy intervention. Since no single medication or medication combination is dramatically and consistently efficacious in the management of SHB, the potential benefits and risks of each play an important role in a drug-selection strategy. For each grouping of psychotropic medications, we describe the known neurotransmitter action, and the potential clinical efficacy and risks. In addition, we overview case reports and/or studies as examples of treatment experience and discuss the practical integration of medications into the treatment process. Finally, we introduce a suggested logarithm for psychotropic medication prescription in this comorbid population.

No single pharmacological agent has been found to be consistently effective among ED self-harmers, which may be explained by the complex neurobiology of self-mutilation (i.e., involvement of the serotonergic, dopaminergic, opioid, and adrenergic neurotransmitter systems [Southwick, Yehuda, Giller, & Perry, 1990; Winchel & Stanley, 1991]) as well as the intricate intrapsychic and interpersonal functions of these behaviors. The majority of studies examining medications in SHB have been undertaken in those diagnosed with borderline personality disorder (BPD), an Axis II disorder characterized by SHB. Collectively, these studies illustrate the possible benefits as well as limitations (e.g., modest treatment effects) of psychotropic medication among self-harming individuals. In this comorbid population (i.e., ED, SHB), the presence of an ED has additional implications for drug selection, particularly with regard to the weight effects of these medications.

Before reviewing the available information on the various classes of medications for SHB, we wish to broach several important caveats regarding the management of SHB in patients with ED. First, medication is conceptualized in this chapter as an adjunct to the overall treatment process, which should include psychotherapy (Grossman, 2002; Soloff, 1994; Soloff, 2000). Second, no medication has been approved by the Food and Drug Administration (FDA) for SHB, with the exception of clozapine (Clozaril) for suicidal ideation in schizophrenic and schizoaffective disorders. Third, there is no clear single drug of choice (Coccaro, 1998; Soloff, 1994); guidelines for medications have been based on small research samples (Soloff, 2000) and there is scant information on drug combinations (Grossman, 2002). Fourth, there appear to be no consistent predictors of drug response (Gardner & Cowdry, 1986). Fifth, medications have had varying degrees of success (Brinkley, 1993); most treatment effects are modest (Soloff, 2000), residual symptoms are the rule (Soloff, 2000), and maintenance studies indicate limited efficacy (Soloff, 1994). Sixth, large and positive placebo effects are observed in most drug studies of SHB, which complicates the interpretation of findings (Moleman, van Dam, & Dings, 1999). Finally, drug treatment may be complicated by the psychology of characterological patients (i.e., their tendency to idealize or negate one treatment over another, regardless of genuine effect; Berger, 1987) and clinicians are cautioned about reinforcing repetitious and misdirected medication changes without factoring in a longitudinal sense of the patient's symptoms. Due to space limitations, we do not review the general side effects or dosage of medications.

Psychotropic Drug Groupings

Antidepressant Medications

Selective Serotonin Reuptake Inhibitors (SSRIs). As the most commonly prescribed antidepressants in the United States, the SSRIs enhance serotonin availability in the central nervous system. Of the six available SSRIs (i.e., fluoxetine [Prozac], sertraline [Zoloft], citalopram [Celexa], escitalopram [Lexapro], paroxetine [Paxil], fluvoxamine [Luvox]), each appears to be acting at a different group of serotonin subreceptors; therefore, each may have a slightly different clinical effect in a given individual. SSRIs are highlighted by their exceptional tolerability in terms of side effects as well as excellent safety profile.

SSRIs have been keen candidates for the treatment of SHB because serotonin appears to be intrinsically related to impulsivity and aggression (Kavoussi & Coccaro, 1999) and, as expected, serotonergic drugs seem to decrease these behaviors (Koenigsberg, Woo-Ming, & Siever, 2002). Fluoxetine is the most studied SSRI in SHB and has been found to decrease impulsivity (Cornelius, Soloff, Perel, & Ulrich, 1991), self-injury (Markovitz, Calabrese, Schulz, & Meltzer, 1991), anger (Salzman et al., 1995), and personality dysfunction (Fava et al., 2002). As an exception to the preceding findings, Dutch investigators (Rinne, van den Brink, Wouters, & van Dyke, 2002) found that fluoxetine was ineffective with impulsivity and aggression in patients with BPD. In addition, fluoxetine has been known to increase SHB in individuals with obsessive-compulsive disorder, Tourette's syndrome, and bulimia (Markovitz, 1995).

As for the remaining SSRIs, Ekselius and von Knorring (1998) found that treatment with sertraline or citalopram resulted in improved personality functioning among those with BPD and comorbid depression, and Markovitz (1995) found that sertraline decreased SHB. Thus, the overwhelming majority of studies with SSRIs indicate some degree of efficacy with SHB.

In addition to their effects on SHB, SSRIs are panoramic in their clinical activity. While most antidepressants alleviate both depression and anxiety, SSRIs are additionally effective in the treatment of social phobia, panic attacks, impulsivity, worry and rumination, post-traumatic stress disorder, obsessive-compulsive disorder, bulimia nervosa, and premenstrual dysphoric disorder (Schatzberg, 2000). Therefore, SSRIs are not only efficacious as first lines of intervention with SHB, but are also excellent choices in ED cases with other psychiatric comorbidity.

In the unique clinical population of individuals with SHB and ED, there are several specific risks with SSRIs. In this regard, citalopram is potentially lethal in overdose because of delays in cardiac conduction and subsequent arrhythmias (Power, 1998). In a British analysis (Buckley & McManus, 2002), both fluvoxamine and citalopram had slightly higher rates of death per million prescriptions than the other SSRIs. With regard to weight effects, paroxetine is characterized by weight gain in a substantial number of individuals (Fava et al., 2000), making the strategizing of weight goals for patients with ED exceedingly difficult. In contrast, weight-neutral SSRIs are sertraline (Fava et al., 2000; Sansone, Wiederman, & Shrader, 2000) and fluoxetine (Fava et al., 2000; Sansone et al., 2000). Because of the possibility of co-administered psychotropic medications in these complex cases, fluvoxamine is problematic because of its potential for extensive drug interactions (Riesenman, 1995). Finally, fluoxetine is characterized by a long half-life (i.e., lengthy washout period if the drug trial is unsuccessful), which may compromise a subsequent drug trial. Fluoxetine may also exacerbate impulsivity in some individuals (Markovitz, 1995). Therefore, among the SSRIs, sertraline appears to be the least complicated to use in this particular population, followed by either citalopram (if the patient has no history of suicide attempts and is not a genuine suicide risk) or fluoxetine.

Venlafaxine (Effexor). In the area of SHB, only two other types of antidepressants have received much empirical attention—venlafaxine and monoamine oxidase inhibitors (MAOIs). Venlafaxine has diverse neurotransmitter effects (i.e., serotonin, norepinephrine, dopamine; Bourin, 1999) and has been found to significantly reduce self-injurious behavior among patients with BPD (Markovitz & Wagner, 1995). While a greater risk in overdose than SSRIs, venlafaxine still is less lethal in overdose than either MAOIs or tricyclic antidepressants (TCAs). (Buckley & McManus, 2002). While we were not able to locate any empirical data, in our experience, venlafaxine appears to be relatively weight-neutral. Therefore, while the data regarding efficacy in SHB are limited, venlafaxine appears to be a promising and practical pharmacological intervention for SHB in this population.

MAOIs. MAOIs inhibit the enzyme that degrades catecholamines, thereby enhancing the effects of these neurotransmitters. While their efficacy is supported by case reports as well as controlled studies (Liebowitz et al., 1990; Gadde & Krishnan, 1999), Markovitz (1995) describes little impact on impulsivity. To complicate matters, MAOIs pose significant risks and are potentially hazardous drugs to use in this population of patients. First, MAOIs are moderately lethal in overdose (Buckley & McManus, 2002), particularly when compared to SSRIs. Second, through their interactions with a variety of tyramine-rich foods as well as various drugs, MAOIs can abruptly precipitate hypertensive crises and subsequent cerebrovascular accidents. Because of this, MAOIs are contraindicated in patients who use illicit substances, specifically stimulants or cocaine (Markovitz, 1995). For individuals with ED, who are already obsessively preoccupied with food amounts and content, the constant monitoring of foods for interactions with these drugs could potentially heighten that focus. For individuals who struggle with SHB, there is also the peril of developing risk behaviors around the ingestion of contraband foods. Indeed, we recall a case in which a patient with ED and with BPD functioned rather well on a MAOI, until she began to intentionally expose herself to tyramine-containing foods in an active effort to hurt herself. Finally, MAOIs are known for causing weight gain (Markovitz, 1995).

Other Antidepressants. Tricyclic antidepressants (e.g., amitriptyline [Elavil], imipramine [Tofranil]) have varying degrees of noradrenergic activity and serotonergic effects. The general opinion is that these drugs have limited efficacy in SHB (Moleman et al., 1999; Soloff, 2000). Indeed, tricyclic antidepressants may increase aggression and hostility in some patients (Markovitz, 1995) and are extremely dangerous in overdose (Buckley & McManus, 2002) because of their effects on cardiac conduction (Sasyniuk, Jhamandas, & Valois, 1986), which may result in lethal arrhythmias. In addition, most tricyclic antidepressants precipitate weight gain (Sansone et al., 2000) as well as orthostatic hypotension, a side effect that can be intensified by dehydration in those who purge, restrict fluids, or use laxatives or diuretics. We are not aware of any efficacy studies with clomipramine [Anafranil], a unique tricyclic antidepressant with anti-obsessional activity.

Among the remaining antidepressants, it is empirically unknown whether they are helpful for SHB in this unique population; however, several have notable concerns. For example, bupropion (Wellbutrin) is *contraindicated* for use in individuals with ED because of the heightened risk of seizures, and is potentially lethal in overdose due to the emergence of conduction delays and cardiac arrhythmias (Bergmann, Bleich, Wischer, & Paulus, 2002). Likewise, mirtazapine (Remeron) is characterized by weight gain and thus may be problematic to use with patients who have ED because of the inability to strategize a weight outcome.

Anticonvulsants

Used for the treatment of epilepsy, anticonvulsants are gaining broader popularity among prescribers of psychotropic medications. While the different anticonvulsant agents have pharmacologically distinct mechanisms (e.g., limiting the spread of discharge from a seizure focus, elevating the seizure threshold, affecting GABA receptors), case reports indicate their usefulness with SHB. Carbamazepine (Tegretol) is the most studied anticonvulsant and has been found to decrease behavioral dyscontrol (Gardner & Cowdry, 1986) as well as violence (Coons, 1992). Valproate (Depakote), the second most studied anticonvulsant (Soloff, 2000), has been found to improve impulsivity (Stein, Simeon, Frenkel, Islam, & Hollander, 1995) as well as reduce aggression (Davis, Ryan, Adinoff,

& Petty, 2000; Soloff, 2000). Lamotrigine (Lamictal) appears to reduce SHB (Daly & Fatemi, 1999) and suicidal behaviors in patients with BPD (Pinto & Akiskal, 1998). Like many other categories of drugs, empirical trials of anticonvulsants have lagged behind their clinical use (Soloff, 2000) and there is little empirical information regarding the newer anticonvulsants such as topiramate (Topamax) or gabapentin (Neurontin) (Grossman, 2002). However, despite modest outcome effects, there do not appear to be any failed empirical trials with anticonvulsants.

There are potential risks with the prescription of anticonvulsants. In overdose, the ingestion of five times the therapeutic dose oftentimes results in toxicity (Mofenson, Caraccio, & Greensher, 1996), usually unconsciousness, seizures, and respiratory depression. Carbamazepine, which is structurally related to tricyclic antidepressants, may cause cardiac arrhythmias (Mofenson et al., 1996) and in one case series, the fatality rate from acute poisoning was 13% (Schmidt & Schmitz-Buhl, 1995). Most anticonvulsants cause weight gain, with the exception of topiramate (Calabrese, Shelton, Rapport, & Kimmel, 2002) and possibly gabapentin (in our clinical experience, low doses have not resulted in weight increases). Topiramate may lower the efficacy of oral contraceptives. With the exception of gabapentin and topiramate, the anticonvulsants require initial and annual laboratory studies as well as follow-up serum levels, adding to the cost and inconvenience of treatment. In addition, many (e.g., carbamazepine, valproate) have a significant number of potential drug interactions and may affect the levels of other prescribed psychotropic medications. Gabapentin is a notable exception in this regard in that it is metabolized and excreted through the kidneys and there are no interactions with drugs metabolized through the liver (about 90% or more of prescribed drugs). While empirical data is not available, like the other anticonvulsants, gabapentin appears to modestly curb impulsivity and aggression, and it is the easiest of the anticonvulsants to use in the outpatient setting.

Lithium

While lithium has a variety of physiological effects, its genuine mechanism of action is largely unknown. Used primarily for the treatment of bipolar disorder, lithium is known to have an overall calming effect on patients and to curb manic as well as depressive symptoms. Although widely used for aggression (e.g., prison settings), clinical trials are lacking (Soloff, 2000). However, lithium genuinely appears to reduce aggression and impulsivity (Links, Steiner, Boiago, & Irwin, 1990). Lithium has distinct drawbacks. It is lethal in overdose and complicated to use in the clinical setting because of the need for initial as well as annual laboratory studies, and follow-up serum levels. Lithium also has a host of troublesome side effects (e.g., frequent urination, thirst, tremor, sedation, diarrhea) and is known for its propensity to precipitate hypothyroidism and cause weight gain.

Antipsychotics

All antipsychotic drugs in the United States have effects on dopamine, and the newer atypical antipsychotics have effects on serotonin as well. These medications have traditionally been potentially hazardous because of the threat of extrapyramidal side effects, most notably tardive dyskinesia. Tardive dyskinesia is a movement disorder that initially manifests as abnormal perioral and/or tongue movements. The disorder may progress into a generalized movement disorder that, in many cases, may not be reversible with the discontinuation of the offending drug. Despite this unusual risk, antipsychotics may be the best-studied medications in self-harming patients (Soloff, 2000).

The typical, or traditional, antipsychotics have been found efficacious with SHB (Grossman, 2002; Moleman et al., 1999; Soloff, 2000) and are reviewed elsewhere (Moleman et al., 1999). With the advent of the newer, atypical antipsychotics (i.e., drugs with significantly less risks of extrapyramidal side effects), clinicians are actively revisiting the use of these drugs in nonpsychotic patients.

Clozapine was the first atypical antipsychotic available in the United States. Clozapine decreases aggression and suicidal ideation (Parker, 2002), impulsivity (Bendetti, Sforzini, Colombo, Marrei, & Smeraldi, 1998), and self-mutilation (Chengappa, Baker, & Sirri, 1995; Chengappa, Ebeling, Kang, Levine, & Parepally, 1999). It was recently approved by the FDA for suicidal ideation. Clozapine can be prescribed only by psychiatrists (i.e., closed prescribing system), requires routine laboratory studies every 2 weeks prior to the dispensing of the drug, and is known to harbor a host of potentially serious complications (e.g., agranulocytosis, significant weight gain, tachycardia, seizures, excessive sedation).

In addition to clozapine, there are several other available atypical antipsychotics (i.e., risperidone [Risperdal], olanzapine [Zyprexa], quetiapine [Seroquel], ziprasidone [Geodon], aripiprazole [Abilify]), each with its own unique chemical structure and pharmacological profile. Risperidone has been found to reduce disruptive behavior (Ad-Dab'bagh, Greenfield, Milne-Smith, & Freedman, 2000), aggression (Rocca, Marchiaro, Cocuzza, & Bogetto, 2002), impulsivity, and self-mutilation (Khouzam & Donnelly, 1997). Olanzapine appears to reduce anger and hostility

(Schulz, Camlin, Berry, & Jesberger, 1999; Zanarini & Frankenburg, 2001) as well as self-mutilation (Hough, 2001). To our knowledge, quetiapine, ziprasidone, and aripriprazole, the newest atypical antipsychotic, have not been examined in patients with SHB.

With considerably lower risks for extrapyramidal side effects, the atypical antipsychotics are not problem-free. As for effects in overdose, clozapine has a significant risk of seizures, olanzapine and quetiapine have intermediate risk, and risperidone has low risk (Schreinzer et al., 2001). All of the atypical antipsychotics demonstrate a heightened risk of lethality in overdose when combined with other psychotropic medications (Schreinzer et al., 2001). During routine use, both olanzapine and clozapine are characterized by potentially significant weight gain in some patients (Volavka et al., 2002), a finding that is also emerging with quetiapine at high doses. However, ziprasidone (Goodnick, 2001) and aripiprazole, and to a lesser degree low-dose risperidone (Volavka et al., 2002), appear to be weight-neutral. Ziprasidone is known to prolong the QT interval, a measure of cardiac conduction, but a heightened risk for cardiac arrhythmias in overdose has not been clearly demonstrated. The only potential clinical limitation with ziprasidone is twice-per-day (versus once-per-day) dosing. Risperidone may cause prolactin elevation, even at low doses, resulting in galactorrhea and sexual dysfunction. Olanzapine, quetiapine, and clozapine may cause increases in serum glucose and lipids, making their prescription in patients with diabetes and those with hyperlipidemia less attractive.

As caveats regarding the use of atypical antipsychotics, there is a paucity of *controlled* trials (Grossman, 2002), low doses are typically recommended (Moleman et al., 1999; Soloff, 2000), and maintenance therapy has not been empirically confirmed, although most clinicians prescribe them long-term (Soloff, 2002).

Opioid Blockers

The theoretical premise of opioid blockers is that they work by blocking the release of an endogenously reinforcing opioid that is released with the execution of SHB. While there have been several studies exploring the use of opioid blockers (i.e., naltrexone [ReVia]) in SHB, there is limited scientific evidence for their efficacy (Grossman, 2002). Indeed, given the complex interpersonal and intrapsychic functions of such behavior, it seems simplistic to expect that opioid blockade, alone, would consistently interrupt SHB.

Psychological Issues in Prescribing Medication

Many patients with comorbid ED and longstanding SHB have characterological disorders, perhaps most frequently BPD. The dynamics of borderline personality include both splitting and crisis behavior to engage others. Indeed, splitting is often found in patients with ED with or without BPD. For the prescriber, splitting may result in the medication being perceived by the patient as the potential cure at the expense of psychotherapy, or vice versa. In addition, the patient's expectations of the medication may be extreme and unrealistic, resulting in, for example, negative perceptions of efficacy despite modest gains. If the prescriber and therapist are not the same, the integration of the two treatment providers may result in interpersonal splitting, manifesting as an unexpected rivalry and tension between professionals, which is covertly being generated by the patient's liaison. Indeed, some characterological patients, for example, will spend inordinate amounts of time focusing on their medications and medication "issues" in therapy. In other instances, characterological patients may use medication crises to foster repetitive contact with the prescriber, resulting in multiple prescriptions, failed trials, and mutual frustration.

Recommendations

We have summarized our impressions of the benefits and risks of these various drug categories in Table 17.1, as well as our recommendations for a prescribing strategy in Figure 17.1. At the initiation of treatment with medications, we suggest an SSRI because of the potential benefits (i.e., broad efficacy) and low risks. Among the SSRIs, sertraline appears to have the most favorable clinical profile. As for a subsequent SSRI choice, citalopram or escitalopram are considerations in the nonsuicidal patient, as is fluoxetine, given careful reflection on the slight risk of increased impulsivity with the latter as well as half-life issues. If SSRIs are ineffective, venlafaxine appears to be the next pragmatic pharmacological option.

Following antidepressants, many authorities recommend an adjunctive antipsychotic as the next level of intervention. However, we suggest anticonvulsant therapy for relatively stable outpatients. Despite the lack of empirical data, gabapentin has been helpful in the outpatient clinical setting and is the easiest anticonvulsant to monitor. Other anticonvulsants may be considered with the recognition of their limitations.

As a final level of intervention, we recommend adjunctive, low-dose, atypical antipsychotics, specifically risperidone or ziprasidone because of their minimal effects on body weight. (With more clinical experience, aripiprazole may be a future option.) These three classes of drugs may be prescribed in combination as well as continued long-term.

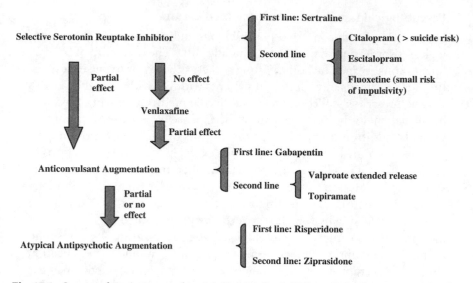

Fig. 17.1 Suggested Basic Approach to Medication for Self-Harm Behavior among Individuals with Eating Disorders

TABLE 17.1 Clinical Comparison of Various Psychotropic Drugs for the Management of Self-Harm Behavior (SHB) among Patients with Eating Disorders

Drug Category	Empirical Evidence in SHB	Laboratory Studies Indicated	Ease of Use	Weight-Gain Risk	Risk in Overdose
Antidepressants					
SSRIs	***	No	****	Variable	Minimal
Venlafaxine	*	No	****	Minimal	*
MAOIs	**	No	*	High	***
Anticonvulsants	***	Yes	**	Moderate (exception: topiramate)	Variable
Gabapentin	—	No	****	Minimal at low dose	?
Lithium	—	Yes	**	Moderate	***
Atypical Antipsychotics	***	No	***	Variable	*
Clozapine	***	Yes	*	Very high	?

Note: **** = high, *** = moderate, ** = low, * = very low; based on the authors' synthesis of empirical data as well as clinical experience; few data allow for direct comparison, such as risk in overdose; when a particular medication within a group has dramatically different properties (e.g., clozapine), it has an individual listing or notation in the table.

Conclusion

Medication management among patients with ED and with SHB is fraught with potential difficulties including the psychology of the patient, the modest beneficial effects of the medication, the risks of particular medications, and the need for adjunctive psychotherapy in all cases. Prescribers must be careful not to align with the patient's impulsivity regarding changes in medication, and to recognize that some patients will use medication dilemmas to secure ongoing contact with the prescriber. Despite these concerns, most patients will modestly benefit from intervention with medications. We have suggested a conservative approach to medications, in keeping with the historic adage, "Do no harm," which seems to especially apply to these difficult and challenging individuals.

References

Ad-Dab'bagh, Y., Greenfield, B., Milne-Smith, J., & Freedman, H. (2000). Inpatient treatment of severe disruptive behaviour disorders with risperidone and milieu therapy. *Canadian Journal of Psychiatry, 45,* 376–382.

Bendetti, F., Sforzini, L., Colombo, C., Marrei, C., & Smeraldi, E. (1998). Low-dose clozapine in acute and continuation treatment of severe borderline personality disorder. *Journal of Clinical Psychiatry, 59,* 103–107.

Berger, P. A. (1987). Pharmacological treatment for borderline personality disorder. *Bulletin of the Menninger Clinic, 51,* 277–284.

Bergmann, F., Bleich, S., Wischer, S., & Paulus, W. (2002). Seizure and cardiac arrest during bupropion SR treatment. *Journal of Clinical Psychopharmacology, 22,* 630–631.

Bourin, M. (1999). Psychopharmacological profile of venlafaxine. *Encephale, 25,* 21–25.

Brinkley, J. R. (1993). Pharmacotherapy of borderline states. *Psychiatric Clinics of North America, 16,* 853–884.

Buckley, N. A., & McManus, P. R. (2002). Fatal toxicity of serotoninergic and other antidepressant drugs: Analysis of United Kingdom mortality data. *British Medical Journal, 325,* 1332–1333.

Calabrese, J. R., Shelton, M. D., Rapport, D. J., & Kimmel, S. E. (2002). Bipolar disorders and the effectiveness of novel anticonvulsants. *Journal of Clinical Psychiatry, 63,* 5–9.

Chengappa, K. N. R., Baker, R. W., & Sirri, C. (1995). The successful use of clozapine in ameliorating severe self-mutilation in a patient with borderline personality disorder. *Journal of Personality Disorders, 9,* 76–82.

Chengappa, K. N. R., Ebeling, T., Kang, J.S., Levine, J., & Parepally, H. (1999). Clozapine reduces severe self-mutilation and aggression in psychotic patients with borderline personality disorder. *Journal of Clinical Psychiatry, 60,* 477–484.

Coccaro, E. F. (1998). Clinical outcome of psychopharmacologic treatment of borderline and schizotypal personality disordered subjects. *Journal of Clinical Psychiatry, 59,* 30–35.

Coons, P. M. (1992). The use of carbamazepine for episodic violence in multiple personality disorder and dissociative disorder not otherwise specified: Two additional case reports. *Biological Psychiatry, 32,* 717–720.

Cornelius, J. R., Soloff, P. H., Perel, J. M., & Ulrich, R. F. (1991). A preliminary trial of fluoxetine in refractory borderline patients. *Journal of Clinical Psychopharmacology, 11,* 116–120.

Daly, K. A., & Fatemi, S. H. (1999). Lamotrigine and impulse behaviour. *Canadian Journal of Psychiatry, 44,* 395–396.

Davis, L. L., Ryan, W., Adinoff, B., & Petty, F. (2000). Comprehensive review of the psychiatric uses of valproate. *Journal of Clinical Psychopharmacology, 20,* 1S–17S.

Ekselius, L., & von Knorring, L. (1998). Personality disorder comorbidity with major depression and response to treatment with sertraline or citalopram. *International Clinical Psychopharmacology, 13,* 205–211.

Fava, M., Farabaugh, A. H., Sickinger, A. H., Wright, E., Alpert, J., Sonawalla, S., Nierenberg, A. H., & Worthington, J. J., 3rd. (2002). Personality disorders and depression. *Psychological Medicine, 32,* 1049–1057.

Fava, M., Judge, R., Hoog, S. L., Nilsson, M. E., & Koke, S. C. (2000). Fluoxetine versus sertraline and paroxetine in major depressive disorder: Changes in weight with long-term treatment. *Journal of Clinical Psychiatry, 61,* 863–867.

Gadde, K. M., & Krishnan, K. R. R. (1999). Current status of monoamine oxidase inhibitors in psychiatric practice. *The Hatherleigh guide to psychopharmacology* (pp. 63–82). New York: Hatherleigh Press.

Gardner, D. L., & Cowdry, R. W. (1986). Positive effects of carbamazepine on behavioral dyscontrol in borderline personality disorder. *American Journal of Psychiatry, 143,* 519–522.

Goodnick, P. J. (2001). Ziprasidone: Profile on safety. *Expert Opinion on Pharmacotherapy, 2,* 1655–1662.

Grossman, R. (2002). Psychopharmacologic treatment of patients with borderline personality disorder. *Psychiatric Annals, 32,* 357–370.

Hough, D. W. (2001). Low-dose olanzapine for self-mutilation behavior in patients with borderline personality disorder. *Journal of Clinical Psychiatry, 62,* 296–297.

Kavoussi, R., & Coccaro, E. F. (1999). Pharmacotherapy. In M. Hersen & A. S. Bellack (Eds.), *Handbook of comparative interventions for adult disorders* (pp. 584–595). New York: Wiley.

Khouzam, H. R., & Donnelly, N. J. (1997). Remission of self-mutilation in a patient with borderline personality during risperidone therapy. *Journal of Nervous & Mental Disease, 185,* 348–349.

Koenigsberg, H. W., Woo-Ming, A. M., & Siever, L. J. (2002). Pharmacological treatments for personality disorders. In P. E. Nathan & J. M. Gorman (Eds.), *A guide to treatments that work* (pp. 625–641). London: Oxford University Press.

Liebowitz, M. R., Hollander E., Schneier, F., Campeas, R., Welkowitz, L., Hatterer, J., & Fallon, B. (1990). Reversible and irreversible monoamine oxidase inhibitors in other psychiatric disorders. *Acta Psychiatrica Scandinavica, 82,* 29–34.

Links, P. S., Steiner, M., Boiago, I., & Irwin, D. (1990). Lithium therapy for borderline patients: Preliminary findings. *Journal of Personality Disorders, 4,* 173–181.

Markovitz, P. (1995). Pharmacotherapy of impulsivity, aggression, and related disorders. In E. Hollander & D. J. Stein (Eds.), *Impulsivity and aggression* (pp. 263–287). New York: John Wiley & Sons.

Markovitz, P. J., Calabrese, J. R., Schulz, S. C., & Meltzer, H. Y. (1991). Fluoxetine in the treatment of borderline and schizotypal personality disorders. *American Journal of Psychiatry, 148,* 1064–1067.

Markovitz, P. J., & Wagner, S. C. (1995). Venlafaxine in the treatment of borderline personality disorder. *Psychopharmacology Bulletin, 31,* 773–777.

Mofenson, H. C., Caraccio, T. R., & Greensher, J. (1996). Acute poisonings. In R. E. Rakel (Ed.), *Conn's current therapy* (pp. 1149–1194). Philadelphia: W.B. Saunders.

Moleman, P., van Dam, K., & Dings, V. (1999). Psychopharmacological treatment of personality disorders. In J. Derksen & C. Maffei (Eds.), *Treatment of personality disorders* (pp. 207–227). New York: Plenum Publishers.

Parker, G. F. (2002). Clozapine and borderline personality disorder. *Psychiatric Services, 53,* 348–349.

Pinto, O. C., & Akiskal, H. S. (1998). Lamotrigine as a promising approach to borderline personality: An open case series without concurrent DSM-IV major mood disorder. *Journal of Affective Disorders, 51,* 333–343.

Power, A. (1998). Drug treatment of depression. Citalopram in overdose may result in serious morbidity and death. *British Medical Journal, 316,* 307–308.

Riesenman, C. (1995). Antidepressant drug interactions and the cytochrome P450 system: A critical appraisal. *Pharmacotherapy, 15,* 84S–94S.

Rinne, T., van den Brink, W., Wouters, L., & van Dyck, R. (2002). SSRI treatment of borderline personality disorder: A randomized, placebo-controlled clinical trial for female patients with borderline personality disorder. *American Journal of Psychiatry, 159,* 2048–2054.

Rocca, P., Marchiaro, L., Cocuzza, E., & Bogetto, F. (2002). Treatment of borderline personality disorder with risperidone. *Journal of Clinical Psychiatry, 63,* 241–244.

Salzman, C., Wolfson, A. N., Schatzberg, A., Looper, J., Henke, R., Albanese, M., et al. (1995). Effect of fluoxetine on anger in symptomatic volunteers with borderline personality disorder. *Journal of Clinical Psychopharmacology, 15,* 23–29.

Sansone, R. A., Wiederman, M. W., & Shrader, J. A. (2000). Naturalistic study of the weight effects of amitriptyline, fluoxetine, and sertraline in an outpatient medical setting. *Journal of Clinical Psychopharmacology, 20,* 272–274.

Sasyniuk, B. I., Jhamandas, V., & Valois, M. (1986). Experimental amitriptyline intoxication: Treatment of cardiac toxicity with sodium bicarbonate. *Annals of Emergency Medicine, 15,* 1052–1059.

Schatzberg, A. F. (2000). New indications for antidepressants. *Journal of Clinical Psychiatry, 61,* 9–17.

Schmidt, S., & Schmitz-Buhl, M. (1995). Signs and symptoms of carbamazepine overdose. *Journal of Neurology, 242,* 169–173.

Schreinzer, D., Frey, R., Stimpfl, T., Vycudilik, W., Berzlanovich, A., & Kasper, S. (2001). Different fatal toxicity of neuroleptics identified by autopsy. *European Neuropsychopharmacology, 11,* 117–124.

Schulz, S. C., Camlin, K. L., Berry, S. A., & Jesberger, J. A. (1999). Olanzapine safety and efficacy in patients with borderline personality disorder and comorbid dysthymia. *Biological Psychiatry, 46,* 1429–1435.

Soloff, P. H. (1994). Is there any drug treatment of choice for the borderline patient? *Acta Psychiatrica Scandinavica, 89,* 50–55.

Soloff, P. H. (2000). Psychopharmacology of borderline personality disorder. *The Psychiatric Clinics of North America, 23,* 169–192.

Southwick, S. M., Yehuda, R., Giller, E. L., & Perry, B. D. (1990). Altered platelet alpha$_2$ adrenergic receptor binding sites in borderline personality disorder. *American Journal of Psychiatry, 147,* 1014–1017.

Stein, D. J., Simeon, D., Frenkel, M., Islam, M. N., & Hollander, E. (1995). An open trial of valproate in borderline personality disorder. *Journal of Clinical Psychiatry, 56,* 506–510.

Volavka, J., Czobor, P., Sheitman, B., Lindenmayer, J. P., Citrome, L., McEvoy, J. P., Cooper, T. B., Chakos, M., & Lieberman, J. A. (2002). Clozapine, olanzapine, risperidone, and haloperidol in the treatment of patients with chronic schizophrenia and schizoaffective disorder. *American Journal of Psychiatry, 159,* 255–262.

Winchel, R., & Stanley, M. (1991). Self-injurious behavior: A review of the behavior and biology of self-mutilation. *American Journal of Psychiatry, 148,* 306–317.

Zanarini, M. C., & Frankenburg, F. R. (2001). Olanzapine treatment of female borderline personality disorder patients: A double-blind, placebo-controlled pilot study. *Journal of Clinical Psychiatry, 62,* 849–854.

Contributors

Charles B. Anderson, Ph.D., is a postdoctoral fellow at the University of North Carolina School of Medicine. His research and clinical interests in the area of eating disorders include treatment outcome, personality functioning, group psychotherapy, and gender differences. His most recent work focuses on gender differences in the genetic epidemiology of eating disorders. He has a forthcoming article with C. M. Bulik (in press), Gender differences in compensatory behaviors, weight and shape salience, and drive for thinness, *Eating Behaviors.*

Cynthia M. Bulik, Ph.D., is the William R. and Jeanne H. Jordan Distinguished Professor of Eating Disorders at the University of North Carolina at Chapel Hill. She has been involved with eating disorder treatment and research for over 20 years. Her most recent work focuses on the genetic aspects of anorexia and bulimia nervosa (Bulik, C. M., Sullivan, P. F., Carter, F. A., McIntosh, W., & Joyce, P.R. [1999]. Temperament, character, and suicide attempts in anorexia nervosa, bulimia nervosa, and major depression, *Acta Psychiatrica Scandinavica, 100,* 27–32; Bulik, C. M., Prescott, C. A., & Kendler, K. S. [2001]. Features of childhood sexual abuse and the development of psychiatric and substance use disorders, *British Journal of Psychiatry, 179,* 444–449).

Laurence Claes, M.A., is researcher and behavior therapist at the Department of Clinical Assessment and Psychopathology, Catholic University of Leuven (Belgium).

Carolyn Costin, M.A., M.Ed., has been a marriage and family therapist and specialist in the field of eating disorders since 1979. She is founder and director of The Monte Nido Residential Treatment Facility and The Eating Disorder Center of California. Her two books, *Your Dieting Daughter* and *The Eating Disorder Sourcebook,* are popular among professionals as well as the lay public.

Ross D. Crosby, Ph.D., is Director of Biomedical Statistics at the Neuropsychiatric Research Institute and is a clinical professor of Neuroscience at the University of North Dakota School of Medicine in Fargo. He received his doctorate in social psychology from the University of Nevada.

Angela Favaro, M.D., Ph.D., is a research scientist in the Department of Neurosciences at the University of Padua, Italy. Her main fields of interest and research are epidemiology, eating disorders, and post-traumatic stress disorder.

Silvia Ferrara, Ph.D., is a clinical psychologist at the Department of Neuroscience, University of Padua, Italy. Her field of interest is epidemiology and clinical aspects of eating disorders.

K. R. Juzwin, Psy.D., is director of the Self-Injury Recovery Services Program at Alexian Brothers Behavioral Health Hospital in Hoffman Estates, Illinois. She is in practice at the Alternatives Center for Counseling and Psychotherapy, specializing in self-injury, trauma, and eating disorders. She is a core faculty member at Illinois School of Professional Psychology, Argosy University–Chicago Northwest.

Marsha D. Marcus, Ph.D., is Professor of Psychiatry and Psychology and Chief of the Eating Disorders Program at Western Psychiatric Institute and Clinic [WPIC], University of Pittsburgh Medical Center. She is also the Co-Director of the WPIC Psychology Internship Training Program and Associate Director of the Pittsburgh Obesity Nutrition Research Center. Dr. Marcus' research interests focus on eating disorders and obesity.

Elizabeth Blocher McCabe, LSW, is Clinical Administrator for Eating Disorders and Behavioral Medicine and Director of Social Work at Western Psychiatric Institute and Clinic at the University of Pittsburgh Medical Center. Her work with eating disorder patients spans the care continuum and includes direct practice, program administration, and program development. She has authored and co-authored articles and book chapters and is a frequent presenter at national and international conferences. She lectures and has published on the use of Dialectical Behavior Therapy with eating disorder patients.

Beth Hartman McGilley, Ph.D., FAED, is a clinical psychologist in private practice, specializing in the treatment of eating and related disorders, body image, trauma, grief, and impaired athletes. A Fellow of the Academy for Eating Disorders, Dr. McGilley has practiced for 20 years, writing, lecturing, supervising, and directing in- and outpatient eating disorders programs. Dr. McGilley is the co-founder and current president of Healing Path Foundation, a nonprofit foundation dedicated to the prevention and treatment of eating disorders.

Tricia Cook Myers, Ph.D., is a research scientist at the Neuropsychiatric Research Institute and a clinical assistant professor of neuroscience at the University of North Dakota School of Medicine in Fargo. She received her doctorate in clinical psychology from the University of North Dakota.

Mervat Nasser, M.B.Ch.B., M.D., M.phil., M.R.C.Psych., is a consultant psychiatrist and senior lecturer in psychiatry at the Eating Disorders Research Unit, Institute of Psychiatry, Kings, Guy and St. Thomas's Medical School, UK. She is known for her research on the role of culture in the field of eating disorders and has various publications in this area, including her two books *Culture and Weight Consciousness* (1997) and *Eating Disorders and Cultures in Transition* (2001). She is also a history analyst and culture critic who writes extensively for literary journals in Egypt and the Arab world.

Margo Norton, Ph.D., is clinical director of the Eating Disorders Institute Hospital Program at Meritcare Medical Center in Fargo, North Dakota. She received her doctorate in clinical psychology from the University of North Dakota.

Monika Ostroff, M.S.W., L.I.C.S.W., is a therapist, author, and consultant specializing in eating disorders. She directed the Eating Disorder Treatment Center at Hampstead Hospital in Hampstead, New Hampshire, for several years before opening her current private practice in Exeter. She co-authored the book *Anorexia Nervosa: A Guide to Recovery* and has appeared on several radio and television broadcasts. Monika has been active in the field of eating disorders for the past 13 years. For the past several years, Monika has been adapting Dialectical Behavior Therapy (DBT), making it more experiential and specific to eating disorders. She presents nationally on this topic.

Lori A. Sansone, M.D., is a board-certified physician in family medicine. Dr. Sansone was the medical consultant for an eating disorders program for two years, has co-authored 70 publications, and is a co-developer of the Self-Harm Inventory. She is currently in private practice with Premier Healthnet in Centerville, Ohio.

Paolo Santonastaso, M.D., is a professor of psychiatry in the Department of Neurosciences at the University of Padua, Italy. He is the director of the Eating Disorders Unit and his main fields of research are eating disorders, psychosomatics, and post-traumatic stress disorder.

Walter Vandereycken, M.D., Ph.D., is professor of psychiatry at the Catholic University of Leuven, and clinical director of the Department of Behavior Therapy at the Alexian Brothers Psychiatric Hospital in Tienen (Belgium). He is senior editor of *Eating Disorders: The Journal of Treatment and Prevention,* and has co-authored several books, including *From Fasting Saints to Anorexic Girls: The History of Self-Starvation* (New York: University Press) and *Trauma, Dissociation, and Impulse Dyscontrol in Eating Disorders* (Taylor & Francis, London).

Hans Vertommen, Ph.D. is a professor of clinical psychology in the Department of Clinical Assessment and Psychopathology at Catholic University of Leuven (Belgium).

Stephen Wonderlich, Ph.D., is a professor and associate chairperson in the Department of Neuroscience at the University of North Dakota School of Medicine & Health Sciences in Fargo. He is also co-director of the Eating Disorders Institute and director of clinical research for the Neuropsychiatric Research Institute in Fargo. He currently sits on the editorial boards for the *International Journal of Eating Disorders* and *Eating Disorders Review.* He is a past board member of the Eating Disorders Research Society and a past president of the Academy for Eating Disorders.

Index